THE
WELL
FAMILY
BOOK

THE
WELL
FAMILY
BOOK

CHARLES T. KUNTZLEMAN
Foreword by Jim Ryun

The Well Family Book
by Charles T. Kuntzleman

Published by
HERE'S LIFE PUBLISHERS, INC.
P.O. Box 1576
San Bernardino, California 92402

Library of Congress Cataloging-in-Publication Data
Kuntzleman, Charles T.
  The well family book.

  1. Family—Health and hygiene.   2. Christian
life—1960–   3. Holistic medicine.   4. Health.
I. Title.
RA777.7.K86   1985   613   85-8754
ISBN 0-89840-092-9

HLP Product Number 951061

Unless otherwise indicated, Scripture quotations are from *The Holy Bible, New International Version*, © 1978 by New York International Bible Society, published by The Zondervan Corporation, Grand Rapids, Michigan, and are used by permission. Other Scripture quotations are from *The Living Bible* (LB), © 1971 by Tyndale House Publishers, Wheaton, Illinois, and are used by permission; the New American Standard Bible (NAS), © The Lockman Foundation 1960, 1962, 1963, 1968, 1971, 1972, 1973, 1975, and are used by permission; and the King James Version (KJV).

FOR MORE INFORMATION, WRITE:

L.I.F.E.—P.O. Box A399, Sydney South 2000, Australia
Campus Crusade for Christ of Canada—Box 300, Vancouver, B.C., V6C 2X3, Canada
Campus Crusade for Christ—103 Friar Street, Reading RG1 1EP, Berkshire, England
Lay Institute for Evangelism—P.O. Box 8786, Aukland 3, New Zealand
Great Commission Movement of Nigeria—P.O. Box 500, Jos, Plateau State Nigeria, West Africa
Life Ministry—P.O. Box/Bus 91015, Aukland Park 2006, Republic of South Africa
Campus Crusade for Christ International—Arrowhead Springs, San Bernardino, CA 92414, U.S.A.

DEDICATION

To my earthly father,
who made it so
easy
to understand my Heavenly Father

Table of Contents

Acknowledgments

I have many people to thank for assistance in writing this book. Mike McGlynn, Debbie Drake and my wife, Beth, spent time helping me with the family activities that are found throughout its pages. I also thank Beth and Debbie for listening to and trying different ideas that I included (or wanted to include) in this book. My sister, Jayne K. Moxey, and father, Walter Kuntzleman, reviewed the manuscript and made many valuable editorial and style recommendations. Barb Robbins and Karen Van Horn spent endless hours at the word processor—both patiently smiled as I gave them reams of paper with my less-than-perfect penmanship. Perhaps my lack of good handwriting was providential since they often guessed at what I was trying to say and, thereby, improved the book with their grammar and vocabulary. I thank Les Stobbe, my editor at Here's Life, for patience and for a letter in which he recommended I let the Holy Spirit be my guide as I fleshed out the pages. It's hard to describe the impact that wisdom had on my writing.

Finally, I thank my family, Beth, Deb, John, Tom, Lisa and Becky, for patience, understanding and support. They were patient when trying recipe and wellness ideas; understanding when things didn't go right; supportive when I spent hours "away" from them reading, writing and thinking.

Thank you all, and God bless you.

Charlie Kuntzleman

Preface

"I pray that you may enjoy good health and
that all may go well with you, even as your
soul is getting along well" (3 John 2).

Good family health. That's a dream of us all. We want our children, spouses and selves to live well, free from runny noses, allergies, tummy aches and athlete's foot. Yet we can deal with these things, and scores of books tell us how.

Heart attacks, cancer, diabetes, strokes and other catastrophic diseases are another story. These strike fear and terror in our hearts. These are diseases that ruin our family's quality of life. These are afflictions that take parents from children. Modern day plagues that kill or maim all family members. Unfortunately, not many books give parents guidelines on how to help their family avoid these dreaded diseases.

As a specialist in exercise, fitness and wellness, I am dismayed at the number of people struck by these afflictions. Dismayed because more than 50 percent of these deaths and ailments could be prevented by a change in living habits. The seeds for these diseases are planted in childhood, nurtured during adolescence and come to full bloom in adulthood.

As a Christian, I also am frustrated, because when I speak or write on wellness, many brothers and sisters in the Spirit argue with me about the value of preaching healthy habits of proper exercise, good food and stress reduction. They note that Scripture says:

"Bodily exercise profiteth little."[1]

"Do not worry about your life, what you will eat or drink; or about your body."[2]

"Who of you by worrying can add a single hour to his life?"[3]

Not surprisingly, many Christians agree with me on avoiding addictions such as smoking and alcohol, but when I talk about overeating, overworking and overusing doctor-prescribed medications, we seem to part company.

The Well Family Book addresses these issues. On the following pages, I plan, with the leading of the Holy Spirit, to show you that from Genesis to Revelation the Bible tells us the body is to be revered as the temple of the Holy Spirit.

The idea that the body is not worthy of care is a heresy as old as Christianity. Some philosophers in the apostle Paul's day preached that the body was worthless. They taught that gluttony, adultery, homosexuality and drunkenness were of no importance because they affected only the body, which was evil. Therefore, Christians were free to do what they liked. Some took an opposing view. Since the body was evil or worthless, Christians were to punish theirs with harsh self-denial—asceticism.

Paul opposed these thoughts. He said our bodies are God's—not ours. They are to be taken care of well. We are to honor God with our bodies.[4]

Just as there are physical laws (gravity, conservation of energy, etc.) and spiritual laws (see appendix A) established by God, there are health laws, which He slowly has been revealing to us. These laws state that you cannot overindulge in food, stress, drugs, sedentary living and personal body fat and expect to maximize your God-given potential for health, vitality and longevity.

When I speak of wellness for your family, I am not speaking of the type of health advocated by many fitness and health magazines that grace our newsstands, fitness that worships thin waistlines, hypes the human body and lauds beautiful legs. I am not advocating a new-age philosophy of worshiping the body and excluding God from our search for better health.

Instead, I want to give you and yours an opportunity to have the best health possible for you, regardless of your current health status. Let me illustrate. One of the "healthiest" persons I've known was a man with terminal cancer. Physically he had difficulty moving from his chair to his bed. But he lived well. He ate well, practiced relaxation techniques, related well to his family and friends, and most importantly, had placed God at the center of his life. *That* is wellness.

To be well, you need to work on a total integration of mind, body and spirit. I have written this book to help you do so. I explore with you how your body relates to your spiritual and mental being. I have applied biblical principles to certain concepts of physical health. I have tried to capture what the Bible says about our physical well-being.

Sometimes Scripture addresses these issues head-on. Other times it is indirect, or silent, not because health is unimportant, but because the Bible deals primarily with spiritual matters. It is God's way of revealing Himself to you, showing you His Son, teaching you how He wants you to live and telling you history and the future. Personal health, education and family life are addressed incidentally or with selected passages. Paradoxically, some Christians embrace the importance of education and family life, but they shove personal health under the table or onto the back burner. I attribute this to the "worthless body" heresy Paul spoke against.

My purpose for teaching you and your family how to be healthy is to help you maximize your potential to:

glorify God;

keep God your top priority;

know and do His will;

have the best health and energy levels possible for you.

You may be asking what qualifies me to write on the importance of physical health (a legitimate question). God has blessed me with many opportunities. He has allowed me to be in the forefront of developing health and fitness programs for groups and organizations across North America.

This book is based on thirteen years of extensive research on Feelin' Good, a cardiovascular fitness program for kindergarten through ninth grade. Feelin' Good teaches public and private school children how to assume responsibility for their own health through regimens of exercise, food, weight, stress management and saying no to smoking and drugs. I call this responsibility the fourth *R* in education.

The program started in 1973. It was field tested by children, teachers and parents in the San Diego Unified School District. In 1976, the program was introduced to hundreds of YMCAs across the United States as part of the nationwide cardiovascular health program. In 1980, a $481,219 grant from the W. K. Kellogg Foundation allowed researchers to evaluate the program's effectiveness in all Jackson County, Michigan, schools. The conclusion: Strategies employed in Feelin' Good teach children how to reduce their risk of cardiovascular disease and body fat, improve their fitness level, increase their activity patterns, improve the quality of their eating, and enhance their self-esteem.

During this same time, I developed and helped evaluate adult health, fitness and wellness programs for the YMCA of the USA, Campbell's Soups, Phillips Petroleum, Ross Laboratories, Rodale Press and other corporations, hospitals, schools and universities. I also developed the Living Well program—a nationwide health enhancement program for corporations and hospitals.

In my work with children and adults, I realized that wellness starts in the home. Health patterns and behaviors established in childhood have a profound effect on adults' exercise, eating, stress, weight and addiction habits and, therefore, upon their current health and vitality.

While many of the ideas presented here are based on experience and ideas used in Feelin' Good, you'll also find experiences and activities that my wife, Beth, and I have used with our five children—ages fourteen to twenty-two. These concepts are reinforced with further views from participants in our health and well-being classes in Jackson County, Michigan, and other fitness professionals around the world.

Now, before you think that I have discovered the secret of raising kids and making them healthy, wealthy and wise, please be assured that the same things do not work with every child. We've had our share of successes and, certainly, our share of failures. My advice is to try the stategies—I think you'll find them effective. But be flexible enough to change and modify if things don't seem to work as outlined.

So let's start a journey. A journey that can be exciting and, yes, at times, frustrating. But a journey that with God's help will make your family feel better. It will enable you and yours to enjoy some of this life's promised fulfillments.

FOREWORD

As a father of four children and husband of one wife, I'm pleased to encourage your involvement with this book. Being well and enjoying good spiritual and physical health requires active participation by the individual. The apostle Paul in 1 Timothy 4:7,8 says, "Train yourself in godliness, For while bodily training is of some value, godliness is of value in every way, as it holds promise for the present life and also for the life to come" (Revised Standard Version). Often as Christians, we have taken the part of Scripture that says "of little value" to mean no value and have neglected our responsibility to care for the Spirit of God that dwells in His temple—our bodies.

I particularly want to challenge the Christian family to read and participate in becoming fit for the King's service. Let's be soldiers who are physically well, that we may be soldiers who are mentally and spiritually prepared for the battle.

Jim Ryun

Chapter 1:
The Well Family

"And Jesus grew in wisdom and stature, and in favor with God and men" (Luke 2:52).

Mary and Joseph must have been delighted. Jesus was maturing as a total person. What an exciting time of joy for his earthly parents.

Things haven't changed much in the past two thousand years. We want our children (and ourselves) to grow in wisdom (mentally), stature (physically), and in favor with God (spiritually) and man (socially).

We want to grow *spiritually* to experience the "abundant life" talked about in John 10:10. So we teach our children about Jesus Christ, God the Father and the Holy Spirit. We go to Sunday school and church. We spend time in family devotions, prayer and Bible study. We teach the importance of daily fellowship with God and the necessity of a personal relationship with Him.

Our relationship can grow and develop, however, only if we are willing to work at it. As Paul tells us in Ephesians 4–6, it is our responsibility to spend time and energy to fulfill God's demands for growth, and we cannot grow by our own strength, but by the strength of God's Spirit within us.

We hope our children and families will grow *socially*. We all want and need strong positive interpersonal relationships. Dr. James Lynch of the University of Maryland has stated that loneliness, a lack of social relationships, and high social mobility are all related to coronary artery disease.[1] Other studies on people who have lived long, healthy lives demonstrate the importance of strong interpersonal relationships.

Social growth also requires effort. Relationships with people don't just happen. They must be cultivated and nurtured. Dr. George E. Vaillant's studies on the personal growth and development of American men showed quite clearly that a person's capacity and ability to love is a key to his or her impact on other people.[2] If we love, share and enjoy life, we give others good feelings about themselves and God's world. Jesus taught us to love our neighbors as ourselves.[3] More importantly, His life showed us how to love other people.

We want our families to grow *mentally*. We send our children to school and teach them to tie shoelaces, read, cook, hammer nails and drive automobiles. We listen to the writer of Proverbs who tells us, "How much better to get wisdom than gold, to choose understanding rather than silver."[4] We know that optimum mental growth does not occur by chance. To help our families grow mentally, we must work on it. We must employ strategies to see that our children reach their mental potentials.

Spending hours playing video games, watching endless soap operas, reading trashy fiction, and daydreaming will not contribute to our mental and intellectual growth. So we encourage our children to read good literature, watch educational television shows, attend lectures and seminars, play problem-solving games, and enjoy stimulating conversation to enhance critical thinking, reasoning skills and relationships. I'm not suggesting that occasional video games and television will stunt intellectual growth, but seven hours of television a day (the average television time in American households) will fry anyone's brain and give him a jaundiced view of life.

We want our children to grow *physically*. We take them to the best doctors we know. They get shots and take vitamins. We read child-care books and magazines that tell us how to meet our children's physical needs—diaper rash, sore throat and poison ivy.

Tragically, we do little to help prevent diseases that may strike them later in life. The results of our studies on seven- to twelve-year-old children in Jackson County, Michigan, are alarming. Their physical activity, eating, and alcohol drinking habits are frightening, as are their feelings about themselves. Their patterns are very similar to their parents', who drink too much alcohol, smoke too much, rarely exercise, eat a diet high in saturated fat, suffer high blood pressure and carry excess body fat.

As parents, we promote the spiritual, mental and social health of our children primarily to prepare them for life's battles, battles they will encounter as adults. We expend a tremendous amount of energy to help them have successful relationships with God, friends and associates. We try to serve as good role models—morally and relationally. We help fine-tune our children's intellectual abilities so they can survive and serve with their God-given talents. That is all good and as it should be.

Unfortunately, when it comes to their skills and abilities to fight heart disease, cancer, diabetes, cirrhosis, emphysema, asthma, arthritis, ulcers, depression, obesity and fatigue, we fall short. We focus on the here-and-now diseases; such non-life threatening ailments as colds, stomachaches and headaches. We fail to give our children a fighting chance to ward off degenerative and debilitating diseases, such as heart disease and cancer, which will rob them and their future families of much joy and happiness. It's almost as if these degenerative diseases are a foregone conclusion. You know, acne at thirteen, a heart attack at fifty-three.

Reasons We Don't Teach Health

I believe that one reason we don't give our children a chance to fight degenerative diseases is that we don't know what kind of family activities to get involved in to encourage good future health.

A second reason is, we view health as the absence of disease. As long as we don't have a cold, chest pain, high blood pressure or ingrown toenail, we are all right. Most of us take our health for granted (although we fear being sick) until it is almost too late. We decide to get well *after* we are too sick to function properly. We watch what we eat *after* we have gained too many pounds. We go to the doctor *after* we develop chronic bronchitis. We start running *after* we have our first chest pain. Then we seek relief or professional help and expect a quick cure—valium to calm down, Dexatrim to lose weight, nitroglycerin to prevent chest pain. These quick "cures" plus billions of dollars spent mask our real problem—our lifestyle. We are not willing to change our way of living and thinking to improve our health and vitality. So we try to repair our health *after* we lose it.

Third, we allow our culture to dictate our living habits, despite the fact that we "know better" and have been deluged with facts and figures on the dangers of smoking, too rich a diet, alcohol and sedentary living.

Fourth, our current lifestyle and habits are convenient, easy and pleasurable. My own experience with people validates a recent poll conducted at Pennsylvania State University on women between the ages of twenty and fifty-nine which illustrates this point. The study revealed that 58 percent of American women haven't changed their eating habits because the emphasis of food selection is based on taste, not nutrition.

Fifth, we assume our children cannot make decisions for themselves. We teach them passivity in health care. We tell them when to go to the doctor. We tell them when to take their shots and medicine. Mom, Dad and the doctor talk while Billy and Suzie stare at the wall or finger a pencil on the desk. Even teenagers are told when to go to the doctor and, again, the adults monopolize the conversation.

Yet a recent study showed that children can help themselves better than an oversolicitous parent, doctor or nurse. Kids actually heal faster if encouraged to help themselves. Studies conducted at the University of Wisconsin Medical School showed that two- to twelve-year-olds recovered quicker from second- and third-degree burns if they cleaned and dressed their own wounds.[5]

Extensive studies on asthmatics showed similar results. Children who were taught what sets off an attack, how to recognize early warning signs, when and how to medicate, and how drugs work had fewer emergency room visits and missed fewer school days.[6]

For these five reasons we, as parents, have been unwilling (or have found it difficult) to change our way of living or to buck the system. The result is poor parent and child health. Look at these facts:[7]

Adults:
—70% drink alcoholic beverages
—30% smoke cigarettes
—53% *never* wear seat belts in a car
—64% do not get enough exercise (24 percent never exercise)
—35% or more are overweight
—50%–80% take a prescription drug every other day

Children:
—98% have at least one heart disease risk factor (high cholesterol, high blood pressure, obesity, etc.); 13 percent have five or more risk factors
—20%–25% carry too much body fat
—28% rarely visit a doctor
—40% *never* wear seat belts in a car
—75% have diets that include too much fat

The Wellness Movement

All this can be depressing, but take heart! Since the late 1970s, things slowly have been changing. A core group of people have realized that what we do for ourselves is far more important than what pills, doctors and hospitals can do for us. These people, which the pollster Daniel Yankelovich calls the "strong formers," have prompted our society to start thinking about self-responsibility for personal health.[8]

Today a concept of wellness has emerged. Wellness means building a lifestyle on a conscious commitment to accept responsibility for your own health. In its broadest sense, it means the healthy development of a person socially, physically, mentally and spiritually.

Unfortunately, the "strong formers" and their wellness concepts have presented substantial problems. First, these people generally are "me" oriented. Consequently, many of their children have been left to flounder. While these parents engage in exercise, try to improve their interpersonal relationships and find themselves spiritually, their children watch television, eat carelessly and fail to deal positively with stress. As a result, their children are not any healthier than those from traditional families.

Second, many have embraced the concept that man is god. They have abandoned the Christian view of a personal God in favor of a "force" or "consciousness." Many hold the belief that people have the answers to all their problems, health included. God is not needed (the tempter's first temptation).[9]

Third, they have emphasized the creation rather than the Creator.[10] Thus the fabric of total wellness is weakened and falls apart. Let me illustrate. Believe it or not, on one occasion I hurriedly made a batch of oatmeal cookies. I followed the recipe, or so I thought. The finished cookies were a fiasco. They slid all over the cookie sheet. They had little form and substance. In my haste, I had forgotten to put in the oatmeal. Nothing held them together. This may be a poor analogy, but it shows what happens when the "me first" philosophy puts in too much creature and too little Creator. The concept of wellness lacks a consistency and something to hold it together.

These "strong formers" preach a message of human potential. They personify the U.S. Army slogan, "Be all that you can be." But an appropriate philosophy of wellness is: Be all that God has in mind for you to be. This is scriptural: "We confidently and joyfully look forward to actually becoming all that God has had in mind for us to be."[11] That means we even see problems as opportunities for God to develop our character, plus perseverence and hope.

I like to take this philosophy of wellness one step further. The apostle Paul tells us to have a realistic view of ourselves from God's point of view. We are not to be prideful, nor are we to have false humility. We should not place ourselves over others and brag about our God-given attributes. Instead, we should look honestly at our gifts from God and use that evaluation as a basis from which to serve others and do His will.[12] Now the philosophy of wellness becomes: Be all that God has in mind for you to be—no more and no less.

This philosophy of wellness eliminates worshipping self or the body. It also eliminates attempts at overachieving. We all can't be marathon runners, great theologians, master teachers, or specimens of perfect health. We should not expect more of ourselves than God does.

This approach to wellness also eliminates low expectations of ourselves. Many people tell me they can't exercise because they are too old, too unfit or too sick. Some claim that preparing good food is too time consuming and expensive. Others say they can't lose weight because that's the way they've always been. These are just excuses. With attitudes like that, how can they be all that God wants them to be? How can they grow and mature as God's unique individuals? These attitudes are as unhealthy as pride. In both cases, people let their wills block their growth as children of God.

"And the child grew and became strong; he was filled with wisdom, and the grace of God was upon Him" (Luke 2:40).

Chapter 2:
The Abundant Life

"I am come that they might have life, and that they might have it more abundantly" (John 10:10 KJV).

As Christians, we all know in part what Jesus meant when He spoke of the abundant life. He was speaking of a life that is full, meaningful and in a right relationship with God; a life and relationship that is enhanced through serving God to the best of our abilities.

Unfortunately, many of us stop there. We fail to (or don't want to) realize that this abundant life (spiritual) can be affected by our physical life (the body). We give lip service to the body as the temple of the Holy Spirit, but we go through life treating it as though it can withstand unbelievable abuse. We carry extra body fat, inhale noxious fumes, eat unhealthy food, expose ourselves to tremendous stresses, and fail to get adequate exercise. Other than preaching against the evils of tobacco, alcohol and drug abuse, we provide little direction to help our children adopt healthier lifestyles to protect their bodies. We think that "God will provide" if we focus solely on our spiritual lives.

One of God's greatest gifts to us is the organization of this universe. Attempt to defy the law of gravity by jumping off a ten-story building, and you will be killed. Swim in icy water for any length of time and you'll freeze to death. Go without air for ten minutes, water for ten days, or food for ten months, and you'll die. You simply cannot go against God's laws of the universe.

The same applies to your body health. Go against God's laws of health, and your vitality and vigor will be affected. And your life may be cut short.

Life is a tremendous gift from God. What are you doing to maximize this precious gift of life? Are you taking care of your body so that you have the energy and vitality to be at your best as a parent, teacher, secretary, boss, truck driver, spouse, friend, Christian? What are you doing to help your spouse and children maximize their precious gift of life?

Taking care of your body or physical wellness can help you in two important areas of your life—your quantity of life and quality of life.

Quantity of Life

In the 1960s and 1970s, Drs. Nedra Belloc and Lester Breslow of UCLA studied 6,928 adults in Alameda County, California. They discovered that people who adopted six or seven basic health habits lived seven (women) to eleven (men) years longer than those people who practiced three or less of these habits. Interestingly, these habits were not complicated. They were things your grandmother probably told you to do: (1) Get regular, moderate exercise; (2) eat breakfast every day; (3) have regular meals with no snacks in between; (4) maintain normal weight; (5) get seven to eight hours of sleep a night; (6) do not smoke; (7) drink alcohol in small amounts (one to two ounces a day) or not at all.[1]

This UCLA study was supported by research done in Wisconsin on 2,000 people and on the health-conscious Seventh Day Adventists, Amish and Mormons in the United States. These studies showed that healthy habits promote longevity.[2]

Studies conducted on other long-lived people in the United States and around the world also have demonstrated that regular exercise, an adequate but meager diet, no smoking, avoidance of alcohol, and a tranquil life all increase a person's lifespan. In other words, fitness, eating the right kinds of foods, keeping your weight under control, avoiding addictions and handling stress problems appropriately will increase your longevity.

You may be thinking, "What about the guy on my street who was overweight, ate fatty meals, smoked big black cigars, drank whiskey, and died at the age of 92?"

This person was an exception. He also probably would have lived even longer if he'd had a healthier lifestyle. The latest research suggests that we inherit our parents' (and their parents') potential for longevity.[3] But our circumstances and daily choices may chop months or years from those God has allotted to us. For example, your parents may have had the capacity to live to be 100. Most likely, their circumstances and habits caused or will cause them to die much earlier than that. In the same manner, you may have inherited the capability to live to be 100. Unfortunately, your living and working environments and your habits—many of which are learned from your parents—may allow you to live only to the age of 70 or 75.

The allotted number of years is an important concept. It explains differences in longevity despite dissimilar health behaviors. One person may be granted a possible lifespan of 100 years and another, 80. The potential 100-year-old may adopt an unhealthy lifestyle and die at the age of 81. The potential 80-year-old may follow so-called well behaviors and live to be 75. The unhealthy person lost one-fifth of his allotted years; the healthy person, one-sixteenth. The former is a travesty of a precious gift.

Some Christians have difficulty with the idea of people living longer by living healthier. They note that Jesus says worry cannot add one day to your life.[4] That is true, but what people fail to realize is that Jesus didn't say anything about cutting your life short. People can and do cut their lives short—by suicide. Some people choose a gun, others may unwittingly choose abusive and/or unhealthy lifestyles.

Quality of Life

But wellness is not necessarily longevity—adding years to your life (or living out your allotted life span). Wellness is, perhaps most importantly, adding life to your years. It can improve your vigor and enthusiasm for life. How many times have you come home from the office and, after working all day, you can't seem to do anything more? The kids want to play, but you're too tired. Your spouse wants to go shopping, but you want to sit. The zing is gone. Aging? Probably not. It's more likely a lack of fitness.

Picture wellness as a continuum. At the far left is a lack of fitness, energy and health. Someone has compared this "living" to being six feet under water—alive but just barely. At the far right is optimum health. You have an excitement and a joy for life. You may even have health problems, but you manage quite well and strive to improve whatever you have. You might be a four-minute-mile runner, an eight-minute-mile jogger, a twelve-minute-mile slogger or a twenty-minute-mile walker.

Most of us are somewhere between these two extremes. It doesn't matter where we are today, as long as we are (or start) working on our health.

This quality of life concept is important. Let's take the examples from the previous section. The person who reached 75 years based on a possible God-given 80 years undoubtedly had a life of vigor, energy and relatively good health. The 81-year-old who had the potential for 100 years probably was plagued with chronic bronchitis or emphysema from smoking, sluggish bowels from a poor diet, low back pain from obesity, headaches from unresolved stress, and a lack of energy because of poor fitness. So the abusive lifestyle cuts deep. It robs a person of longevity and *joie de vivre*.

I don't mean to imply that if you're fit you won't have health problems or disappointments or down periods. Most of us carry within us the microbes that cause influenza, tuberculosis, staph infections and other illnesses—including the common cold. When we get into a family or office argument, stay up late, eat poorly, or overdo work or some chemical, our resistance is lowered. When that happens repeatedly, these microbes can take hold. But improved health habits and well-being help you roll with the blows you receive in life, reduce your chances for or severity of disease, keep the microbes in check, and help you experience the wholeness promised in the New Testament.

Adding life to your years and years to your life without adding difficulty is the aim. This involves integrating concepts of well-being that are possible for all members of the family, without creating significant stress or distracting from your quality of life. The goal is for you and your family to see, apply and internalize the connection and interrelationship between physical well-being and your spiritual, mental and emotional well-being. Then you can maximize your God-given physical potential and learn how to grow physically whether you are a superb athlete, significantly ill, wheelchair bound, or Ms./Mr. Average.

Spiritual Reasons for Better Health

Adding life and years to you and yours is vital for several reasons.

First, God has given us the gift of life. It is our responsibility to maximize our potential for longevity and vitality for living.

Second, God honors us by allowing His Spirit to live within our bodies. It is therefore an overwhelming privilege and responsibility to improve our health and bodies.

Third, God wants us to know His fullness and to share Him with others. It is of paramount importance that we have the energy, desire and capacity to be all that God has in mind for us to be, no matter what the task—big or small.

Fourth, God wants us to be good stewards of the time, money and talents He graciously has given to us. Jesus said, "If you have not been trustworthy in handling worldly wealth, who will trust you with true riches?"[5] It is important that we improve our health. In this land of milk and honey, self-responsibility for our health would go a long way in reducing the $355 billion spent each year on health; the more than 130 million workdays we lose each year due to heart disease alone; the more than $200 billion lost on employee productivity due to illness; and the $25 billion lost on premature death, to say nothing of the heartache and pain that accompanies the death and disability.[6]

From a purely secular point of view, think how a 50 percent reduction in the $355 billion spent on health care each year in this country would affect our economic vitality. In ten years, our $1.6 trillion national debt would be eliminated. That's staggering, yet as Christians, the results of wellness are even more significant.

". . . so that now as always Christ will be exhalted in my body, whether by life or by death" (Philippians 1:20).

Chapter 3:
Technology—America's Modern-Day God?

". . . And God saw everything that he had
made, and, behold, it was very good" (Genesis 1:31).

The word "good" in the above verse sums up every creative action of God in
the story of creation. In fact, the "good" is repeated at least seven times in
Genesis 1. Yet it didn't take man long to relate to all things created and misuse
them to his own hurt and harm. Sadly, we continue to misuse and abuse God's
created gifts. With all our advancement in knowledge, technology and development of skills, we often turn the good into a nightmare of destruction. An example
of this is modern technology.

It is phenomenal how science, industrialization and modern technology have
transformed our 20th century living. We stand in awe of moonshots, nuclear
power, CAT scans, the eradication of smallpox, lasers, computer chips, cloning,
high-tech automobiles, 100-story buildings, microwaves and food technology. Our
doctors transplant organs, bone marrow and artificial hearts. Food is enhanced
with vitamins and minerals, and sweetened without the dangers or calories of
sugar. Even our exercise has become high-tech, with machines that count the
calories used, heart rates and blood pressures. Literally everything you touch has
been touched by high-tech.

But modern technology has a flip side. Our dependence and worshiping of
technology has caused things to run amok. The result is decreased fitness, es-
calated weight, polluted food, abused drugs and unrelenting stress.

Fitness and Weight

Industrialization—automobiles, suburbia and automation—help us enjoy life
more. Gardens and yards often are maintained by power mowers, tillers and cul-
tivators. Leaves are scooped up with power-driven vacuum cleaners. The house
is heated by gas or oil—no more chopping wood or shoveling coal. Clothing is
washed in automatic washers and dried in dryers, rather than by hand-scrubbing

11

and hanging it on the line. Rugs are vacuumed, replacing the annual spring ritual of beating the carpets. The list is endless. Modern technology has created a life-style of convenience. Most of us do little physical work, at home or on the job, supposedly increasing our energy and free time.

Sadly, our fitness and health slip with the easy life. Sixty-six percent of us do not get the minimum amount of exercise recommended by the President's Council on Physical Fitness and Sports. Thirty-nine percent of the American population reports that they do not get regular exercise at least once a month.[1] Unfortunately, our children mimic our behaviors. As they watch us sit and use labor-saving devices, they, too, get caught in a life of ease and low fitness. The die seems cast. Since World War II, each generation has done fewer physical things at home or on the job.

Consequently, about a third of us are carrying too much body fat.[2] For the average male, more than 20 percent of his weight is fat, and for the average female it is more than 30 percent. The ideal would be 15 percent for the male and 19 percent for the female. A study of Canadian women ages twenty to twenty-nine showed that over one-half were well below what was considered average fitness for their age group.[3] We can assume that United States women are the same.

This lack of fitness and too much body fat contribute to low back pain, fatigue, heart disease, cancer, diabetes, ulcers and obesity.

Food

The technology that makes us inactive also has altered our food, positively and negatively. The good news is that freezing and refrigeration permit us to enjoy a variety of foods year-round and to eat foods indigenous to one area of the world, such as kiwi fruit or garbanzo beans. Food additives increase shelf-life, help prevent botulism, and enhance the flavor of bland foods. Food technology can heighten the nutritive value of products and give us new foods, such as tofu, and egg and butter substitutes. At one time, supermarket shoppers had 3,000 or so choices of food products. Today they have 20,000 selections.

The bad news is that most of these 17,000 recent products are highly processed and high in sugar, white flour, saturated fat and salt. The packaging, storage and selection procedures have lowered the nutritional value of food. In the United States, where the problem is perhaps most advanced, health-oriented people have long objected to some of these procedures, but their arguments have been countered by industry claims that Americans are well-fed.

Solid scientific evidence indicates that this may not be the case. In 1971, Dr. Edith Weir of the U.S. Department of Agriculture declared that if all Americans ate just the recommended daily alllowances of nutrients recommended by the USDA—amounts now considered sub-optimal by many nutritionists—the result would be a dramatic improvement in at least nineteen major health problems and the saving of 500,000 lives a year. A slight shift in eating habits to less cholesterol, fat, sugar, salt and calories would result in:[4]

—1.2 million fewer cases of heart and vascular disease each year
—64,000 fewer cancer deaths, and 120,000 fewer cases of cancer each year
—49 million fewer cases of respiratory infection
—3 million fewer cases of birth defects
—3 million fewer cases of arthritis
—3 million fewer cases of osteoporosis (thinning of the bones)
—16,200 fewer cases of blindness
—3 million fewer cases of allergies
—2.5 million fewer mental health problems requiring hospitalization

The United States' food supply is also seriously jeopardized by pollutants. One government survey disclosed that 14 percent of the meat and poultry examined contained illegal and potentially harmful residues, many of which came from acid rain, pesticides, herbicides, fertilizer run-off and toxins from landfills.

Other pollutants in our food include the lead passed into it from canned goods, which constitute 20 percent of the American food supply. New lab studies suggest that the lead content in tuna and other foods in lead-soldered tins may be a thousand times greater than the non-canned samples. This lead poses a major health threat.[5]

Then there are the thousands of little-tested food additives that each of us consumes at a rate of three to six pounds a year. As microbiologist Michael F. Jacobsen, of the Center of Health Science in the Public Interest, has noted, "The list of ingredients on food labels read like the index of a chemistry textbook."[6]

The biggest fear is that all these pollutants and additives increase you and your family's chances of developing cancer, respiratory problems, cirrhosis, allergies, auto-immune disease, head pain and fatigue.

Drugs

Technology has allowed us to do amazing things with drugs. Drugs arrest cancer, control diabetes and regulate heart rates. Medications hold back virulent infections and keep age-old plagues in check. Mental disorders are controlled with pharmacology.

With all these benefits, it is no wonder that we have developed casual attitudes toward drugs. Of course, we worry about our children being addicted to the "life robbers" of cocaine, marijuana and speed. So we try to give them all the facts on their dangers. We strongly preach against their usage.

We send mixed messages to our children, however, by using drugs ourselves. The average non-hospitalized, "healthy" American adult is estimated to take three to four different drugs a day, either by prescription or self-medication. Former Surgeon General Julius B. Richmond reports that about 24 million Americans take either prescription or over-the-counter medications to induce sleep.[7]

An estimated 100,000 to 200,000 non-prescription drugs cram the shelves of our drugstores and supermarkets. The FDA has tested relatively few of these drugs and has found only 50 percent to be safe and effective. Yet Americans can't seem to get enough of them, and are said by experts to be caught up in "an orgy of self-medication."[8]

Prescription drugs also are abused by doctors and patients. Medical maverick, Robert S. Mendelsohn, M.D., flatly states that doctor-prescribed drugs kill more people than illegal street drugs. He cites a national survey of medical examiners, which revealed that prescription drugs such as valium and barbiturates cause 23 percent of drug abuse deaths. He says another 20,000 to 30,000 Americans die each year from adverse reactions to drugs prescribed by their doctors.[9]

It is sad that more than 35,000 prescription drugs are available in the United States. Every twenty-four to thirty-six hours, 50 to 80 percent of Americans take one of these prescribed chemicals.[10]

Yet most drugs, over-the-counter and prescribed, are ineffective. They mask the symptoms and fail to treat the cause. Fully 80 percent of all our ailments can be treated with methods other than drugs. In other words, we usually depend upon a pill to solve ailments that will go away with or without medication. Our God-given immunity system coupled with other appropriate health measures will help us overcome most ailments. Or we can prevent the diseases by adopting a healthier lifestyle.

No wonder our admonitions to our children not to do drugs fall on deaf ears. They are rejecting a value system that condemns one form of drug usage and accepts another.

Stress

At the start of this chapter, I highlighted the changes that science and technology have brought to the American way of life in the past 100 years. We have first-class entertainment, incredible communication, convenient travel and luxurious living. Curiously, this same technology has created unbelievable stress for most of us. We compete for jobs and agonize over shortages (food and fuel) and sky-rocketing prices. We must cope with noise, traffic jams, polluted air and water, industrialization and other headaches of a technological society. Moreover, our private lives are becoming increasingly unstable. The family composed of a husband, wife and a few children, which was once the norm of industrial society, now is breaking down. In 1982, one of every four Americans lived alone, and an estimated two-thirds to three-fourths of our population no longer fit within the traditional pattern of family life.[11]

By 1990 there will be greater changes, according to a report prepared by the Joint Center for Urban Studies of Massachusetts Institute of Technology and Harvard. Among its findings:[12]

—14% of the husband/wife households will have only one working spouse (Compared to 43% in 1960).

—Wives will contribute about 40% of the family income (compared to 25% in 1980).

—At least thirteen separate types of households will eclipse the conventional family, labeled with terms such as "female head"; "widowed with children"; "male head, previously married with children."

—More than one-third of the couples first married in the 1970s will be divorced.

—More than one-third of the children born in the 1970s will have spent part of their childhood living with a single parent (the emotional and financial consequences of this trend will be huge).

Corporations have imposed extraordinary stresses on their workers. These stresses contribute to the break-up of families, decreased worker productivity, feelings of poor self-worth, and destruction of personal health.

Regrettably, we have taken this stress home. Our children are stressed. Over half feel it. Many react violently with drugs, alcohol, hostile behavior and suicide.

The industrial revolution, which has heightened our interdependence, drives directly against our God-given ability to survive a host of diseases. Stress overloads our nervous and endocrine systems, which in turn overload our bodies. In time, our bodies cannot handle the pressure, and we reach a breaking point. Everything from heart disease to cancer to the common cold has been attributed to excessive stress or our inability to handle it properly.

The Question: "How?"

How did all of this happen? To answer that question we must go back to the beginning of the sixteenth century. At that time, the Western world started to move from a conservative, feudal system of government and work to the liberal ethic of democracy and/or socialism and economic self-determinism. Fueled by the Reformation and the Renaissance, a philosophy of hard work matured. You worked hard to show God's goodness and grace to you. This philosophy of industriousness became deeply embedded in the fabric of society. Hard work and godliness became almost synonyms, even to the secular world.

This attitude, along with an opportunity for a person to have his own place in the new world, a feeling that the resources of this planet were infinite, and an expanding world economy, caused the industrialization of society to take hold. Yet, survival was pretty basic—the people's needs were food, water and shelter.

Late in the nineteenth century, the phenomena of industrialization gained a secure foothold. Then early in this century Henry Ford built his assembly line and paid his employees five dollars a day, thus helping to create a middle class that would buy his assembly line built Model Ts and As. As expected, other corporations soon followed suit. Then the revolution was on. The middle class became a dominant force in American and Western society. This large segment of the population had money and more free time. People wanted more than food, water and shelter. They started to search for higher human needs.

During this time, the smokestack industries flourished. Some historians call the period of 1950 to 1973 the Golden Age of Industrialization. These twenty-three years were the longest sustained period of prosperity, work and productivity. Goods became cheaper and cheaper, because salaries continued to rise faster than prices. Things looked rosy. There was plenty for everyone. With hard work and a little luck, you attained the American dream. Each generation planned for their children to have the better life. More opportunities. More education. More money. This was a time, as Daniel Yankelovich says, of finite choices and infinite resources. The finite choices were:[13]

—Converse basketball shoes
—Meat and potato sports—football, basketball, and baseball
—The Big 3 auto companies—low-priced, mid-priced and high-priced cars in grey, black, maybe white
—Chocolate, vanilla and strawberry ice cream
—CBS, ABC and NBC television or radio
—Life, Look, and Post magazines
—Gray sweatsuits
—Sports for males only in high school and college

The infinite resources were:

—Cheap oil and gas and enough for everyone
—Enough coal to last five hundred years or more
—Nuclear energy is just around the corner, and it will be cheap
—Plenty of wood from our boundless supply of forests—minerals galore
—A new country where the air was clean, water pure and the land undeveloped
—A country that was number one in resources, wealth and strength—we had an industrial base second to none

Throughout this era of expansion, optimism and infinite resources, something else happened. People dropped God. They no longer worked to demonstrate God's grace and goodness. They did not work to glorify God. People worked to get to the top of the heap, reach the American dream and fulfill their desire to have the "finer things in life" for themselves. Work became a means to have a chicken in every pot, and peace and prosperity. Americans wanted an opportunity to have their gold at the end of the rainbow. They wanted the cars of Hollywood, the residential homes of Westchester County, the leisure of Maui and the independence of the Rockefellers. They worshiped the "good life," not God.

Upon achieving these goals, people continued to want more, more and still more. Their primary concern was finances. Several years ago, the Wall Street Journal reported that, according to studies, executives who made $200,000 a year or more worried most about their incomes and meeting monthly bills. Materialism became God. Yet one thing did not really change—the work ethic.

Today, we all know people who are workaholics, well-ordered, disciplined and very busy. When we ask why they are that way, most say "I don't know." They don't know because the work ethic that grew out of the Reformation has been woven into the fabric of our society. It's almost as if our drive to work and be successful has been encoded in our genes. We are afraid of idle time. We always must be doing something—working, playing, reading, watching television, listening to music. Work and material benefits have become our gods.

Our passion for material goods and technology has contributed to turning our world upside down. Instead of the finite choices and infinite resources of the first half of the century, we now have infinite choices and finite resources. A few infinite choices are:[14]

—More than 50 athletic shoe companies and infinite styles

—Wrestling, running, aerobics, fencing, sailing, water skiing, wind surfing, running and cross-country skiing are a few of our new favorite sports

—More than 75 different models of cars and trucks, plus an infinite variety of colors and pricetags from $5,995 to more than $250,000 are available

—More than 100 kinds of ice cream, including licorice, rainbow, and Oreo cookie

—In addition to network television, 5,000 cable companies with as many as 100 different channels

—The demise of general magazines and upsurge of specialty magazines on running, boating, outdoors and cooking

—Running suits of every color; velour jogging suits; Gore-Tex® suits that breathe

—Sports for male and female—from 6 to 106

All our technology, our passion for work, material goods, plus the opening of other countries to the twentieth century lifestyle have pushed the world's resources almost to the point of exhaustion. At least we know that they are finite:[15]

—Oil and gas are in jeopardy of being depleted in thirty to fifty years. Prices have skyrocketed.

—We are running out of coal.

—Nuclear energy may not be an alternative. If it is, it won't be cheap.

—We are running out of wood and minerals.
—We are polluting our air.
—We have fouled our waters.
—We have raped our land.
—We have lost much of our industrial lead to other countries.

This passion for work, technology and material goods also has ruined our health. It has made us fatter and less fit. We have created an array of unhealthy foods and have been driven to use alcohol, drugs, caffeine and tobacco in order to cope. We are stressed. We have created a Catch-22 syndrome. More technology means less health, which means more technology, which means . . . so the circle whirls and widens.

Worship of Creation

In short, we came to worship the creation rather than the Creator. We worship the false gods of work, technology and industrialization. They do god-like things—they heal the diseased, feed the hungry, provide warmth and shelter, save lives and give freedom. It all sounds so good. We are solving so many problems. But, like all false gods, they take us down a primrose path. For each new problem solved, we give ourselves two more. For example, food technology has found methods of preventing botulism with sodium nitrate. But the compound sodium nitrate causes high blood pressure (sodium) in salt-sensitive people and the nitrates combine with our digestive system to form nistrosamines, which are cancer producing.

We have managed to misuse and abuse God's gifts to us. Our love for the good life, rich food and fast-lane living has overwhelmed our bodies. We are overloaded with too much of a good thing. We are beset with self-inflicted plagues that grip our hearts, livers, brains, kidneys, lungs, bowels and backs. Look at these tragic facts:[16]

Ten Modern Plagues
   —1 of 2 will die of heart disease
   —1 of 4 will die of cancer
   —1 of 20 have diabetes
   —1 of 5 have upper respiratory problems such as emphysema, asthma, chronic
     bronchitis
   —1 of 20 have cirrhosis
   —1 of 4 have allergies or autoimmune disease
   —1 of 2 have ulcers, colitis or irritable bowel syndrome
   —9 of 10 suffer from low back, neck or head pain
   —3.5 of 10 are obese
   —8 of 10 suffer from emotional fatigue

To overcome this tragedy, we must get back to basics. First, we must drop the false gods of work, industrialization and technology. We must stop worshiping them. Industrialization extracts a heavy toll. It promises the good life only to deliver modern diseases that rob us of joys, opportunities and our potential. We must get our spiritual lives in order and worship the Creator. The sooner we do that, the sooner our children will see the futility of worshiping science and high-tech. They will see that God provides solutions to humans' problems. This change in attitude will give us and our children a fighting chance against these dreaded diseases.

Second, we must change our ways of living. I'm not asking you to change a society that has developed over the past five hundred years. Instead, I want you to recognize that we must exercise more, eat healthier, lose body fat, and control our addictions and stress. These five things will help get our physical lives in order. They will help family members feel better, live longer, get along better, have more zing in their lives, and most importantly be able to be and do more for the Lord and others.

"Be very careful, then, how you live—not as unwise but as wise, making the most of every opportunity" (Ephesians 5:15, 16a).

Chapter 4:
How Well Is Your Family?

"And he said unto them, Is he well? And they said, He is well: and, behold, Rachel his daughter cometh with the sheep" (Genesis 29:6, KJV).

When Jacob was traveling, after his dream, he came to a watering place. There he met some shepherds with their sheep. Jacob asked them, "Do you know Laban, the son of Nahor?"

Their reply was very encouraging. "Of course we know him."

"Well, how is he?" Jacob asked.

"He is well and prosperous," the shepherds answered.

The story of this meeting in Genesis 29 unfolds a tale of important relationships and positive change in Jacob's life.

Today, as you and I come together on the pages of this chapter, I ask, "How well is your family?"

I ask because I am concerned about the well-being of you and yours. I would like to offer a few suggestions and strategies, which, if followed, will help you and your family achieve a greater degree of wellness (especially physical wellness).

I refer to *you,* since you are reading this book, and because someone must take the lead in achieving family well-being. Our experiences with motivating children clearly show that if parents are committed to and have formulated a healthy wellness philosophy, their children are more apt to do the same. So *you* will be asked to do many things. You will learn about good fitness, food and stress management. Then you will be able to apply the information and strategies to your family.

Moving into Action

To be healthy and to maximize your family's and your own physical potential, you must make a personal decision to improve family health. No one on earth can move you to action. To paraphrase the old adage, I can lead you to water, but you must decide to drink it. Improving your health is your responsibility. Once you understand that, you can take action.

First, you must take stock of how you're doing. That's what this chapter is all about—showing you areas of need and ways to improve your family's health. A checklist and some guidelines will help you pinpoint problems, know what concerns you the most, and develop a plan of action.

Avoid Making Many Changes at Once

Avoid the pitfall of trying to change all your behaviors at once. People who try to give up smoking and coffee at the same time, and then start exercising as well, usually are not successful. It's best to do one thing and do it well. When you've experienced success and feel good about that area, then move on to another area of concern. There is nothing like success to bring more success.

In Spring Arbor, Michigan, where I live, one family used to start each new year with a grand resolution to improve their health. They planned to exercise (walk) five times a week, thirty minutes at a crack. Desserts were given up (except for once a week). Mom and Dad promised to cut down on coffee, if the kids would not drink cola. Television was to be watched only one hour a day. Mom promised not to talk on the phone more than twenty minutes a day, and Dad vowed to lose twenty pounds.

The family did great for ten days to two weeks. Then things started to fall apart. It snowed and got icy outside, so walking was difficult. Dad enjoyed that morning cup of coffee, and the son had a cola after school. Television was watched for four to six hours on Super Bowl Sunday. Soon they realized that dieting was no fun. Slowly, the old habits crept back, and by February 1, everyone was back doing their old thing.

In 1984, I convinced this family to pick one area to work on. They chose "no more than an hour of television a day." That was manageable and agreeable to all. There were some slip-ups, but the family started to win the battle of television time. After three months, the father told me that he was convinced the family had beaten the television. They felt they had freed up some time.

For April, they sponsored a family fitness contest called "The Body Beautiful." Four times a week, each family member exercised for thirty minutes. The father and mother chose to walk, the daughter selected aerobics, and the son started to run and lift weights. As their fitness improved, they added "no-sugar days" to their family commitments. This year (1985), coffee and cola were confined to once-a-day beverages, rather than the normal three to five times a day. As I write this book, they're thinking about a "new behavior." One member suggested: "Let's all eat breakfast together four times a week."

This approach is logical and successful. Trying to do everything at once is counter-productive. It's like trying to learn several new languages at one time.

You Never Graduate

Another important point is that you never graduate from the school of health and well-being. It is a lifelong, evolving process, and dynamic as well. You make commitments, evaluate changes, and then decide to keep, change or modify as you experience new healthful techniques.

Here is a summary of my family's commitment to building better physical health, with an emphasis on some of my personal decisions.

Age	Health Stage
21	Married.
22	Debbie born.
	Cut back on salting my food.
23	John born.
27	Reduced personal sugar consumption.
	Thomas born.
29	Reduced children's salt intake.
	Reduced saturated fat/cholesterol in my diet.
	Started taking vitamins.
	Rebecca born.
31	Increased my distance running to four to five miles a day (five days a week).
32	Developed and practiced neuromuscular relaxation techniques.
	First wife died.
	Had children reduce their saturated fat/cholesterol intake.
33	Personally decided not to use medicine of any type.
34	Remarried.
	Increased long-distance mileage to six miles (five to six days a week).
	Set up reward system for children to exercise.
	Reduced children's sugar intake.
	Cut way back on processed foods.
35	Supplemented family diet with vitamins.
36	Took the television out of the house.
37	Dropped neuromuscular techniques and picked up relaxation response and body-scanning techniques.
	Cut back on red meat consumption for all family members.
38	Decided to use medicine for allergies.
39	Started mineral supplementation for family and personal use.
	Flirted with vegetarianism.
40	Brought television back into the house.
	Returned to eating meat one to two days each week.
41	Gave up fruit during ragweed season to reduce allergies.

42   Two daughters highly allergic, so rotational diets established for them.
44   Created a family fitness room in the basement.

As you see, we made health changes when we were ready. Also, we sometimes made changes when we re-evaluated previous decisions. For example, I went off all medication, yet my allergies plagued me, so I resorted to over-the-counter medication to help me through extremely difficult times. I also discovered that cutting back on fruit during the ragweed season helped me tremendously, so much so that one season I didn't take any medication. The television was taken out of the house for a period of at least three years. We brought it back in because some family members like to watch certain shows (besides, the children lobbied for it).

The point is, building personal health is not something you do overnight. It's a maturation process. Making changes is a dynamic and lifelong process, one that can go in any direction. You gradually understand or realize what does and does not work for you. My personal changes and those of the family came slowly; yours must too. Don't try to do everything at once. It won't work.

As our children reach adulthood, they are adopting certain habits themselves. Some are similar to ours. They have rejected others that we established. But, no matter. They are experimenting for themselves and trying to do the healthy things that work best for them.

The Checklist

Table 1 has five checklists, one for each of the five areas of well-being that I have talked about—fitness, food, weight, addictions and stress. These will help you define the area of health that you or members of your family should work on. It gives you an idea of where you are in terms of wellness. It can tell you what you should work on, where you can expect the greatest success, and where you then can move on to. I wish I had seen one of these lists when I started on the road to well-being. It would have kept me from going down many blind alleys.

Once you've identified your major area of concern, you can help your children and spouse do likewise. Have them take the test. You will need to read and/or answer the questions for children under nine or ten years of age.

To get started, look over Table 1. After each entry, you'll find six statements. Read each one carefully, and circle the number on the left that best describes your level of achievement. Be truthful, but fair. Then check the box on the right that indicates your level of satisfaction. Are you pleased with your level of achievement, or do you think you need to improve? Again, be honest. If you scored poorly in a given area, yet you are really satisfied to stay at that level, admit it. Remember, this is only for you and your family. No one has to know what you think of yourself except you.

TABLE 1

Enjoying Exercise (Fitness)

Level of Achievement	Level of Satisfaction		

Low High		OK	*Needs Improvement*	*Could be Improved but Not a Concern at This Time*
1 2 3 4 5	a. I bike, swim, run or walk for at least 30 minutes, three or mores times a week.	☐	☐	☐
1 2 3 4 5	b. Whenever possible, I walk or ride a bike instead of using cars, elevators, escalators.	☐	☐	☐
1 2 3 4 5	c. I do some form of stretching several times per week.	☐	☐	☐
1 2 3 4 5	d. I work on muscle fitness three times a week.	☐	☐	☐
1 2 3 4 5	e. It is fun for me to be physically active.	☐	☐	☐
1 2 3 4 5	f. I try to learn one new sport every two years.	☐	☐	☐

Eating Well (Food)

Level of Achievement	Level of Satisfaction		

Low High		OK	*Needs Improvement*	*Could be Improved but Not a Concern at This Time*
1 2 3 4 5	a. I eat a balanced diet and enjoy a variety of fresh, natural foods.	☐	☐	☐
1 2 3 4 5	b. I try to eat foods with little added sugar, salt, and/or saturated fat.	☐	☐	☐
1 2 3 4 5	c. I take time to relax and enjoy my meals. I also eat my food in one location (at a table).	☐	☐	☐
1 2 3 4 5	d. I consume very little coffee, colas, or other foods high in caffeine.	☐	☐	☐
1 2 3 4 5	e. I eat three well-balanced meals a day—breakfast, lunch and dinner.	☐	☐	☐
1 2 3 4 5	f. I do not eat in fast food restaurants more than one to two times a month. When I do, I'm careful to select the most healthful foods.	☐	☐	☐

TABLE 1 — Continued

Staying Slim (Weight)

Level of Achievement			Level of Satisfaction		
					Could be Improved but
				Needs	Not a Concern
Low	High		OK	Improvement	at This Time
1 2 3 4 5	a. I bike, swim, run or walk for at least thirty minutes, three or more times a week.		☐	☐	☐
1 2 3 4 5	b. I eat foods high in nutrients and low in calories three times a day.		☐	☐	☐
1 2 3 4 5	c. I don't eat when I'm bored or under pressure.		☐	☐	☐
1 2 3 4 5	d. I cannot pinch more than an inch of fat on my body.		☐	☐	☐
1 2 3 4 5	e. I am satified with the way my body looks.		☐	☐	☐
1 2 3 4 5	f. I do not worship my body by attempting to be excessively slim or exceptionally well-built.		☐	☐	☐

Taking Care of Yourself (Addictions)

Level of Achievement			Level of Satisfaction		
					Could be Improved but
				Needs	Not a Concern
Low	High		OK	Improvement	at This Time
1 2 3 4 5	a. I don't smoke cigarettes, cigars, pipes or pot.		☐	☐	☐
1 2 3 4 5	b. I drink one to two ounces of alcohol or less daily.		☐	☐	☐
1 2 3 4 5	c. I rarely (not more than once a month) take self-prescribed medicine—over-the-counter-drugs, i.e., aspirin or aspirin type products, hay fever medication, etc.		☐	☐	☐
1 2 3 4 5	d. I do not need colas, coffee or caffeine to get my day going or give me a lift during the day.		☐	☐	☐
1 2 3 4 5	e. I am not addicted to work or television. I need not watch a certain soap opera; I need not get to work at a certain time to keep my day from falling apart.		☐	☐	☐
1 2 3 4 5	f. I am not addicted to exercise, i.e., running. If I miss a day or two of exercise, I am not easily upset.		☐	☐	☐

TABLE 1 — Continued

Enjoying Life (Stress)

Level of Achievement						Level of Satisfaction		
Low				High		OK	Needs Improvement	Could be Improved but Not a Concern at This Time
1 2 3 4 5					a. I like to find time to be quiet and relax.	☐	☐	☐
1 2 3 4 5					b. I do not feel hurried or pressured during most of my day.	☐	☐	☐
1 2 3 4 5					c. I can accept my feelings, such as being mad, sad, glad and frightened.	☐	☐	☐
1 2 3 4 5					d. I am often happy, and I find it easy to laugh.	☐	☐	☐
1 2 3 4 5					e. When I make mistakes, I admit them and learn from them.	☐	☐	☐
1 2 3 4 5					f. I can tell when I am reacting to stress, and I have a plan for reducing that stress.	☐	☐	☐

Now go over your responses on the right and pinpoint those areas where you feel you need improvement. That's where you need to start in your quest for a healthier life. Just remember, you can't attack everything at once. Pick one and go from there. (Tables 1 and 2 may be photocopied for your personal use.)

Planning for Better Health

After you complete this checklist, have the other members of your family do the same. First, however, discuss with your spouse the questions on Table 2 on the next page.

If you checked all ten as YES, congratulations! Wherever there is a NO, you and your spouse need to look at techniques to improve your responses.

In addition to these questions, ask each other, "Are we willing, with God's help, to do what it takes to improve our family's health? Are we willing to affirm each other's efforts and those of our children?" If the answer is no, close this book now. If it is yes, read on.

Admit Your Problem

This is perhaps one of the most difficult steps in any plan of action. It's also the most necessary. Unless you admit that you or your family have a problem, you never will solve it. Tables 1 and 2 are good places to start. They help you see those areas in which you think you have a problem. The right-hand column of Table 1, labeled "Level of Satisfaction," is the most important part of that survey.

TABLE 2
Family Wellness Checklist

	Circle One
As parents, we actively, constructively and consistently:	
a. Engage in and provide opportunities for our family to get regular physical exercise.	YES NO
b. Engage in and provide opportunities for our family to walk or ride bikes, rather than use motorized vehicles.	YES NO
c. Provide nutritious meals that are low in salt, fat, cholesterol and sugar.	YES NO
d. Provide snacks that are healthy and nutritious, i.e., fruit, vegetables, fruit juices, whole grain breads, etc.	YES NO
e. Reinforce positive pictures of the children's bodies and avoid put-downs such as, "You're fat" or "You've put weight on lately, haven't you?"	YES NO
f. Support our spouse's or children's attempts to control their weight through proper exercise and appropriate eating habits.	YES NO
g. Discourage smoking, abuse of alcohol and drugs (legal included), overwork, caffeine, candy, and overuse of television. This is done without nagging.	YES NO
h. Support our spouse's or children's attempts to cut down or eliminate use of items mentioned in item *g* by affirming their efforts and personhood.	YES NO
i. Eliminate unnecessary stressors on children and each other. We do not unnecessarily dump our stress on other members.	YES NO
j. Provide opportunities for family members to relax and enjoy each other and provide strategies to teach them how to do these things.	YES NO

You may score yourself rather low in the area of food selection, but as far as you're concerned, that's fine. You see no reason for improvement. You must *admit* that you weigh too much, eat poorly, don't exercise enough, are over-stressed, or whatever, before you can successfully correct any of these areas. Once you can admit a problem comfortably, you're ready for the next step.

Decide to Change

It's one thing to admit your problem, it's another thing to decide to do something about it. How many times have you heard one of your smoking friends declare, "One of these days I've got to quit smoking"? That's also a common attitude about improving health. You may know you need help in some areas. Now you need to consciously decide to do something about your health.

Take Stock of Your Condition

The survey gave you a general idea of what areas may contribute to your lack of energy, health and excitement for life. Once you admit that a certain area presents a problem to you and decide to do something about it, you need to be specific. For example, let's say you are not satisfied with your eating patterns and you decide to change the way you eat. You select item c under "Eating Well" as an area that needs improvement because you do not take time to relax and enjoy your meals. You eat your food on the run or in front of the television.

Taking stock of that problem involves a closer look at mealtime. Why don't you take the time to relax and enjoy meals? What causes you to hurry? How much time is actually spent at the table? What sort of activities are taking place while you are eating? Answering these questions will help you pinpoint why this is a problem. The key to this step is determining how it developed into a problem. Once you see the causes, you can devise ways to minimize it.

Now you're ready. Read each of the following chapters. Don't skim over any unless you now know exactly what you want to change in your life. If you know, go to the section that deals with that area. After you've completed reading this book, answer the questions in Tables 1 and 2 again. New information may have changed your opinion about what area you need to emphasize. After re-evaluating carefully read the pertinent chapters again. Then review chapter 15—Managing Time, Setting Goals and Getting Started—and get going. When you achieve a desirable level, move to a new area of concern.

On the following pages, you will find the theory and strategies to improve your personal and family health in five areas—fitness, food, weight, addictions and stress.

Chapters 5 and 6 cover the "why" and "how" of physical fitness.

Chapters 7 and 8 discuss how and why your family should eat better.

Chapters 9 and 10 highlight the problem of weight control.

Chapters 11 and 12 provide information on addictions and what to do about them.

Chapters 13 and 14 discuss stress and its implications for your family's pattern of living and health.

At the end of each section, you will find a series of family strategies to improve your family's fitness and eating, and help control your weight, addictions and stress. These strategies are designed to make health fun, achievable, effective and family-oriented.

Family Cooperation

It's much better if everyone is pushing for a common goal. That is, all are attempting to eat better, lose weight or exercise more. If the husband goes off in one direction, the wife in another and the children in a third, things can get a little rough. That is especially true if the children are teenagers. If they are under ten, Mom and Dad pretty well control their habits. If you serve bean sprouts and artichokes, the younger kids may squawk, but they will tend to go along. With teenagers, things can get pretty tricky.

Personally, I find it easiest to start off with a new habit myself, or my wife, Beth, will initiate the idea. We'll talk about it and see if the other wants to go along. Then we will try it for a period of time. After observing us, some of the children decide to participate, without direct encouragement. Other times, they need to be coaxed.

Sometimes family members never join in on an activity, however, and you need to respect their right to pass. Forcing your child to run three miles will be as effective in the long run as my forcing you to run three miles against your will. Personal example, excitement for a habit, reward for involvement, the majority of the family participating, and making health habits fun are better motivators than nagging.

> "Let us consider how we may spur one another on toward love and good deeds . . . let us encourage one another" (Hebrews 10:24,25).

Chapter 5:
Fit For Life

"I praise you because I am fearfully and wonderfully made; your works are wonderful"
(Psalms 139:14).

Your body is magnificent! Regardless of whether you are muscular or obese, well
or sick, strong or weak, your body allows you to do many things for enjoyment,
pleasure and work. You most likely can use your legs to run, walk, jump and
swim. You can use your arms to climb mountains, carry boxes and answer tele-
phones. Your fingers and eyes work in such close harmony that you can thread
the tiniest needle, draw the most beautiful picture, or bat a baseball traveling
ninety miles per hour. You, or someday your child, may use legs to run a marathon, fingers and eyes to perform microsurgery, or arms to build a mission hospital in Haiti.

The human mind can comprehend complex thoughts, explore difficult philo-
sophies and speak eloquent thoughts. Humans, because of their physical and mental prowess, have subdued the earth, changed its face considerably since its
creation, and built magnificent, although many times tragic, civilizations. David
was right. We are fearfully and wonderfully made.

In earlier times, humans lived by their strength and endurance alone. Every
daily task required the vigorous and dynamic use of their bodies. Survival meant
being able to run fast and long if attacked. Muscle, tendon, bone and nerve were
needed to lift, carry, till, strike and hold. Endurance, strength and fitness were
necessary for survival.

I will be the first to admit that the Bible says little about physical exercise,
other than Paul's recommendation to Timothy, ". . . physical training is of some
value, but godliness has value for all things, holding promise for both the present
life and the life to come."[1]

Paul used several illustrations of athletes to drive home points, but the necessity
of exercise is not mentioned in the Bible. Why not? Because there was little need
for deliberate exercise two thousand years ago. People were fit because of the
demands of working, walking and existing. Consider these examples: Moses, at
120 years of age, climbed Pisgah Peak in Mount Nebo.[2] Elijah ran about twenty

miles, then fled another ninety. He finally left his servant and went into the wilderness, traveling all day.[3] Jesus was a carpenter in His younger days, an extremely demanding occupation when power tools did not exist. Jesus also walked fifty miles to Tyre and Sidon.[4] His entire ministry involved extensive walking, much over difficult terrain. The two disciples walked seven miles to Emmaus, ate supper and hurried back (was this a fast jog?) to Jerusalem that same night.[5] Mary ran to Jerusalem from outside the city, a trip of one to two miles.[6] The herculean feats of Samson and David delight young and old alike. What about John the Baptist? He apparently was a rugged, outdoor person, strong of limb and spirit. Consider Peter's occupation—fisherman. A hard, demanding job.

But in the years since Peter, things have changed. We use tools and machines, or some other form of energy, to do most of our work. We survive with our wits. We have shifted from brawn to brain. In the past thirty years, the industrial/technological revolution has accelerated. The automobile is king. Most people live in suburbia. Shopping centers abound. Interstate highways connect cities. Walking is abandoned. Ranch homes are convenient—too convenient. We no longer need to use our legs, arms or backs.

As I explained in chapter 3, our "automatic this" and "power that" have made us physically unfit. We no longer need to move our bodies. Modern technology has created a lifestyle in which the majority of people do not have to do much physical work at home, on the job or in their recreation.

These changes affect children as well. We think that kids are full of enthusiasm, vitality, energy and "vinegar." You wouldn't think they'd need fitness programs. But our research on 24,000 children in Jackson County, Michigan, suggests that they are not as fit or active as you might think. Their profile is very similar to their parents'.[7]

> —96% of the 7- to 12-year-old child's time is spent doing sedentary or mild activities.
> —Only 10 minutes of a child's day is devoted to appropriate levels of exercise.
> —The average child carries too much fat—20% for boys, 23% for girls (12% or so is desirable).

Other studies on children have shown that:[8]
> —The children of the 1980s are fatter than the children of the 1960s.
> —United States children are less fit than children in the less-developed countries of the world.

Benefits of Exercise

Since we don't struggle physically for our survival, as we did a few generations ago, we have no outlet for the natural physical tensions that build up inside us. Tensions, left unchecked, ultimately affect our muscles, nerves, stomachs, hearts and brains. As a result, we lose our vitality. We are tired before the end of the day. Our waistlines sag, our hips spread and we suffer heart attacks while shoveling snow. We are short of breath after two flights of stairs. We are uptight and nervous. We are fearful, and we wonder if our mysterious ache or pain is a foreboding of some serious disease. We are not physically fit.

What is physical fitness? It is the capacity of your body to meet the demands of your day (or any unexpected emergencies) without undue fatigue. The demands might include shoveling snow for thirty minutes, climbing thirty flights of stairs, putting shrubbery in the yard, or playing basketball with the kids.

To meet these demands without fear of overexertion, you must develop four major components of physical fitness: cardiovascular endurance, proper body composition/weight ratio, muscle fitness and flexibility.

Cardiovascular Endurance

Cardiovascular endurance is the fitness of your heart, blood, blood vessels and lungs. A high level of cardiovascular endurance means that your body can transport and use oxygen efficiently.

Improving your cardiovascular endurance definitely will improve your stamina and energy level. In fact, without a good level of cardiovascular endurance, you

---

Plague #1

Heart Disease

The major killer and crippler in the United States is heart disease. Almost 50 percent of all Americans die of heart attacks, strokes and kidney failure. Many are stricken in the prime of life (thirty-five to fifty-five years of age. The 50 percent who survive the first heart attack have a life expectancy of five to seven years.[12] Often these are years of disability, marred by reduced productivity and curtailed activities.

Heart disease takes many forms. Degenerative coronary artery disease is the most insidious. It is a degeneration of the heart's blood vessels, caused by a build-up of fats on their lining. The build-up, if uncontrolled for a period of time, eventually will block blood circulation with the formation of a clot, called a thrombosis. If the blood vessel is completely blocked, the tissue around it dies.

This blockage may occur anywhere in the body. In the heart it is called a heart attack; in the brain, a stroke; in the kidney it is called kidney failure.

Modern science is making long strides in treating heart disease, but the key is in preventing or slowing the disease. Heart disease appears to be caused by our lifestyle. At least 50 percent of all heart attacks and strokes could be prevented by:[13]

• stopping smoking
• reducing elevated blood pressure
• reducing blood fats (blood cholesterol)
• modifying the diet (reduction in cholesterol, saturated fat, salt and sugar consumption)
• increasing physical fitness
• reducing weight and body fat
• dealing positively with stress

almost always will feel below par, too tired to do family chores or be involved in family fun.

Good cardiovascular endurance seems to play a role in reducing your risk of heart disease, as well. In 1976, Dr. Kenneth H. Cooper and some of his associates presented research that compared cardiovascular risk factors and fitness levels of 3,000 men who had come to the Cooper Clinic between 1971 and 1974. The study results showed striking consistencies. Men who were in very poor and poor condition showed uniformly poor results. Predictably, their cholesterol, triglyceride, glucose, uric acid, systolic and diastolic pressures and body fat values were substantially poorer than the men who had good to excellent cardiovascular endurance.[9]

Intrigued by Dr. Cooper's research, we did a similar study with children ages seven to twelve. Our results were almost identical. As the children's cardiovascular endurance levels increased, their cardiovascular risk factors decreased significantly. The risk factors most affected were HDLs (a type of cholesterol), HDL/TOT-C (the ratio of cholesterol to HDLs), triglycerides, skinfolds, systolic and diastolic blood pressures (see Table 3).

TABLE 3
Physical Fitness of Children Compared to Heart Disease Risk Factors

Physical Fitness Level	Risk Factors					
	HDL	HDL/TOT-C	Triglycerides	Skinfolds	Blood Pressures	
					Systolic	Diastolic
Very Poor	38	18	122	125	121	86
Poor	45	24	86	81	106	65
Average	49	26	77	46	99	65
Good	50	27	72	36	95	60
Excellent	50	30	74	33	92	62

NOTE:
For HDLs and HDL/TOT-C, higher scores are better.
For triglycerides, skinfolds and blood pressures, lower scores are better.

The results of this study showed that improved physical fitness of children reduced their heart disease risk factors.

Improved physical fitness is important for children, especially since researchers believe that heart disease begins in childhood. Fat deposits are found early in life. By age three, nearly *all* American children have some fat deposits on the inner surface of the aorta (the body's largest artery). These deposits increase rapidly after age eight, and at age fifteen have affected 15 percent of the aorta's surface. Yet children in primitive countries do not have these fatty deposits. It seems, therefore, that these blood vessel changes are due to habits. Research we conducted on school-aged children in our county supports that view, since:

—41% had cholesterols considered to be too high
—29% had elevated triglycerides
—12% had low levels of HDLs (high levels are a good sign)
—15% had excessively high systolic blood pressures
—28% had diastolic blood pressures that were too high

Exercise is also important for the heart health of adults. Since the early 1950s, numerous studies have been conducted to determine the effects of exercise on a person's chance of having a heart attack. The evidence is almost overwhelming. Active people have only about one-half the chance of having a heart attack as inactive people. Furthermore, if an active person has a heart attack, his survival chances are two to five times greater than the inactive person.

Why is this so? Dr. Samuel Fox, professor of cardiology at Georgetown University in Washington, D.C., and Dr. William Haskell, assistant professor at Stanford University in Palo Alto, California, have presented several possible reasons. According to these experts, exercise may:[10]

1. Increase the number and size of your blood vessels (causing better and more efficient circulation).
2. Increase the elasticity of blood vessels (less likelihood of breaking under pressure).
3. Increase the efficiency of exercising muscles and blood circulation (muscles and blood are better able to pick up, carry and use oxygen).
4. Increase the efficiency of the heart (able to pump more blood with fewer beats—better able to meet emergencies).
5. Increase tolerance to stress and give you more joy of living (so you will be less likely to be caught in the stress/pressure syndrome).
6. Decrease clot formation (less chance of blood clot forming and blocking blood flow to the heart muscle).
7. Decrease triglyceride and cholesterol levels (less likelihood of fats being deposited on the lining of the arteries).
8. Decrease blood sugar (reduce chances of blood sugar being changed to triglycerides).
9. Decrease obesity and high blood pressure (most people who are obese and have high blood pressure are more prone to heart disease).
10. Decrease hormone production (too much adrenalin can cause problems for the arteries).

Good cardiovascular endurance also has been shown to help people relieve headaches, reduce anxiety, lift people from depression, and stimulate creativity and confidence.

My daughter, Deb, is a case in point. Seven years ago, at the age of fifteen, she started to run. Two years later, during an enjoyable father and daughter run,

I said, "Deb, when you were fifteen you seemed more moody. If things didn't go your way, you'd get real quiet and sulk. Maybe even go out in the middle of the yard and sit for an hour or so. You don't do that any more. How come?"

"Oh that's easy," she said. "My running changed all that. Maybe I'm more mature, too, but I noticed that about six months after I started running, I lost some of my tension and anger. It relaxed me."

That reinforced my opinion of the value of exercise. It said more than all the research studies I've read on the mental benefits of exercise.

Cardiovascular exercise is not a panacea, but the evidence is clear. Good cardiovascular endurance benefits your heart, mind and energy levels. And cardiovascular endurance is improved with exercises such as walking, running, biking, swimming, cross-country skiing, rowing and aerobic dancing.

Body Composition/Weight Ratio

This aspect of physical fitness will be discussed in greater detail in chapters 9 and 10.

Muscular Fitness

Muscle fitness refers to the strength, endurance and appearance of the various muscles of the body. A reasonable degree of muscle strength is needed for moving and lifting heavy objects—everything from pianos to groceries. From a health perspective, muscle fitness is necessary to avoid low back pain. In a study of 3,000 back pain patients at Columbia Presbyterian Medical Center, Al Melleby, director for the YMCA's Healthy Back Program, found that 83 percent of the back problems were of muscle origin.[11]

According to experts, our sedentary life heads us into back trouble. A lack of physical activity causes abdominal muscles to weaken and sag. In addition, we accumulate too much fat around our waists. To compensate for the sagging waistline, we arch our backs. Consequently, the pelvis tips forward. Our derriere sticks out. The last joints of the spine require a lot of muscle to hold them up. Eventually, the muscles in the lower back tire of carrying the load and they ache a bit. Most backaches with children are due to this poor posture or weak abdominal muscles.

With adults, the low backache syndrome starts with the same problems—weak muscles and too much fat. That is then aggravated by day to day tensions, which make the back muscles contract. When the muscles contract beyond a certain point, significant back pain occurs.

Flexibility

Flexibility is the range of motion possible at each of your joints. It is important for your good health because it helps prevent muscle pulls and strains. Improved flexibility results in fewer injuries and more freedom of movement. A lack of

---

Plague #2

Back, Neck and Head Pain

Back or neck pain is a problem for about 80 percent of our population. Approximately seven million Americans are off work at any one time because of aching backs.[14]

Why are our backs in such horrible condition? One explanation is that back pains arise from a problem with the facet joint (it connects the back of each vertebra to the vertebrae above and below), the soft tissue around the joint, or the disk ("pads," which serve as "shock absorbers" between vertebrae).

The back pain originating from these structures usually is mechanical. In the case of the facet joint, the bones that meet at the joint can become locked or irritated and inflamed. The intervertebral disk also may be the culprit in low back pain when, as a result of acute trauma, it begins to "bulge" out of shape. Occasionally the disk may even protrude enough to press against the spinal nerves, or it may rupture (herniate).

To prevent or reduce back pain, do the following: 1) have proper posture when lying, sitting or standing, 2) use proper lifting techniques, 3) keep your weight under control, and 4) exercise properly.

Ninety percent of the population suffers from headaches sometime in their lives, 20 percent of which need treatment. Most headache sufferers are women between the ages of fourteen and forty-five. Dr. Harold G. Wolff of New York Hospital, a pioneer student of headaches, notes that 95 percent of all headaches are caused by what he calls biological reprimands.[15] These reprimands tell you that something in your body is off balance. Your body makes adjustments to compensate for this lack of balance. These adjustments include tightened muscles and expanded blood vessels in the head and neck. Tightened muscles and enlarged blood vessels then press upon and irritate neighboring tissues. In short, you get a headache.

The causes of headaches are endless and, unfortunately, different for practically everyone. Contributing factors include too much of the following: alcohol; chemicals in food, air or water; light or glare, causing you to squint; caffeine; pain-killing drugs; stress and tension; anger and frustration; and repressed anxiety. Headaches also may be caused by hunger, the lack of oxygen in high altitudes, and a very low barometric pressure. Preventing headaches is best done by practicing stress management techniques, exercising regularly, eating a proper diet, and avoiding alcohol, caffeine, drugs and tobacco.

---

flexibility can contribute to low back pain and those maddening muscle and joint injuries that occur when you attempt to reach for an object underneath a desk or on top of a shelf.

Generally, flexibility is not a problem with children. The loss of flexibility starts during the teen-age years and becomes obvious at about age thirty-five.

There is no such thing as a flexible person; there are only people with flexible joints. To improve your overall flexibility, you must work on each part of your body. Exercises best for this are those of the slow stretch nature. Yoga-type exercises are also advantageous.

There you have it! To be physically fit you must work on the four essentials of fitness—cardiovascular endurance, body composition/weight ratio, muscular fitness and flexibility. Neglect of any essential element may cause injury, an imbalance in physical appearance, or lack of the potential benefits outlined here.

Let's move on to find out how you can be fit for life.

"Offer your bodies as living sacrifices, holy
and pleasing to God" (Romans 12:1).

Chapter 6:
Strengthening Your Fitness

"Enlarge the place of your tent, stretch your tent curtains wide, do not hold back; lengthen your cords, strengthen your stakes" (Isaiah 54:2).

As the nomads moved from place to place, there was wear and tear on their tents. The people had to spend time keeping their tents strong to withstand the elements. As families grew, tents had to be enlarged.

To improve their living quarters, and thus their life within them, they needed to strengthen their stakes and drive them farther in the earth. The cords that held the tents secure had to be lengthened and strengthened. This was done regularly and routinely, according to the need of each family.

Our bodies are somewhat like those tents. The parts that keep the body strong and alive need constant strengthening and development.

Strengthening Your Heart

The amount of heart exercise you need depends upon your personal goals. Physiologists talk about the intensity (how hard), duration (how long) and frequency (how often) of exercise. They also recognize the interaction between intensity, duration and frequency. That interaction creates a fourth factor—total work—which is the real key to fitness.

Let me explain. Total work is a combination of how hard, how long and how often a person exercises, regardless of age. Training requires a *minimum* heart rate threshold (somewhere between 40 and 50 percent of maximum), a minimum number of minutes (about 15 to 20), and a minimum number of days per week (two to four). These factors can be adjusted so that if a person works harder (more intensely), he or she does not need to exercise as long. If a person works at less intensity, he or she needs to exercise longer.

How Hard?

The best way to determine how hard you should exercise is to measure the maximum amount of oxygen your body is capable of using. To do this, you can ride a specialized bicycle or walk or run on a treadmill (stress test). While you give an all-out effort, a doctor measures the amount of oxygen you use. Since it is a maximum effort, it is called maximum oxygen uptake (max VO$_2$). With this information, the physician can prescribe how hard to exercise. In school, your children may be asked to run a mile or so as a fitness test. That test can give the teacher an estimate of your child's maximum oxygen uptake.

If you don't want to go through a stress test, you can use your heart rate as a worthy alternative. Simply reach for your wrist and count your heart rate (see box). Then make sure you exercise at a level that keeps your heart beating at the proper rate, which will differ for different people.

Everyone has a maximum heart rate. Your maximum heart rate is the number of beats per minute when you are exercising as hard, as fast and as long as possible. Although it varies from person to person, your maximum heart rate is roughly 220 minus your age. If you are 20 years old, your maximum heart rate is about 200. If you are 40, it's about 180 (see table 4).

HEART RATE

The number of times your heart pumps blood each minute is your pulse rate or heart rate. To feel your pulse, sit quietly for three to five minutes. Then turn the palm of your hand up and place two or three fingers of your right hand on the thumb side of your left wrist. This point is called the radial pulse.

When taking your pulse, you should feel a push or thump against your fingers. Each push is one heart beat, which is called your pulse. The number of pushes each minute is your heart or pulse rate.

After locating your pulse, look at the sweep second hand on your watch. Starting with zero, count the number of beats for a 10-second interval. Multiply that number by 6. This represents your resting heart rate per minute. A normal heart rate for adults after sitting quietly one to five minutes is 54 to 82 beats per minute. With children, heart rates are usually between 72 and 100 beats per minute. Children under 10 often will have resting heart rates of 86 to 100.

TABLE 4
Maximum Heart Rate

Age	Maximum Heart Rate (bpm)*	Age	Maximum Heart Rate (bpm)*
10 or less	210	45	175
15	205	50	170
20	200	55	165
25	195	60	160
30	190	65	155
35	185	70 or more	150
40	180		

*bpm = beats per minute

Do not try to exercise at your maximum heart rate level. That is not necessary for general fitness. A safe and more appropriate level is between 40 and 75 percent of your maximum. That is your ideal heart rate range.

To find your ideal heart rate range, check your resting pulse (see box). Subtract the number of resting beats per minute from your maximum heart rate (on table 4). That gives you your heart rate range. Multiply your range by 40 to 75 percent and add that number to your resting heart rate. For example, the calculation for a 40-year-old who has a resting heart rate of 60 will look like this:

$$180 \text{ Maximum heart rate}$$
$$- \underline{ 60} \text{ Resting heart rate}$$
$$120 \text{ Heart rate range}$$

$$120 \times 40\% = 48 + \text{ resting heart rate } (60) = 108$$
$$120 \times 75\% = 90 + \text{ resting heart rate } (60) = 150$$

This person's ideal heart rate range would be 108 to 150 beats per minute.

To save you all this math, look at Tables 5 to 8. All the calculations are done for you. First, locate your age chart. Then find your resting heart rate at the top of your age chart. From this you will find your ideal heart rate range for exercise.

To use these charts when exercising, check your pulse after you have walked, run, biked, swum, cross-country skied, rowed or aerobicized for at least ten minutes. Count your pulse beats for ten seconds and multiply the number by six to determine your heart beats per minute while exercising. Then locate your resting heart rate column (across the top) and find your exercise pulse in the vertical column. Look at the far left column for the percent of maximum heart rate (fitness category). Remember that category; you'll need it in the following section.

If your heart rate is higher than the range provided, slow your pace or reduce the resistance, if riding a bike or rowing. If your heart rate is lower than the

TABLE 5
Exercise Heart Rate
Age 20 and Under

Percent of Maximum Heart Rate	Resting Heart Rates					
	54 or less	55–64	65–74	75–84	85–94	95 or more
1. 40%	110–115	116–122	122–127	128–133	134–139	140–144
2. 45%	116–122	123–129	128–134	134–139	140–144	145–149
3. 50%	123–129	130–136	135–141	140–145	145–149	150–154
4. 55%	130–136	137–141	142–147	146–151	150–155	155–159
5. 60%	137–143	142–147	148–153	152–157	156–161	160–164
6. 65%	144–150	148–153	154–157	158–161	162–164	165–170
7. 70%	151–156	154–160	158–162	162–165	165–168	169–174
8. 75%	157–163	161–166	163–168	166–171	169–173	175–179

TABLE 6
Exercise Heart Rate
Age 20 to 39

Percent of Maximum Heart Rate	Resting Heart Rates					
	54 or less	55–64	65–74	75–84	85–94	95 or more
1. 40%	106–111	112–116	118–122	124–128	130–134	136–140
2. 45%	112–118	117–123	123–128	129–134	135–140	141–145
3. 50%	119–125	124–130	129–135	135–140	141–145	146–150
4. 55%	126–132	131–137	136–142	141–146	146–150	151–155
5. 60%	133–140	138–144	143–148	147–152	151–156	156–160
6. 65%	141–148	145–151	149–154	153–158	157–162	161–165
7. 70%	149–153	152–156	155–159	159–162	163–166	166–170
8. 75%	154–160	157–162	160–165	163–167	167–170	171–175

TABLE 7
Exercise Heart Rate
Age 40 to 59

Percent of Maximum Heart Rate	Resting Heart Rates					
	54 or less	55–64	65–74	75–84	85–94	95 or more
1. 40%	98–102	104–108	110–114	116–120	122–126	128–132
2. 45%	103–108	109–114	115–120	121–125	127–130	133–136
3. 50%	109–115	115–120	121–125	126–130	131–135	137–140
4. 55%	116–122	121–126	126–130	131–135	136–140	141–144
5. 60%	123–128	127–132	131–136	136–140	141–144	145–148
6. 65%	129–134	133–138	137–142	141–145	145–148	149–152
7. 70%	135–140	139–144	143–148	146–150	149–153	153–156
8. 75%	141–145	145–150	149–154	151–155	154–158	159–162

TABLE 8
Exercise Heart Rate
Age 60 and Above

Percent of Maximum Heart Rate	Resting Heart Rates					
	54 or less	55–64	65–74	75–84	85–94	95 or more
1. 40%	89– 94	96–100	102–106	109–112	115–118	122–124
2. 45%	95–100	101–105	107–111	113–116	119–122	125–127
3. 50%	101–106	106–110	112–115	117–120	123–125	128–130
4. 55%	107–111	111–116	116–120	121–124	126–129	131–134
5. 60%	112–117	117–121	121–125	125–129	130–133	135–137
6. 65%	118–122	122–126	126–129	130–133	134–136	138–140
7. 70%	123–126	125–130	128–132	132–137	137–140	141–144
8. 75%	127–130	137–133	133–136	138–140	141–144	145–148

range provided, pick up your pace or increase your resistance during the next exercise session. You should push yourself, but not too hard. You should be breathing deeper than usual, and you probably will perspire. The exercise should be pain-free, however, and you should be able to talk to someone next to you (real or imagined).

With children, you can expect the pulse rates of those over ten years old to vary substantially. It also is normal for children under ten to want to stop and go when exercising. That is, run, walk, skip, throw and go back to running. Let them. The key is to keep their interest. Give them the freedom to move as they want at their own rhythm, but encourage them to keep moving. Additionally, you will need to check their heart rates for them.

How Long?

When training your heart and lungs, most experts agree that at least 20 minutes of exercise at 60 to 65 percent of heart rate range is necessary. Of course, the intensity may be increased or decreased. Maybe 50 percent is more comfortable for you. Therefore, you must exercise longer to adjust for the reduced intensity. Table 9 shows how long to exercise, based on pulse rates.

TABLE 9
Number of Minutes of Recommended
Exercise at Different Training Heart Rates

Percent of Maximum Heart Rate	Number of Minutes To Exercise—Heart/Lung Fitness
50%	45:01–52:30
55%	37:31–45:00
60%	30:01–37:30
65%	25:01–30:00
70%	20:01–25:00
75%	15:00–20:00

If you are exercising and your heart rate is at 60 percent of maximum, you should exercise for 30 to 37½ minutes; if you are exercising at 50 percent of your maximum heart rate, you'll need to exercise for 45 to 52½ minutes. Exercising at 75 percent of your maximum heart rate is necessary for only 15 to 20 minutes.

Two notes of caution: First, for healthy, normal people, the training effect on the heart and lungs usually does not occur below 45 percent of a person's maximum heart rate. Second, 30 minutes can be an eternity for children. When exercising as a family, keep their interest by playing games, such as those recommended after this chapter. Also, any efforts to increase the amount of time exercising should be gradual. And if it is clear that 15 minutes is their current attention span, so be it. Take that and don't force them to exercise for longer periods of time.

How Often?

Exercise a minimum of three to five times a week. Studies show that this provides a reasonable and optimum frequency of exercise.

Summary

Now you have it! Walk, run, bike, swim, aerobicize, row or cross-country ski about an hour at 50 to 75 percent of your maximum heart rate range. Doing this for 15 to 50 minutes 3 to 5 times a week will train your heart and lungs, reduce selected cardiovascular risk factors and energize your body and mind.

Strengthening Muscle Fitness

To improve your muscle fitness, you need to overload your muscles with specific exercises, such as calisthenics (push-ups and sit-ups), weight training (free weights), training with equipment (Universal- or Nautilus-type machines), or isometrics. Select whatever approach you prefer.

Because of individual preference, I've selected two muscle fitness programs—calisthenics and free weights. You and your family can decide which is best for you. Maybe Mom will prefer weights and Dad, calisthenics, or vice versa. It doesn't matter. Either will improve your muscle fitness. Some people are turned off to women lifting weights, but I assure you, the bias is purely cultural. Men, women, boys and girls can enjoy the benefits of muscle fitness through weight training.

I caution you, however, that children who have not reached puberty should avoid training with weights. Some experts feel that young children's bones, tendons and ligaments are not fully developed. Therefore, they should wait until they are 14 or so before they begin weight training. Calisthenic training is O.K. for children 8 and above, but those under 8 tend not to like it. They are best encouraged by watching Mom and Dad exercising. If they want to jump in and exercise for five minutes, great! Encourage, but don't force.

Plan 1: Calisthenics Program

Below are ten basic exercises. They are set up in rotation to strengthen each main part of your body—the upper third, the middle third, and the lower third. To obtain the greatest benefit from them, do them in sequence as listed. For instance, after you do number 1, the upper third of your body can rest as you move to number 2 for the middle part. Then while you do number 3, both the upper and middle thirds of your body rest. When you move to number 4, you are ready to exercise the upper third of your body again.

If you don't feel you can do all of the exercises listed, you can group them as follows and choose one or two from each group, depending on how much you want to work on a particular part of your body.

> Upper third: numbers 1, 4, 7, 10
> Middle third: numbers 2, 5, 8
> Lower third: numbers 3, 6, 9

1. *Push-Ups.* Lie face down on the floor with your feet together and your hands beneath your shoulders. Keeping your body straight, extend your arms fully, then return to the starting position. This exercise helps develop the shoulders, chest and arms.

   Modified Push-Ups. Lie face down on the floor with your feet together and your hands beneath your shoulders. Your body weight should be distributed between your knees and hands. Keeping your trunk straight, extend your arms and return to the starting position. This exercise strengthens the shoulders, chest and arm muscles.

2. *Curl-Ups.* Lie flat on your back with your lower back touching the floor and your legs bent. Curl your head and upper body upward and forward to about a 45-degree angle. At the same time, contract your abdominal muscles. Return slowly to the starting position. Be certain your back is curled up so that the lower back is not aggravated. Place your arms across your chest or on your thighs. This exercise is excellent for firming and strengthening the stomach muscles.

3. *One-Half Knee Bends.* Standing, bend your knees to a 45-degree angle. With arms extended or hands on hips, bend your knees. Heels are allowed to come off the floor. Return to the starting position. This exercise strengthens the thigh muscles.

4. *High Hips.* Put your right hand on the floor, palm down, and keep your arm straight. Keeping your body rigid, extend your legs as far as they will go. Your body weight should rest entirely on your right foot and right hand. Now lower your hips to the floor, and then raise them again as high as possible. Do these on one side; repeat on the other side. This is a good exercise for strengthening the muscles of the arms and shoulders and for improving trunk flexibility.

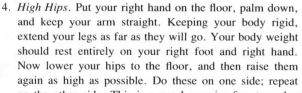
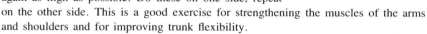

5. *Curl Down*. Sit on the floor with your knees bent and hands folded across your chest or on your ankles. Slowly lower your upper body to a 45-degree angle. Hold the position and return. This exercise strengthens the upper portion of the stomach muscles.

6. *Straddle Hops*. Stand with your feet together and hands on your hips. Hop off the ground so that your feet are spread about three feet apart. Then return to the starting position. Continue. This exercise is a cardiovascular conditioner and strengthens the calf muscles.

7. *Arm Flex*. Stand with your feet apart and your arms extended to your sides at shoulder height. Palms should be up. Flex the arms inward as though making a muscle. Touch your fingertips to your shoulders. This exercise strengthens the upper arms and shoulders.

8. *Side Double Leg Raises*. Lie on your right side, legs extended, head supported by your right arm. Raise both legs together as high as possible, then lower to the starting position. Repeat on the opposite side. This exercise helps firm the lateral muscles of the trunk and hips.

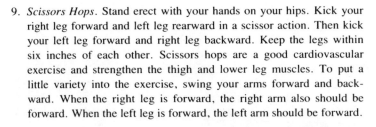

9. *Scissors Hops*. Stand erect with your hands on your hips. Kick your right leg forward and left leg rearward in a scissor action. Then kick your left leg forward and right leg backward. Keep the legs within six inches of each other. Scissors hops are a good cardiovascular exercise and strengthen the thigh and lower leg muscles. To put a little variety into the exercise, swing your arms forward and backward. When the right leg is forward, the right arm also should be forward. When the left leg is forward, the left arm should be forward.

10. *Hip Lift/Kicks*. Sit on the floor with your arms by your sides and your palms flat on the floor. Bend your knees and place your feet flat on the floor. Raise your buttocks off the floor so that your trunk is parallel to the floor. Kick the right leg, and then kick the left leg. Alternate kicking the right and left legs for a specified number of beats. Return to the starting position. This exercise strengthens the thighs and the shoulders.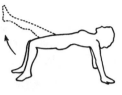

Schedule

Three to four exercise sessions a week are recommended, with one day of rest between each session. Do all selected exercises at each session.

Overload

Do three to 10 repetitions of each exercise. Start on the low side if you are unfit, on the high side if you are in good physical condition. After your repetitions, rest, and repeat two more times. That is, three sets of 3 to 10 repetitions each.

Program

1. You should be able to do an exercise the specified number of repetitions (3 to 10). Do the exercise correctly. Do not race against time.
2. After each set of 3 to 10 repetitions, rest for 30 seconds by walking, shaking your arms and legs.
3. When you have completed 3 sets of 3 to 10 repetitions, rest for 30 seconds to one minute, again by walking and shaking the hands and legs. Then move on to the next exercise on the list.

Adaptation and Progression

In one to three weeks, your body will adapt to the overload of the exercise. When it feels as though your body can do more exercise, increase the number of repetitions by one. If you were doing three sets of 5 repetitions of an exercise, now do three sets of 6 repetitions. Continue to increase in this manner until you can do three sets of 25 repetitions if you are under 60 years of age, or three sets of 15 repetitions if you are over 60.

Plan 2: Weight Training Program

Below are ten basic weight training exercises.

1. *Arm Press*. Develops and firms muscles of the shoulders, upper back, upper chest, and back of the upper arms. Aids in the prevention of round shoulders.

   1. Stand with your feet shoulder-width apart. Hold barbell in front of your chest, overhand grip, hands slightly more than shoulder-width apart.
   2. Extend barbell overhead, until arms are straight.
   3. Return barbell to the starting position. That is one repetition.
   4. Repeat.

2. *Curl*. Firms the abdominal muscles.

   1. Lie flat on your back, knees bent, hands and arms off the floor but parallel to it.
   2. Tighten your abdominal muscles and push the small of your back to the floor.
   3. Bring your knees to your chest; simultaneously tuck your chin down onto your chest and curl upward as far as possible. Return. That is one repetition.
   4. Repeat.

3. *One-Half Squat*. Develops and firms the muscles in the front of the thigh and lower leg.

   1. Stand with your feet comfortably spread.
   2. Hold the barbell in an overhand grip behind your neck, resting on your shoulders.
   3. Bend your knees to perform a half-squat (thighs no more than parallel to the floor). Return to the starting position. That is one repetition.
   4. Repeat.

4. *Barbell Curls*. Develops and firms the muscles of the upper arms and the forearms.
   1. Stand with your feet apart, arms at sides. Hold the barbell against your thighs in an underhand grip.
   2. Flex your forearms, raising the barbell to your shoulders.
   3. Return to the starting position. That is one repetition.
   4. Repeat.

5. *Curl and Cross Touch.* Firms the abdominal muscles.
   1. Lie flat on your back, your knees bent, hands alongside your neck, and elbows bent.
   2. Tighten your abdominal muscles and push the small of your back to the floor.
   3. Bring your left foot off the floor so that your lower leg is parallel to the floor. Simultaneously curl upward and touch your right elbow to the inside of your left knee. Return. That is one repetition.
   4. Repeat with the left elbow to right knee.

6. *Lunge.* Develops and firms muscles in the front of the thigh and buttocks.
   1. Stand erect, feet together, the barbell balanced across your shoulders.
   2. Take a giant step forward, bend your knees, and touch your trailing knee to the floor.
   3. Push up to the starting position. That is one repetition.
   4. Repeat with the opposite leg.

7. *Forward Raise.* Develops and firms muscles of the upper chest and shoulders.
   1. Stand with your feet waist-width apart. Hold dumbbells down at your sides (or resting on your thighs) in an overhand grip.
   2. Raise the dumbbells forward to shoulder height, keeping your arms straight.
   3. Lower the dumbbells to the original position. That is one repetition.
   4. Repeat.
      Variation: Do one arm at a time.

8. *Side Sit-Ups.* Firms the muscles of the waist.
   1. Lie on your side, body straight, hands clasped behind the neck.
   2. Have a partner hold your feet down for support, or put them under a loaded barbell.
   3. Raise your upper body off the floor, bending directly toward your side. Slowly lower back down. That is one repetition.
   4. Repeat.
      Do on the other side.

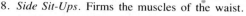

9. *Calf Raise*. Develops and firms the muscles in the front and the back of the lower leg.
   1. Stand with the balls of your feet on a one- to two-inch block of wood or weight plate, with your heels on the floor.
   2. Hold the barbell in an overhand grip behind your neck, resting on your shoulders.
   3. Raise up on your toes as far as possible. Return to the original position. That is one repetition.
   4. Repeat.

10. *French Press*. Develops and firms the muscles on the back of the arms and shoulders.
    1. Assume a standing position with your feet shoulder-width apart and your body erect. Hold a dumbbell in both hands with your arms fully extended overhead.
    2. Lower the dumbbell behind your head as far as possible by bending the elbows.
    3. Raise the weight back to the starting position. That is one repetition.
    4. Repeat.
       Remember to keep your elbows pointed straight up and close to your head throughout the movement.

Schedule

Do three exercise sessions a week, with at least one day of rest between each session. You should do all selected exercises (minimum of four) at each session.

Overload

Training weights are 30 to 50 percent of your maximum for each exercise. To find your maximum weight, lift what you think is your maximum for each exercise. This may take a week or so to determine for each lift. That time is well spent, however, since it will help condition your muscles and prepare them for more demanding exercise. If your maximum weight tested out at 100 pounds for a particular exercise, you will train with 30 to 50 pounds. Start out on the low side if you are unfit, on the high side if you are in good physical condition. Do the exercise 15 times, rest, and repeat two more times—that is, do three sets of 15 repetitions each.

Program

1. Lifting the training weight, you should be able to perform a maximum of 15 repetitions. You're not racing against time, but the repetitions must be consecutive. If you can do more than 15 repetitions, the weight is not heavy

enough. If you cannot do 15, the weight is too heavy. Adjust the weight upward or downward accordingly.
2. Rest one minute after the repetitions. A good way to relax is simply to shake your arms and legs.
3. Repeat the 15 repetitions—no more. Because of fatigue from the previous repetitions, you may be able to do only 10 to 12.
4. Rest one minute.
5. Repeat the exercise. Again, because of fatigue from the previous two sets, now you probably can do between 7 and 10 repetitions.
6. After a rest of 1½ to 2 minutes, proceed to the next exercise in your program, following the same procedure for each exercise.

Adaptation and Progression

In one to three weeks, your body will adapt to the overload of the weight and repetitions. When you can do 15 repetitions of each of the three sets for any given exercise, add 2½ to 5 pounds to the barbell or dumbbell and repeat the cycle of attempting three sets of 15 repetitions for each exercise. After several weeks, when you can do three sets of 15, again increase the weight by 2½ to 5 pounds. After several months of training, the increments of increase may be only one to two pounds.

Flexibility: Lengthening for Fitness

Stretching Exercise

The key ingredient in flexibility exercise is a slow, sustained stretch. This type of movement is *very* important. Fast, jerky and bouncy movements cause the muscle you are attempting to stretch to contract at the same time. The contraction reduces the effectiveness of your stretch and often causes muscle soreness. By using a slow, sustained stretch, the nerve endings cause the muscle to relax and lengthen. The lengthening increases your flexibility.

To do stretching exercises, assume the position called for in the description. Then move in the direction recommended until you feel a tug or pull on the muscles, or a general resistance to stretching further. Hold that position and concentrate on the tug and pull. Visualize the muscle stretching or relaxing. (This may require intense concentration.) As the muscle or tendon relaxes, continue to stretch farther until you feel a second tug. Hold that position for 10 to 20 seconds. Then relax and move on to the next exercise.

When selecting the various exercises, pick a minimum of two for the upper third, two for the middle third, and two for the lower third.

Young children seem to enjoy doing these exercises with their parents. It's a great family activity.

Upper Third

Elbow Special. Benefits the muscles of your chest and upper back.

1. Stand with your hands behind your head, fingers interlocked.
2. Draw your elbows back as far as possible and hold.
3. Draw the elbows forward and try to touch them together.
4. Hold and repeat.

Kneeling Shoulder Stretch. Stretches the shoulders and upper back.
1. Kneel on the floor, sit back on your heels, and look at your knees as you reach forward with your hands. Keep your seat down and continue to focus on your knees.
2. Once you have reached as far as possible, press down against the floor with your hands. You will feel your shoulders stretch.
3. Hold and repeat.

Lateral Neck Stretch. Stretches the side of the neck.
1. Lie on your back with your knees bent and your hands at your sides.
2. Keep the back of your head on the floor and turn your chin toward one shoulder. Be sure to keep your head on the floor.
3. Hold and repeat to the other side.

Middle Third

Knee Raises. Stretches your gluteus maximus.
1. Lie on your back with your legs bent.
2. Hold your right knee with both hands and pull it toward your chest.
3. Hold and repeat with the left knee.

Side Stretch.

1. Stand with feet shoulder-width apart, legs straight. Place one hand on your hip and extend your other hand up and over your head.
2. Bend to the side on which your hand is on your hip. Move slowly. Hold 6–10 seconds.
3. Repeat on the other side.

Single-Leg Tuck. Stretches the muscles at the back of your thighs (hamstrings) as well as the lower back.

1. Sit on the floor with your left leg straight and your right leg bent. Tuck your right foot into your groin.
2. Bend from the waist, reach forward, and clasp your left ankle. Pull your chest toward your left knee. Hold.
3. Repeat with the right leg.

Sitting Stretch. Benefits the muscles of the lower back and those behind the thighs (hamstrings).

1. Sit on the floor with your legs extended.
2. Bend slowly at the waist and bring your head toward your knees, as close as possible. Keep your legs extended and your head down. Try to touch your toes and hold. Be sure to stretch slowly.

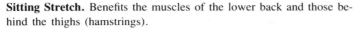

Lower Third

Calf Stretch. Stretches the calf muscles and Achilles tendon.

1. Stand with your right leg forward and your left leg back. Keep your left leg straight and bend the right leg. Keep both feet pointed straight ahead.
2. Lean forward, keeping your left heel on the ground. Hold.
3. Repeat with the right leg.

Crossed-Leg Hamstring Stretch. Stretches the hamstring muscles.

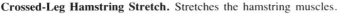

1. Sit on the floor with one leg straight. Cross your other leg over the top of the straight leg. This helps stabilize the leg and prevents you from bending it during the stretch.
2. Place both hands on the straight leg and, bending slowly from the waist, walk your fingers down the leg as far as possible and hold.
3. Repeat for the other leg.

Quadricep Stretch on Side. Stretches the muscles at the front of your thighs (quadriceps).

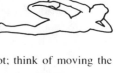

1. Lie on your left side. Hold your right ankle with your right hand. Keep your knees together.
2. Slowly pull your right thigh back. Do not just pull on the foot; think of moving the entire thigh. Hold.
3. Repeat for the left thigh.

Sitting Groin Stretch. Stretches the muscles of your inner thighs (groin) and lower back.

1. Sit on the floor and place your heels together.
2. Grasp your ankles and pull your feet in toward your groin.
3. Push your knees toward the floor, using your elbows.
4. Hold, straighten legs and repeat.

Putting it All Together

Doing all the things recommended in this chapter may seem overwhelming. Fortunately, it's not. The cardiovascular endurance, muscle fitness and flexibility can be incorporated into a 30- to 45-minute workout.

Just remember the following four points about each exercise session.

1. The 5- to 10-minute warm-up should include:
   - 2½ to 5 minutes of walking, easy running or doing your cardiovascular exercise at a slow pace;
   - 2½ to 5 minutes of stretching exercises.

2. Exercise aerobically
   - 15 to 52½ minutes of your aerobic exercise (training heart rate), depending upon your exercise intensity.

3. Muscle fitness
   - 10 to 15 minutes of muscle fitness is sufficient. This is an optional aspect of the workout. If you find your muscle fitness to be good, you can skip this part of the workout.

4. The 5- to 10-minute cool-down should include:
   - 1 to 5 minutes of slower walking.
   - 4 to 5 minutes of stretching exercises.

The minimum amount of time for workouts is 25 minutes three times a week; the maximum is 1½ hours five times a week. That means you will spend 1 to 4 percent of your time each week exercising. Most people will exercise 2 to 2½ percent of their time. If properly orchestrated, the exercise can double as family time, or one-to-one time with your spouse or one of your children. Some of my best conversations with my wife and children have been on long runs or when lifting weights, riding a bicycle or cross-country skiing.

Often you will find that the children will want to do only one of the four stages of a workout. Or they may do only a few minutes of each. This is fine, since you are planting the seeds for an active lifestyle later on.

On the following pages you'll find strategies to strengthen you and your family, to improve your fitness, to increase your vigor and stamina, and to make physical fitness fun for all of you.

> "Do you not know that your body is a temple of the Holy Spirit, who is in you, whom you have received from God?" (1 Corinthians 6:19).

FAMILY FITNESS ACTIVITIES

The recommendations in the previous chapter usually are adopted by the parents and older children, fourteen and up. Children under fourteen do not always respond to these ideas, however, as they tend to have a "play orientation" toward fitness. Therefore, I've included the following activities, which are designed to create a positive environment for improving younger children's physical fitness.

After the title of each game, I've given the ages for which it is best suited, but there are exceptions. Also, parents are to do all the activities with the children.

The entire family can benefit from these games. They will help younger children internalize more sophisticated and possibly regimented activities. And they will stretch parents and older children to have more play in their fitness.

I. *Activities to Understand Pulse Rate*

● Children's Pulse Rates (Ages 3–16)

Children's pulse rates are much faster than those of adults, since they are more excitable and have a higher metabolic rate because they are growing. Have your child take his own pulse rate, then have him take yours. Compare the two. Yours probably will be much slower. Do an activity together—anything from raking the lawn, chasing each other around the house, going for a bike ride, or climbing stairs. Have him take his and your pulses. Notice that both have increased, but the child's is still at a faster rate. Talk over the ways in which your bodies are similar and different.

● Pulse Rates and Eating (Ages 3–16)

Take your child's and your pulse just before eating dinner. After finishing dinner and the dishes, sit down and take your pulses again. Lie down, wait a few minutes, and check again. Point out to each other the changes in pulse rates, and talk about why you think these changes happened.

● Number of Heartbeats (Ages 9–14)

To determine how many times your heart beats each day, take your pulse for one minute. Multiply that by 60 minutes, then by 24 hours (i.e., 50 beats per minute times 60 equals 3,000; three thousand times 24 equals 72,000 beats per day). Compare this to your child's. Whose heart is working harder? If you exercised 30 minutes every day, you probably could lower your pulse by 10 beats per minute

55

for 23 hours a day. How many beats would you save? A fit heart uses fewer beats to do the same work as an unfit heart.

● Caffeine and Pulse Rates (Ages 9–16)

If there is a coffee drinker in the house, have him refrain from drinking anything for approximately three hours. Take his pulse, then have him drink a cup of coffee. Record his pulse one minute, five minutes, ten minutes, and twenty minutes after having the coffee. Caffeine is a stimulant. It affects the nervous system, causing the person's heart to beat quicker. Determine the extra heart beats of a coffee drinker in a day, week, month or year.

● Finding Pulse Rates (Ages 5–14)

How many places can you find your pulse? Start by finding your pulse in your wrist. Your child finds his or her pulse at the wrist, and then in another place. You must find your pulse in the same place, then find a new spot. If you cannot find a pulse where your child found one, he gets a point. Keep going until you cannot find any more pulse points.

II. *Activities to Understand the Benefits of Exercise*

● Changes in Physical Activity (Ages 3–10)

Tell your child about the things you liked to do physically when you were a child. You might even pass on stories your parents or grandparents told about how things were before we had automobiles, electric lights, and supermarkets. Discuss with your child what it must have been like to split your own wood, grow your own garden and walk to town. Explain that because our modern conveniences eliminate these activities, it is important for us to get physical exercise in other ways to keep our hearts healthy.

● Favorite Activities (Ages 9–16)

You probably know what your child's favorite activities are: basketball, tiddly-winks, mowing the lawn, softball, washing dishes or whatever. (Interestingly enough, of these activities, mowing the lawn is by far the best aerobic activity, provided that you use a push mower that is not self-propelled.) For each activity that your child enjoys, figure out how much aerobic exercise it provides. Help your child make a list with the best aerobic activities at the top and increasingly less aerobic activities below. Playing tiddlywinks definitely would be at the bottom of the list. Make a list for yourself as you help your child prepare his or her list.

● My 10 Most-Favorite Physical Activities (Ages 8–16)

Have your children list their ten favorite physical activities on a sheet of paper. Then have them do the following:

a. Put *F* next to their most favorite activity.
b. Put *L* next to their least favorite.
c. Indicate with a *B* the activity that they think is best for them.
d. Put 5's next to those activities they think they will be able to do when they're 50 years old.
e. Put a 2 next to those activities that take two or more people to participate.

Ask your children to write answers to the following questions on the back of their paper after they study the above coding.

a. What did the "Ten Most-Favorite Activities" exercise tell you about your activity selection?
b. Did you select a cardiovascular exercise?
c. What, if anything, do you plan to do as a result of this exercise?

● Being Well and Fit (Ages 8–16)

Being free from disease and being well are not the same thing. A person can be in terrible condition and still be labeled "healthy." At annual checkups, many businesspersons have been told by their doctors that nothing is wrong, even though it probably would be all they could do to walk up a couple flights of stairs.

People in this condition are not healthy, they are just free from disease. The following Wellness Chart shows the difference between being ill, having "nothing wrong," and being in excellent condition. Have each family member decide where he or she is on the Wellness Chart. Think of one thing each of you can do to become even more well.

III. *Games*

● Excuses and Answers (Ages 9–14)

Play this like a game. Have each family member write down three or four common excuses of why they don't exercise. Example:

Don't have time
Don't know how
Too dark
Nowhere to exercise
It hurts
Costs too much
Don't have the equipment
Too cold outside

Put the excuses in a hat and have family members take turns drawing them. Each person has ten seconds to think about why the selected excuse is not very good. After he or she answers, other family members can add their comments.

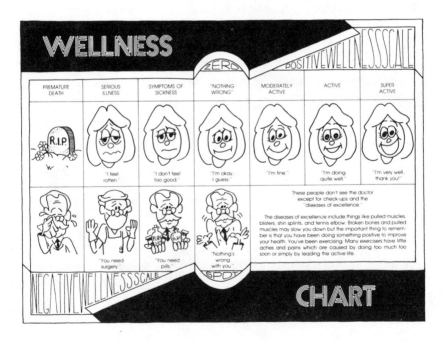

● Exercise Monopoly (Ages 8–14)

If you have the popular board game Monopoly, you can adapt it to reinforce exercise concepts. Change all the properties to exercise facilities or places synonymous with fitness. Half the fun will be thinking up new names for the properties (i.e., Fred's Fantastic Fitness Facility, Boston Marathon Route).

You may wish to change the cards as well, to require participants to be active (i.e., run around the room three times, do five push-ups). Every time a person passes "Go," to collect $200 they must do ten sit-ups.

The object of the game is to gain control of all the fitness facilities.

● Clue (Ages 8–14)

Again, use the board game, but adapt as follows:

Weapons
Change the weapons to fitness equipment (i.e., running shoe, hockey stick, baseball bat, football) or risk factors (i.e., not enough exercise, too fat, smoking).
Personalities
Use athletes—hockey player, baseball player, football player, and so forth.
Rooms
Change the rooms to sports or exercise facilities, such as a gymnasium, hockey arena, baseball park and rollerskating rink.

● Family Fitness Cheer (Ages 7–14)

Have a "Family Fitness Cheer" contest to see who can come up with a funny and creative family cheer. You might use the cheer to help motivate family members to get out of bed in the morning.

Sample cheer:

> Hey Kuntzlemans
> We like the gyms.
> Run, jump and roll;
> Fitness is our goal.
> Feelin' good, feelin' spry,
> That's the way to really try.

● Pie of Life (Ages 12–16)

Ask your children to list all the things they do during a typical weekday. Draw a pie, and section off pieces for the various activities of the day (i.e., sleeping ⅓, eating ⅛, reading ⅛, television ⅛, exercise ¹⁄₂₄, and so on). Have them list the things they would like to do but never seem to have time to accomplish. Draw a new pie, divided for how they would like to spend their time.

IV. *Analyzing Your Activity Level Strategy*

Many people think they are active. The Activity Index below gives you important guidelines for determining your true activity level. On this chart, circle the appropriate number for intensity, duration and frequency. (For example, if you play tennis for 30 minutes two times a week, circle *3* under intensity, *4* under duration, and *3* under frequency.)

	Score	**Activity**
Intensity:	5	Sustained heavy breathing and perspiration—as in jogging.
	4	Intermittent heavy breathing and perspiration—as in racquetball.
	3	Moderately heavy—as in recreational sports such as tennis.
	2	Moderate—as in volleyball, softball.
	1	Light—as in fishing or mowing the lawn.
Duration:	4	Over 30 minutes
	3	20 to 29 minutes
	2	11 to 19 minutes
	1	Under 10 minutes
Frequency:	5	Daily or almost daily.
	4	Four to five times a week.
	3	Two to three times a week.
	2	One time a week or a few times a month.
	1	Less than once a month.

Multiply your intensity rating (1–5) by your duration rating (1–4) by your frequency rating (1–5). (In our tennis example, intensity 3 × duration 4 × frequency 3: 3 × 4 = 12 and 12 × 3 = 36. This total falls under the "Need more activity" category in the following evaluation list.)

EVALUATION CATEGORY

Score	Evaluation
81 to 100	Very active lifestyle
61 to 80	Active and healthy
41 to 60	Acceptable (could be better)
21 to 40	Need more activity
Under 20	Sedentary

● **Measuring Your Family's Fitness** (Ages 6 and up)

Flexibility

Sit and Reach

Put a piece of tape on the floor. Sit perpendicular to it, with your legs extended and heels about five inches apart, just touching the inside edge of the tape. Place a yardstick between your legs, with the 15-inch mark on the inside edge of the tape. As your partner holds your knees straight, reach forward with both hands as far as possible (don't lunge) and touch the stick.

Sit and Reach Test Norms (inches)

Age	Sex	Excellent	Average	Improvement Needed
6–9	F	23+	17–22	0–16
	M	22+	13–22	0–12
10–13	F	23+	17–22	0–16
	M	22+	13–21	0–12
14–29	F	23+	17–22	0–16
	M	22+	13–21	0–12
30–39	F	23+	17–22	0–16
	M	22+	13–21	0–12
40–49	F	22+	15–21	0–14
	M	21+	13–20	0–12
50–59	F	21+	14–20	0–13
	M	20+	12–19	0–11
60 and over	F	21+	14–20	0–11
	M	20+	12–19	0–11

Muscle Fitness

Push-Ups

Women: Keep your shoulders, back and buttocks straight and your knees bent. Place your hands directly under your shoulders. Bend your elbows until your chest touches the floor. Without pausing, do as many as you can.

Men: Ditto, but with straight legs. Lower yourself till your chest touches a friend's upright fist on the floor.

Push-Ups Test Norms (Number completed)

Age	Sex	Excellent	Average	Improvement Needed
6–9	F	16+	9–15	0–8
	M	16+	16–30	0–8
10–13	F	31+	0–8	0–15
	M	31+	0–15	0–15
14–29	F	46+	17–45	0–16
	M	51+	25–50	0–24
30–39	F	41+	12–40	0–11
	M	46+	22–45	0–21
40–49	F	36+	8–35	0–7
	M	41+	19–40	0–18
50–59	F	31+	6–30	0–5
	M	36+	15–35	0–14
60 and over	F	26+	5–25	0–4
	M	31+	10–30	0–9

Curl-Ups

Lie flat with your knees bent and heels six inches from your buttocks. Place your hands on your thighs. While a partner holds down your feet, curl up your head, then shoulders, then upper trunk. Come up until your fingertips touch the middle of your kneecaps, then return. Do as many as you can without pausing.

Curl-Ups Test Norms (Number Completed)

Age	Sex	Excellent	Average	Improvement Needed
6–9	F	15+	10–14	0–5
	M	15+	10–14	0–5
10–13	F	41+	21–40	0–20
	M	41+	21–40	0–20
14–29	F	46+	25–45	0–24
	M	51+	30–50	0–29
30–39	F	41+	20–40	0–19
	M	46+	22–45	0–21
40–49	F	36+	16–35	0–15
	M	41+	21–40	0–20
50–59	F	31+	12–30	0–11
	M	36+	18–35	0–17
60 and over	F	26+	11–25	0–10
	M	31+	15–30	0–14

Cardiovascular Fitness

Step Test

Facing a 12-inch high bench, step one foot on top, then the other, then down with one foot and then the other. Pace is critical—do 24 full steps a minute. Go for three minutes, then sit down immediately. Have your partner count your heart rate for one minute starting five seconds after you finish the exercise.

3-Minute Step Test Norms (Heart rate)

Age	Sex	Excellent	Average	Improvement Needed
6–9	F	100 or less	100–119	120+
	M	100 or less	100–119	120+
10–13	F	92 or less	93–113	114+
	M	92 or less	93–113	114+
14–29	F	to 79	80–110	111+
	M	to 74	75–100	101+
30–39	F	to 83	84–115	116+
	M	to 77	78–109	110+
40–49	F	to 87	88–118	119+
	M	to 79	80–112	113+
50–59	F	to 91	92–123	124+
	M	to 89	85–115	116+
60 and over	F	to 94	95–127	128+
	M	to 89	90–118	119+

V. *Special Events*

● **Birthday Walk** (Ages 1–16)

Children love to do things with their parents. What better way is there to celebrate your child's birthday than to go for a walk together? You may wish to try the following:

1. When the child turns one year old, walk 1 kilometer (.624 miles) together. You may have to push your child in a stroller. If he or she can walk, you might want to walk ¼ kilometer in the morning, ¼ at noon, ¼ before dinner and ¼ in the evening.
2. When your child is two years old, walk 2 kilometers together. (Again, you may not want to do the entire two kilometers at once.)
3. When the child is three years old, walk 3 kilometers together.
4. Continue until your child is five, or even until he or she is 21.

To add fun to the walk, bring along a ball and kick or throw it. If you live in a cold climate, you can use shopping malls for winter walks.

● **Valentine's Day** (Ages 5–16)

Everyone associates the heart with Valentine's Day. How about doing something that will strengthen the heart and improve cardiovascular fitness?

Challenge your family to a "hearty" Valentine's Day. Between 8 A.M. and 8 P.M., family members try to obtain as many heart points as possible. (Select a weekend day close to Valentine's Day, or disallow activity during Mom's or Dad's working hours.)

Walking	1 point for every 10 minutes
Jogging	1 point for every 10 minutes
Cycling	1 point for every 10 minutes
Swimming	1 point for every 10 minutes
Skipping	1 point for every 10 minutes

You may wish to give younger children a handicap and make it harder for teens. For example:

Children 5–7	Multiply total score by 2
Children 8–10	Multiply total score by 1.5
Children 11–19	Multiply total score by .75
Adults 20 and up	Multiply total score by 1

The winner at the end of the day receives a token prize (e.g., shoelaces for their running shoes).

• Easter (Ages 8–16)

Organize an Easter egg hunt for several neighborhood families. Color and number the eggs. (Use as many eggs as you wish, at least two for every child.) Prior to the hunt, keep the children in an area where they cannot see the eggs being hidden. Hide the eggs in a large yard, playground or schoolyard. Once the eggs are hidden, bring the children to a starting line.

On the signal, the children search the field for eggs. Each time someone finds an egg, he or she returns it to the designated area, where the child's name and the number of the egg is recorded. After children find two eggs, they can help others find their eggs, until everyone has found two (or the number you hid for each).

When all the eggs are found, you may want to give the children prizes, such as coloring books, crayons, balloons, frisbees, puzzles or comic books (no chocolate or candy).

• Mother's Day or Father's Day (Ages 8–16)

Children, provide Mom or Dad with a list of clues as to where to find a gift. Perhaps the gift will be at a neighbor's home, but Mom or Dad will have to walk one or two miles before finding it. Clues may be hidden all over the neighborhood, and the whole family will want to accompany Mom or Dad on the hunt. For example:

1. Your next clue can be found where you meet the 7:05 A.M. (bus stop near home).
2. Your next clue can be found beside the neighbor's hound (beside neighbor's doghouse).

● Television Time (Ages 5–16)

If you are concerned about and want to limit the amount of television your children watch, tell them that viewing time must be earned. Establish guidelines, such as:

One hour of reading or studying earns ½ hour of television
One hour of active play earns ½ hour of television

You may want to keep a tally sheet for each child, but be careful not to make other activities appear to be punishment. Instead, explain that you want them to enjoy some of the many other fun things to do, besides watching television.

● Christmas (Ages 3–16)

Have everyone attach a note to each gift they give. The note should describe an exercise that the recipient must do before opening the gift. The exercises should be unusual, but not too difficult. For example: Gift for Dad, "Do five sit-ups with hands in pockets." Gift for Mom, "Lift Junior off the ground five times."

VI. *Exercise*

● Family Superheart (Ages 7–16)

Ground Rules:
1. Contest starts ____(date)____ and ends ____(date)____ .
2. Be positive and avoid unhealthy competition. Have each person strive for personal goals weekly. Participation is the key; reward anyone who exercises three times a week.
3. Only Training Heart Rate Exercises qualify. That is:

a. Bicycling	f. Rowing
b. Brisk walking	g. Running
c. Cross-country skiing	h. Running in place
d. Aerobics	i. Swimming
e. Rope jumping	

Sports such as basketball, aerobics, fencing, field hockey, football, gymnastics (floor exercises only), ice or roller skating, ice hockey, martial arts (Judo and

Karate), racquet games (tennis, etc.), soccer, wrestling, and volleyball also qualify, but you receive only ½ credit for participation. So double the time to get full credit—40 minutes of basketball will give you 20 minutes of aerobic exercise, etc. This method allows for rest periods, coaching and slow play.

4. When a family member logs 20 minutes of Training Heart Rate Exercise (or forty minutes of the other listed exercises) for a particular day, the person gets a checkmark on a chart. Sample chart:

Name	M	T	W	Th	F	Sa	Su	Total
Deb	X	X		X		X		4
John	X	X	X			X		4
Tom	X		X	X	X	X		5
Lisa	X			X	X	X		4
Becky	X		X	X			X	4
Dad	X			X				2
Mom	X	X		X				3

Beginning Date _____ Ending Date _____
Number in family getting 20 minutes of Training Heart Rate Exercise (or forty of other) three times a week __6__
Percent   86%

● Something New (Ages 9–16)

Have family members write down an activity they would like to do but never have had the chance to do (i.e., hiking, bowling, and so on). Once every month or every two weeks, place these activities in a hat and draw one. Plan to do this activity with the whole family.

● How Low Can You Go? (Ages 5–16)

Have family members record the number of hours of television they watch in one week. The following week, ask them to cut one hour of television. Each week, cut another hour. See who can go the lowest. You also might provide a reward. For example, for every three hours of television time cut out, allow your child to purchase a book or some active equipment.

● No-Car Day (Ages 9–16)

Pick a day and try to make it through the whole day without using a car. Bicycles are O.K.; so are buses. How much more activity do you engage in when you don't use the car? Discuss the effect of labor-saving devices on activity patterns in your lives.

● Family Fitness (Ages 3–14)

Select one hour a week that you will devote to family fitness. Have each member select three activites; then schedule a different activity for each week. You may want to state that the activities cannot require a great deal of skill, and all family members must be able to do them.

● Name in a Hat (Ages 9–14)

Have each family member place his or her name in a hat. Everyone then selects a name from the hat. Design three exercises for the person whose name you drew to do daily for a week. Each day the person does one more repetition (i.e., one push-up on day one, seven push-ups by day seven.) The person who drew the name makes sure that the other person does his or her exercises every day.

● No-Sit Day (Ages 5–16)

Select one day (i.e., Saturday) as a no-sitting day. The object of this contest is to go through the whole day, from 9:00 A.M. to 5:00 P.M., without sitting. This activity is fun, but it is tiring (no sitting means no lying down, kneeling, etc.— only standing, walking or running). See how many family members make it through the day. Discuss the adventure at the evening meal, while sitting.

● Nine to Five (Ages 5–16)

Select one day to go from 9 A.M. to 5 P.M. without using any labor-saving devices—nothing electric or motorized. (This means you must cook without electricity or not cook.) Have the family set the rules for the day. Discuss at the evening meal how times have changed and how much less active we are today.

● Activity Day (Ages 3–16)

Plan an activity day for the whole family. Friends, neighbors and relatives can be invited. Have each family member plan one activity. The younger children can work with an older sibling or a parent; others should not reveal their plans until the day comes. Some examples are: a scavenger hunt, a neighborhood walk, fun relays, a handicap run, a treasure hunt.

● Mileage Plot (Ages 4–16)

The further you go, the fitter you get. Each week, have the children plot their mileage on a map, following roads and highways. (It is best if the entire family does this.) Mileage equivalents for activities are as follows:

Aerobics	8–12 minutes	= 1 mile
Bicycling	3 miles	= 1 mile
Cross-Country Skiing	¾ mile	= 1 mile
Jogging	1 mile	= 1 mile
Rebounding	8–12 minutes	= 1 mile
Rope jumping	8–12 minutes	= 1 mile
Rowing	8–12 minutes	= 1 mile
Running in place	8–12 minutes	= 1 mile
Swimming	450 yards	= 1 mile
Walking	1 mile	= 1 mile

For personal mileage, use a state or county map. For family mileage, use a state or national map. You may want to aim for a destination, such as a relative's home.

Place the map in an obvious place—a refrigerator door, family bulletin board or family-room wall.

● Fitness Rewards (Ages 3–16)

When the children reach certain goals, reward them. A few ideas from the Kuntzleman family include:

—Running shoes when they accumulate 1,000 miles
—10-speed bike when they reach 10 years of age
—Allowance based on mileage achieved
—T-shirts, shoelaces for minor goals
—Running suits for performance goals, 10K times
—Cross-country skis as Christmas gifts
—Family Fitness Vacations—backpacking, mountain climbing
—Graduate from High School—graduate's choice of what to do with Mom or Dad:
  ● Debbie—Climb Long's Peak in Colorado
  ● John—A week of deer hunting with Dad (I don't hunt) in the wilds of Michigan's upper peninsula
  ● Tom—He's planning to hike for one week on the Appalachian Trail
  ● Lisa and Becky—ninth and eighth graders who are undecided
—Seven cent allowance: When the children were really small, seven cents was put in the family jar each week for each family member (forty-nine cents a

week). Each day we exercised, we got a penny. If we missed, the penny stayed in the jar. At the end of the week, the extra pennies were handed out among the children. Those who exercised the most days had the most money.

Our basic philosophy is: reward with physical activity, not food. Unfortunately, Americans tend to think the opposite: reward with food, punish with physical activity. No wonder, as a society, we're addicted to food and turned off to physical activity.

● President's Council Award (Ages 7 and up)

Have school-aged children ask their physical education teachers if they can participate in the President's Council on Physical Fitness and Sports Fitness Award.

Those aged 15 and older (including parents) can participate in the Presidential Sports Award. There are 43 qualifying sports, from archery to weight training. You select one (or more) sport and keep your own personal fitness log. For information, write:

> Presidential Sports Award
> PO Box 5214
> FDR Post Office
> New York, NY 10150–5214

Chapter 7:
The Good News of Nutrition

"[I pray] that you may be able to discern what
is best and may be pure and blameless until the
day of Christ" (Philippians 1:10).

Paul spent quite a bit of time with the people of Philippi. He gave them a message
of comfort, hope and healing. His message was "good news," the story of the
life, death and resurrection of the Lord Jesus Christ. The hearers of the gospel
grew strong in faith toward God and love toward each other.

During his time there, some other teachers appeared on the scene. They looked
good; they sounded right; they had an appealing message about Christ; but their
message was false.

Paul had some strong words to say about these false teachers. He warned the
people of the harm they were bringing. He prayed that the Christians would discern
and grow in the truth.[1]

Today *nutrition* has become a kind of gospel word. Good nutrition is a lifesaver,
a blessing to good health. But, too often, confusing messages about food and
drink bombard us. They look good; they sound right; they are very appealing;
but alas, they may be bad news, indeed. Again, we need knowledge and
discernment.

This section can help you discern, as it offers helpful information about nutrition. Chapter 7 deals with the good news; chapter 8 gives some bad news. And
"Family Food Activities" explains fun ways to improve your eating habits.

Nutrients

Nutritionists tell us there are six basic nutrients: carbohydrates, fats, proteins,
vitamins, minerals and water. All six nutrients are essential for your family's
health, vitality and appearance. Each has a specific task. Carbohydrates and fats
supply you with energy. Proteins build tissue. Vitamins and minerals help regulate
your bodily functions and cooperate with carbohydrates, fats and protein. Water
provides a medium for the other nutrients to do their jobs.

Plague #3

Cancer

One out of every four Americans will develop some kind of cancer. Barring new breakthroughs in cancer research, about 60 percent of these people will die of this dreaded disease.

Cancer takes many forms. Essentially it is a degenerative disease of the cells. The DNA (the material coded with the information as to what the cell can do and its offspring can become) changes, causing the growth regulation of the affected cells to go haywire. These cells divide abnormally. The cancerous cells, as they are called, injure the body by crowding out normal cells and robbing the normal cells of their nutrients. The abnormal cells tend to form masses called tumors.

Malignant solid tumors are named for the kind of tissue from which they originate. Carcinomas occur in the skin, glands, or respiratory or gastrointestinal membranes. Carcinomas spread to other parts of the body, mostly through the lymph system. Sarcomas develop in connective tissues or in membranes covering muscles and fat. They travel through the bloodstream. Lymphomas occur in the lymph nodes, while leukemia arises in the blood-forming tissues. Both lymphomas and leukemia are characterized by the increase of abnormal white blood cells.

As in the case of heart disease, the medical profession has made long strides in battling cancer. But the key seems to be in preventing the disease. Researchers say that 60 percent of all cancers could be prevented if people:[3]

● stopped smoking
● avoided over-exposure to sunlight
● dropped their weight and body fat
● ate foods rich in fiber and vitamins C, A and E
● ate less sugar and fat
● avoided alcohol and drugs
● reduced their stress
● avoided unnecessary X-rays and exposure to noxious gases, nitrates and nitrites (found in hotdogs, bacon and luncheon meats), selected chemicals (plastics, coal tar, dyes, arsenic and pesticides)

Foods are composed of these nutrients. For example, a piece of beef includes proteins, fats, small amounts of carbohydrates, vitamins, minerals and water. Carrots contain carbohydrates, vitamins, minerals, water and a trace of proteins. Table sugar is almost 100 percent carbohydrates (it may include a trace of minerals, but no fats or proteins).

Let's look at the six nutrients.

Carbohydrates

Carbohydrates are your body's most preferred nutrient. They are also the most maligned. Most of us think of them as the tempting, good-tasting treats from Grandma's kitchen. But they also are found in fruits; vegetables, including beets, onions, carrots, turnips, sweet potatoes; grains and grain products, such as breakfast cereals, noodles and pastries.

Carbohydrates are the easiest foods for your body to digest. Aside from providing energy, high-quality carbohydrate foods contain important minerals and vitamins, and they often come packaged with proteins.

When the carbohydrate stored in your body become inadequate, such as from prolonged, strenuous physical activity or starvation, your body can adjust and allow you to use fats and, infrequently, proteins to fill your energy needs. Unfortunately, the use of fats and proteins in place of carbohydrates is less-efficient and chemically more complex. The use of proteins can continue for only a limited amount of time before other body functions begin to suffer.

Carbohydrates come in the form of sugars, starches or cellulose. Sugars sometimes are called simple carbohydrates, which include: fruits (apples, oranges, cherries, grapes, pears, bananas), foods made with sugar (cakes, pies, jam, crackers, cookies, chocolate syrups), table sugar and honey.

Simple carbohydrates are the children's favorite. Heavy advertising on television, accessibiity through vending machines and stores, and parents' feelings that love is a chocolate chip cookie, heighten consumption of these sweets. Conversely, among young children, the vegetables become the quiet corner of their plate. Therefore, parents must be innovative to get children to eat vegetables instead of snacks. "Family Food Activities" can help.

Starches are called complex carbohydrates. On Table 10, you'll find a listing of many of these carbohydrates.

TABLE 10
Complex Carbohydrates and "Healthful" Simple Carbohydrates

Fructose (Healthful Simple Carbohydrates)

Apples	Figs	Mangoes	Plums
Apricots	Gooseberries	Muskmelons	Pomegranates
Bananas	Grapefruit	Nectarines	Quinces
Blackberries	Grapes	Oranges	Raisins
Blueberries	Guava	Papayas	Raspberries
Breadfruit	Kumquats	Peaches	Strawberries
Cherries	Lemon juice	Pears	Tangerines
Cranberries	Loganberries	Persimmons	Watermelon
Dates	Lychees	Pineapple	

Complex Carbohydrates
Grains

Barley	Cornmeal	Popcorn	Rye
Buckwheat	Oatmeal	Rice	Wheat

Vegetables

Artichokes	Carrots, raw	Legumes (dried)	Pumpkins
Asparagus	Cauliflower	Lentils	Radishes
Bamboo shoots	Celery	Lettuce	Rutabagas
Beansprouts	Chives	Mustard greens	Squash
Beans, snap green	Corn kernels	Okra	Sweet potatoes
and yellow	Cucumbers	Onions	Swiss chard
Beans, lima	Eggplant	Parsley	Tapioca
Beans, pinto	Endive	Parsnips	Tomatoes
Beets	Garbanzos	Peas	Turnips
Broccoli	Garlic	Peppers	Water chestnuts
Cabbage, raw	Leeks	Potatoes	

Cellulose is a complex carbohydrate that is difficult to digest. Cellular material must be cooked to be digested at all, and even then, most of it remains indigestible. It often is called fiber and is important as a bulk source for the digestive tract. Fiber helps in elimination and keeping the digestive tract healthy and possibly free from cancer, hemorrhoids, diverticular disease, appendicitis, colitis and bowel polyps. High cellulose foods include bran, whole grains, and vegetables and fruits with seeds and skins.

Fats

Fats are a class of nutrients made up of fatty acids and glycerin (an organic alcohol). They are found in foods such as butter and other dairy products, fatty meats, fish, poultry, salad and cooking oils, margarine, chocolate, nuts, and peanut butter. Pound for pound, fats provide more usable energy than carbohydrates or proteins. They also take longer to digest, so you feel fuller after a meal or a snack that contains some kind of fatty component. Foods containing fat tend to be high in vitamins A, D and E and the minerals phosphorus and sulfur.

The fatty acids that constitute fats are of three general kinds: saturated, unsaturated and polyunsaturated. These terms refer to the manner in which the hydrogen and carbon atoms of the fat are fastened together. If you could look at a saturated fat under a microscope, you would see the hydrogen and carbon atoms linked together (see Table 11). With a little imagination, it is possible to visualize each carbon atom as having four hands—one on each side, one at the top and one at the bottom. The carbon atoms would be holding hands like a human chain, leaving

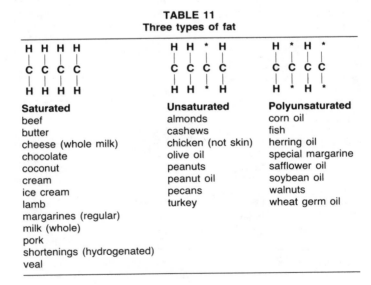

TABLE 11
Three types of fat

Saturated	Unsaturated	Polyunsaturated
beef	almonds	corn oil
butter	cashews	fish
cheese (whole milk)	chicken (not skin)	herring oil
chocolate	olive oil	special margarine
coconut	peanuts	safflower oil
cream	peanut oil	soybean oil
ice cream	pecans	walnuts
lamb	turkey	wheat germ oil
margarines (regular)		
milk (whole)		
pork		
shortenings (hydrogenated)		
veal		

each carbon atom with two hands free. If the free hands of the carbon atom held onto the hands of the hydrogen atoms, all the carbon atom's hands would be occupied. When this is the case, the fat is saturated with hydrogen. If a carbon atom does not hold hands with the hydrogen atom, it is unsaturated. If some carbon atoms are holding hands with the hydrogen, but some are not, the fat is polyunsaturated or less-saturated. In short, the less hydrogen present, the more unsaturated the fat is. More on these fats and your family's health in chapter 8.

Proteins

Proteins are present in all living tissues. They make up vital parts of cells and are the main constituents of muscles, nerves, glands and many hormones. Protein molecules are large and composed of many nitrogen-containing components called amino acids. Individual protein molecules may consist of several different amino acids. Before your body can use these proteins, your digestive system must break them down into their component amino acids. There are twenty-one amino acids, of which your body can manufacture eleven. They are called nonessential. The other ten, called essential amino acids, can be obtained only by eating the right foods.

Your body uses proteins to build and repair body tissues. Only proteins can supply the amino acids that your body needs. If your protein supply is not sufficient to offset the daily destruction of cells, your body begins to waste away. So, a poor protein diet has serious effects on growth and development.

Proteins are crucial, but they are not required in large amounts. Parents tend to push protein on children, yet our studies and those of others show that in America a protein deficiency among children is very unlikely. It's important to get protein from a wide range of sources, however, particularly during periods of rapid growth and cell formation, as in adolescence, pregnancy and convalescence.

Meat, fish and eggs, are rich in complete protein. They contain all the essential amino acids. Dry cereals, breads, nuts and most fruits and vegetables contain lesser amounts and incomplete proteins, which means that they do not contain all ten essential amino acids. They do contain some and are good foods, but for most effective use by our bodies, they should be combined with other proteins (see Table 12). Many of these foods also provide some minerals and vitamins.

Vitamins

Vitamins are not food energy sources, per se. That is, they don't provide calories. But vitamins are very important. They make it possible for you to use appropriately the food you eat. They provide for chemical control of our body functions and play an important role in energy production, normal growth, resistance to infection, and general health. Most vitamins act as catalysts that initiate or speed

TABLE 12
Protein Foods

Animal Products (Complete Protein)

Beef	Duck	Fish	Pork
Cheese	Eggs	Milk	Turkey
Chicken			

Grains (Incomplete Protein)

Brown rice	Corn	Oats	Rice

Legumes (Incomplete Protein)

Garbanzo beans	Lima beans	Peas	Soybean flour
Kidney beans	Mung beans	Soy sprouts	Soybeans

Nuts and Seeds (Incomplete Protein)

Cashews	Peanuts

Vegetarian Dishes* (Complete Protein Dishes)

Barley and yogurt soup	Middle Eastern hummus (sesame and chick-peas)
Bean or pea curry on rice	Milk in legume soups
Blended dip of garbanzos, sesame, lemon, garlic, oil	Pasta with milk or cheese
Bread made with milk or cheese	Pea soup and toast
Breads with added seed meals	Rice and milk pudding
Breads with sesame or sunflower seed spread	Rice-bean casserole
Cereal with milk	Rice-cheese casserole
Cheese sandwiches	Rice with sesame seeds
Cheese sauce, garbanzo beans	Sesame salt on legume dish
Corn-soy bread	Sesame seeds in bean soups and casseroles
Corn tortillas and beans	Sunflower seeds and peanuts
Legume soup with bread	Wheat berries with cheese sauce
Lentil curry on rice	Wheat bread with baked beans
Macaroni and cheese	Wheat-soy bread

Source: Based on Frances Lappe, *Diet for a Small Planet* (New York: Ballantine, 1975).
*These dishes show how you can combine nonmeat protein foods (those not containing all ten essential amino acids) to make a complete protein dish. That is, barley and yogurt soup provide all the essential amino acids, as does macaroni and cheese, and sunflower seeds and peanuts.

up the rate of chemical reactions. Life cannot continue without these biochemical catalysts.

Most plants manufacture the vitamins they need. For the most part, your body can't do that. You must get your vitamins from the foods you eat. The highest sources of vitamins are meats, particularly the liver and kidneys; fruits; vegetables; milk; eggs; fish; and certain cereals. Vitamin deficiencies can result in night blindness, poor bone and tooth formation, scurvy, stunted growth, lack of vitality, poor condition of skin and mucous membranes, and a loss of appetite and weight.

Vitamins are designated by a letter of the alphabet because at one time scientists did not know their chemical structure and could not give them proper scientific names. There are two basic kinds of vitamins: water-soluble and fat-soluble. The fat-soluble vitamins are A, D, E and K. The water-soluble vitamins are vitamins C and B, in particular B_1 and B_2 and niacin, pyridoxine, B_{12}, folic acid, biotin and pantothenic acid.

When most people talk about nutrition, they think only of vitamins. Parents feel secure that their children are getting adequate nutrition because they eat a cereal fortified with eight essential vitamins plus iron. Yet, if your chidren ate nothing but cereal every day for the rest of their lives, they probably wouldn't live very long. They would get some carbohydrates and vitamins, but an inadequate amount of proteins, selected minerals and other essential vitamins.

There is much controversy regarding the amount of vitamins needed by Americans. On one side of the coin, the traditional medical establishment advocates the United States government recommended daily allowances (RDA) on vitamins (see appendix B). On the other side of the coin, some famous biochemists, such as Drs. Linus Pauling and Roger Williams, recommend megavitamins. Megavitamins are large doses of certain vitamins to reduce the incidence of disease— everything from the common cold to cancer. Quite frankly, the vitamin story is far from complete. Research findings have not been definitive. Most of the studies show that supplementing an already well-balanced diet will not improve health. But, and it's a big one, most of these studies have been conducted over relatively short periods of time. We don't know what effect vitamin supplementation has (good or bad) over a ten-, fifteen-, or twenty-year period of time.

I subscribe to what Dr. Williams calls biological individuality. Each person is different. What is appropriate for one person may not be appropriate for another. Even traditional scientists and physicians are starting to accept this concept. They recognize that medication must be adjusted for each person, so why shouldn't vitamin requirements vary?

Research has demonstrated that certain people need extra vitamins. Heavy alcohol drinkers, heavy smokers, and women who are using a birth control pill seem to have difficulty securing enough vitamins from food. Appendix B includes a list of people who are apt to be deficient in certain vitamins.

You cannot assume, however, that if a little of a vitamin is good for you, a lot is better. When your cells are vitamin-saturated, additional vitamins are worthless.

I recommend that you make sure that you and your children get your RDA. If you are having some of the problems listed in Appendix B under the "Known Health Roles" of vitamins or are showing signs of deficiency, then you could try taking additional amounts of the vitamin. One of our daughters supplements her diet, but, through a nutrition study at the University of Texas, she was found to be deficient in choline, folic acid and vitamin B_{12}. Naturally, we upped her intake of foods high in these vitamins and increased her supplementation.

Minerals

Minerals are unique, inorganic chemical substances. Like vitamins, they are important in regulating body functions and are essential to the structure of bones and other body tissues. They are vital to your family's energy and health.

Minerals are part of the cell membrane, cell nucleus and other cell structures, such as the mitochondria, or powerhouses, of the cell, which convert food nutrients to energy. For example, selected minerals help break down glucose, fatty acids and amino acids into energy. All other minerals build up the glucose, fatty acids, and amino acids into glycogen, fats and proteins, respectively. Minerals also serve as important parts of the structure of various hormones, enzymes and other substances that help regulate the chemical reactions within cells.

For years, nutritionists have emphasized the major minerals, such as calcium, magnesium, phosphorus, potassium, sodium and sulfur. These have been considered essential. Appendix C gives you an idea of the role and sources of these important elements.

More recently, the trace elements or minerals have been brought to the fore. Work begun by Dr. Henry A. Schroeder, professor emeritus at Dartmouth Medical School, has demonstrated that trace elements, although present in minute amounts, are essential for normal metabolism. Trace minerals include chromium, copper, fluorine, iodine, iron, manganese, selenium, zinc and a few others.

Water

Water accounts for about 70 percent of the body's weight. All body fluids are basically watery solutions and are found in three main forms:

1. Intracellular fluid, which exists within the cells.
2. Extracellular fluid, which exists between the cells and provides the environment in which they exist and perform their respective functions.
3. Plasma, the fluid part of blood or lymph, which is 92 percent water.

These fluids consist of water and dissolved inorganic mineral substances. The chemistry of animal life involves exchanges between these fluids and combinations of the various solutions.

Water is acquired in three ways: taken as drink, contained in foods we eat, and formed within the body as a result of the oxidation process. Water is lost from the body through urination, defecation, perspiration and evaporation. In the average adult, the daily water loss amounts to about three quarts, so we must replace that amount daily. Two quarts of that requirement are provided by the food we eat. We must drink the other quart. Ordinarily, the thirst mechanism is sufficient to induce us to take enough water. Also, the fluid requirement varies from day to day depending on certain factors, the most important of which are perspiration, temperature, and exercise or strenuous work. Under conditions of extreme exertion, heat and excessive perspiration, we must make a special effort to meet the water (and mineral) loss.

The Basic Four

Nutritionists have reduced all of this information into a palatable approach for the average family by creating the four basic food groups:

Group 1 The vegetable-fruit group. Rich in vitamins, minerals and carbohydrates.
Group 2 The bread-cereal group. Rich in vitamins, minerals, and carbohydrates; contains some amino acids.
Group 3 The milk group. Rich in vitamins, minerals, protein and fat; contains some carbohydrates.
Group 4 The meat group. Rich in fats, protein, vitamins and minerals.

To insure adequate intake of the six nutrients, they recommend eating daily:

- Four servings of group 1(vegetables-fruits)
- Four servings of group 2(breads-cereals)
- Two or three servings of group 3 (milk)
- Two servings of group 4 (meat)

Alas, this plan is unsatisfactory. Suppose you ate four servings of fruit from group 1. You would get plenty of carbohydrate and vitamin C, but your vitamin B and mineral intake would be too low. The plan does not provide diversity.

According to Jean Mayer, Ph.D., world-famous nutritionist and currently president of Tufts University, this classification system is misleading and not satisfactory. Mayer states, "There is no reason, for example, to classify potatoes and spinach together. It would make more sense to gather the main sources of animal protein and good quality vegetable proteins (milk, meat, fish, eggs, peas, and beans) and separate starch fruits (bananas) and roots (potatoes) from green leafy vegetables and other foods."[2]

Because of Dr. Mayer's criteria and my own work with helping people eat a more healthy diet, I propose the following food classification system (which will be further refined in the next chapter):

Group 1 Non-starchy vegetables (basically, green or leafy vegetables)
Group 2 Starchy vegetables (basically, white and yellow vegetables)
Group 3 Fruits
Group 4 Milk and milk products
Group 5 Protein foods
Group 6 Grain foods
Group 7 Fats, sweets and alcohol

To insure adequate intake of the six nutrients, you should eat daily:

- Two servings from group 1
- One serving from group 2
- One serving from group 3
- Two servings from group 4
- Two servings from group 5
- Four servings from group 6
- Zero servings from group 7

This approach allows you to obtain a wide source of vitamins and minerals. It also requires you to be more diverse in your eating plan.

Your Family's Eating Habits

Many people think their family eats well. The "Nutrition Guide" (Table 13) gives you important guidelines for determining your family's and your own eating habits. The guide is simple to use. If you eat what is recommended for each group, you receive the maximum number of points. For example, if you eat two servings of non-starchy vegetables, you receive 20 points. If you eat one serving, you get 10 points. If you don't eat any, you get zero. Follow this pattern for all the groups. After you finish for the day, total your score. The score is pass or fail. One hundred points is the maximum number you can receive. If you get 100, you will be getting the recommended daily allowance for vitamins, minerals, fats,

TABLE 13
Nutrition Guide

Group	Score	Food Groups & Number of Servings	Day 1	Day 2	Day 3
1	20	Two servings (about 1 cup) of non-starch vegetables (basically leafy/green, such as asparagus to zucchini).			
2	10	One serving (about ½ cup) of starch vegetables, such as corn and potatoes.			
3	10	One serving (about ½ cup) of fruit—citrus or non-citrus.			
4	20	Two cups of milk or milk products. One-inch cube of cheese is equivalent to ½ cup of milk.			
5	20	Two servings (total: approximately 4 oz.) of protein food (meat, poultry, fish, dried beans, peas, nuts, eggs, or vegetable dishes listed on table 14).			
6	20	Four or more servings of grain products (breads, cereals, or noodles).			
7	0	Zero servings of fats, sweets and alcohol.			

proteins and carbohydrates. If you fall below 100 points, you are deficient in one or more of these categories.

Take the test now, using what you think is a typical day.

After you take the test, have your spouse and children do likewise. If the children are too young or you anticipate resistance, do it for them. Watch their eating for a day (don't tell them what you're doing). You may be surprised at your family's results.

While this guide gives you an indication of whether or not you are getting a sufficient amount of nutrients, it has its limitations. It does not take into account the saturated fat, sugar, fiber, caffeine and salt in your diet. That will be discussed in the next chapter.

"He makes grass grow for the cattle, and plants for man to cultivate—bringing forth food from the earth" (Psalm 104:14).

Chapter 8:
The Bad News of Nutrition

> "Their destiny is destruction, their god is their stomach, and their glory is in their shame. Their mind is on earthly things" (Philippians 3:19).

Many Christians believe that we are permitted to eat what we want. Peter was told in a dream that he could eat whatever God made clean.[1] Paul told Timothy that everything God created, including food, was good, so it should be received with thanksgiving.[2]

All that is true. But, it does not give us license to consume an excess of real or imitation foods. Our stomachs should not be our god. We must be careful about what we eat. Yes, if God made it, it is good. But if man has tampered with it, beware.

Just 100 years ago, bread, the staff of life, had a protein rating of 18 to 20 percent. Today, it has dropped to 9 to 12 percent. Technology has decreased the nutritive value of certain foods and defiled others with too much salt, sugar, fat, cholesterol, caffeine and certain additives. The technology that protects us from botulism, scurvy, and protein deficiencies has contributed to the development of heart disease, cancer, arthritis, obesity, stroke, colitis, high blood pressure and fatigue, to name a few maladies.

In Peter's and Paul's day, there were no food companies, food technology and refining processes that provided people with food in boxes, bottles and bags. Foods were not stripped of vital nutrients and "enhanced" with sugar, salt and fat. There were no agribusiness, supermarkets, butylated hydroxyanisole (BHA), carrageenan or monosodium glutamate (MSG). The Israelites lived close to the land. They raised crops, herded sheep and fished the waters. They ate from this bounty. If they wanted more, they bartered, traded and purchased from other merchants. Food was available, yet the average Israelites scraped and saved tiny morsels.

America's land of milk and honey is significantly different. The availability of food is incredible. We have sugar-coated cereals, saccharin-and aspartame-sweetened pop, cocktail puffs, egg substitutes, decaffeinated coffee, imitation cream, pretzels, potato and tortilla chips, vegetable protein meats, Big Macs, colas and Hostess Twinkies.

The significance of this food is understood when you realize that the average American has more than 3000 calories cross his or her plate every day. That breaks down to 1500 to 2000 pounds of food a year. Specifically, 16 pounds of

---

Plague #4

Allergies and Other Disorders of the Immune System

Our ability to stay alive and healthy in a world teeming with disease organisms and other toxins is a tribute to God's wisdom in providing us with defense and repair mechanisms. The most sophisticated aspect of the defense network is the immunological mechanisms. These mechanisms enable the body to identify and destroy invading viruses and bacteria or other threatening foreign substances. Basically, the immune system brings together molecules of protein that will attack a specific foreign substance identified by the body as hostile to it. The defensive molecules are called antibodies; the foreign molecules that incite an immune system to create antibodies are called antigens.

Unfortunately, the very complex immune system can go awry in many ways. In so-called autoimmune diseases, such as multiple sclerosis, lupus erythematosus and rheumatoid arthritis, the body turns against parts of itself. It creates antibodies that attack its own cells. These healthy cells multiply to compensate for the injury and tissues are inflamed or damaged as a result.

More common still is the immune malfunction called allergy, which is believed to torment 20 to 60 million or more Americans. In these cases, immune system becomes intolerant of ingested, inhaled or touched substances that the majority of people find harmless.

Virtually any natural or synthetic substance in the environment can cause allergic reactions. A few frequent offenders are pollens, molds, dust, animal dander, drugs, cosmetics, foods (such as cows' milk, wheat, eggs, white potatoes, chocolate, tomatoes and oranges), food additives, fabric softeners, gas from vehicles or ovens, and odorless emissions of mercury and other substances from incinerators. Allergic reactions also are caused by chemical fumes given off by various plastics and commonly used products, such as disinfectants, paint and floor wax.

If the offending substance strikes the lungs or bronchial tubes, asthma or bronchitis result. Allergic skin reactions include hives or eczema. The upper respiratory system may react with allergic rhinitis or hayfever, or perhaps sinus problems. Housemaid's knee or other joint problems also may be an expression of allergy. The gastrointestinal tract can be a target, too, resulting in cramps, diarrhea, constipation or colitis.

---

boxed cereal, 280 eggs, 175 pounds of fruits, 70 pounds of bread, 250 pounds of vegetables, 230 pounds of meat and fish, 430 gallons of soft drinks, 2 gallons of wine, 24 gallons of beer, 2 gallons of liquor, 144 gallons of milk and cream, 560 cups of coffee, 150 cups of tea, 130 pounds of fat, more than 100 pounds of sugar and 6 pounds of salt![3] The tragedy is that despite all of this food, we are not eating well.

Table 14 (see next page) offers a close look at what has happened to American family eating habits in my lifetime.

This pattern of living has created a diet that is much too rich. Our diet is 42 percent fat; 12 percent protein and 46 percent carbohydrates. The United States government recommends 30 percent of a diet coming from fat, 12 percent from protein, and 58 percent from carbohydrates. To achieve these goals, we need to follow the guidelines at the end of this chapter.

TABLE 14
Family Dietary Changes

Before World War II	Today
1. Meals from scratch	1. TV Dinners and meals
2. Almost all meals at home	2. One-third of meals eaten outside of the home plus many fast-food restaurants
3. Complex carbohydrates (potatoes, peas, whole-grain products)	3. Simple carbohydrates (sucrose, highly refined diet)
4. Fresh vegetables	4. Canned and frozen vegetables
5. Fresh fruits	5. Canned (heavy syrup) and frozen fruits
6. Fresh fruit as dessert	6. Pastry desserts
7. Water/milk beverages	7. Coffee/soda pop beverages
8. Occasional alcoholic beverages	8. Alcoholic beverages at most meals, snacks, or bedtime
9. Low-salt, low-additive diet	9. High-salt, high-additive diet
10. Low-fat diet	10. High-fat diet
11. Moderate beef intake	11. High beef intake
12. Butter	12. Margarine
13. High-calorie breakfast and lunch, relatively low-calorie dinner	13. Low-calorie breakfast (if any), moderate- to high-calorie lunch, very high-calorie dinner
14. Little snacking	14. High degree of snacking
15. High activity (3000 calories, men; 2400 calories, women) per day	15. Low activity (2200 calories, men; 1500–1600 calories, women) per day

Data from a 15,000-household study done in 1977–1978 by the USDA suggested that Americans seemed to be getting more vitamins A, B and C and iron than in a 1965 survey, but less calcium and too much sugar, fat and salt. In 1909, 32 percent of the average American's calories were from fat. In 1976, fat had increased to 42 percent of his calories. Between 1909 and 1976, the amount of carbohydrates eaten stayed the same, but the type changed. In 1909, 68 percent of our carbohydrates were from starches and 32 percent from sugars. Today, 47 percent come from starches and 53 percent from sugars. Salt consumption also has skyrocketed over the past seventy years.[4]

As nutritionist Jean Mayer has pointed out, less than 10 percent of American food was processed in 1941. As of 1970, 50 percent was processed, engineered or synthesized.[5] Today, the figure must be 70 percent or more. If you doubt that, check the shopping carts next time you shop. Someone has estimated that seventy cents of every food dollar is spent on processed items.

Sugar

"Just a spoonful of sugar" may not harm your fitness and energy levels, but eating 100 to 120 pounds a year (as the average American does) is energy suicide. Some investigators say that preteens may eat as much as 150 pounds a year![6]

The problem is the amount eaten, rather than sugar, or sucrose, itself. If you eat only a few pounds of sugar a year, or a fraction of an ounce a day, it should not harm your fitness. But the average American adult eats 2 to slightly less than 2½ pounds of sugar a week, which breaks down to 500 to 600 calories per day of pure sugar. That is too much. It amounts to 18 percent of their total calorie consumption. Our studies on children in grades two through seven showed that the average child eats 25 percent of his or her calories from simple carbohydrates, mostly from pop, candy, donuts, "ade" drinks, pre-sweetened cereals, etc.

All of this is particularly serious because a diet high in sucrose usually tends to be low in other basic nutrients—especially the B vitamins and several essential minerals. Additionally, the sugar comes highly refined and stripped of any fiber, which is necessary for a healthy intestinal tract. A diet high in sugar has been linked to heart disease, tooth decay, diabetes, hypoglycemia, fatigue, obesity, cancer, arthritis and hyperactivity.

While sugar may taste good, moderation is the key. Intead of 500 to 600 calories a day, a more reasonable intake is 200 to 250 calories a day or about a pound of sugar a week.

Fats

We Americans consume more fat per person than any other nation in the world. In fact, we eat 80 percent of the world's foods that are high in saturated fat.

Fats can be a source of energy, but when eaten to excess, problems occur. According to many scientists, the fats you eat actually can suffocate your tissues by depriving them of oxygen. Saturated and unsaturated fats form a film around the red blood cells and platelets in your blood, causing them to stick together. This is called sludging. Sludging causes the red blood cells to carry less oxygen and makes it more likely that they will plug your tiny blood vessels (capillaries). Because the capillaries get blocked, the watery part of the blood is forced through the capillary walls, causing edema (swelling), which reduces the amount of oxygen available to the cells. Some experts say that plugging in this manner can affect 5 to 20 percent of your body tissue.

A diet high in fat also can raise blood cholesterol levels. This cholesterol tends to be deposited on the lining of the arteries. When these linings become partially blocked, less oxygen gets to the heart and you become a prime candidate for heart disease.

In chapter 7, I told you about saturated, unsaturated and polyunsaturated fats. Now this distinction becomes important.

Saturated Fat. Saturated fats are usually solid at room temperature. They are found primarily in food of animal origin (meat fat, cheese, cream, butterfat), but are also found in a few vegetable fats (coconut, coconut oil, palm kernel oil, cocoa butter). Unsaturated liquid fats can be converted to solid partially saturated fats (shortening, margarines) by the chemical process of hydrogenation. Excessive intake of saturated fat tends to raise the level of cholesterol in the blood.

Unsaturated Fat. Unsaturated fats are considered "neutral fats," since they neither raise nor lower the level of cholesterol in the blood. Olive oil, olives, peanut oil, peanuts and avocado contain unsaturated fat.

Polyunsaturated Fat. Polyunsaturated fats (safflower, sunflower, corn, cotton-seed and soybean oils) are liquid at room temperature. Polyunsaturated oils tend to lower the level of cholesterol in the blood by an unknown mechanism.

While saturated fat is the least desirable of all fats, experts tell us to reduce the total amount of fat eaten. The average American gets 42 percent of his or her calories from fat. Children get almost as much—38 percent.

Cholesterol

No discussion of dietary fat is complete without addressing cholesterol foods. Cholesterol is a fat-like substance present in all animal tissues, such as blood, muscle, liver and brain. It is manufactured by the body and found in all foods of animal origin. Eggs, organ meats and shrimp contain more cholesterol than any other animal products.

Keeping blood cholesterol levels low is important for your children. Dr. Gerald Berenson of Louisiana State University Medical College in New Orleans has traced children's blood cholesterol levels over the past fourteen years. He started testing children when they were five to ten years of age. Now some of the children are in their early twenties. Not surprisingly, about one-half of the children who had high blood cholesterol levels as children have elevated blood cholesterol levels later in life.[8] These findings, coupled with research that shows that a 1 percent reduction in blood cholesterol reduces the risk of heart attack by 2 percent, demonstrates the necessity for you to keep your child's and your blood cholesterol levels low.[9] Our studies on children suggested that girls tended not to eat much food cholesterol, but boys (who could afford it least) exceeded the recommended 300 milligrams per day.

According to Dr. Berenson's studies, desireable blood cholesterol levels are:

TABLE 15
Desirable Blood Cholesterol Levels

Age	Cholesterol Levels
Birth	65–70
1–2 years	145–155
2–10 years	160
10–16 years	140
16–50 years	170–230
Over 50 years	170–230

Source: Gerald S. Berenson, *Cardiovascular Risk Factors in Children* (New York: Oxford University Press, 1980), 3–18.

To keep your blood cholesterol levels low, follow the guidelines at the end of this chapter and the family fitness, food, and weight control activities on pages 55 to 69, 96 to 122, and 140 to 156.

Table 16 is a list of the cholesterol content of many common foods. People often are surprised to see that liver, which is "nutritious," has a very high cholesterol content.

TABLE 16
Cholesterol Content of Common Foods

Foods	Amount (Cooked)	Cholesterol (mg)
Brains	3 oz.	2000
Kidney, all kinds	3 oz.	683
Liver, chicken	3 oz.	634
Liver, beef	3 oz.	372
Egg yolk	1	272
Heart, beef	3 oz.	233
Shrimp	3 oz.	128
Cream cheese	3 oz.	94
Cheddar cheese	3 oz.	90
Veal	3 oz.	86
Crab	3 oz.	85
Beef, lean	3 oz.	77
Chicken drumstick, without skin	3 oz.	77
Pork, lean	3 oz.	75
American cheese	3 oz.	75
Lobster	3 oz.	72
Chicken breast, without skin	3 oz.	67
Clams, canned	3 oz.	54
Flounder	3 oz.	50
Oysters	3 oz.	50
Milk, whole	1 cup	34
Milk, lowfat (2%)	1 cup	18
Milk, lowfat (1%)	1 cup	10
Milk, nonfat (skim)	1 cup	5
Fruits, vegetables and grains	Any amount	0

Source: Jane Brody, *Jane Brody's Nutrition Book* (New York: W. W. Norton, 1981), 83–84.

Fat and Food Preparation

In addition to understanding the rationale for keeping blood cholesterol levels low and knowing which foods contain high levels of cholesterol and fat, you should be aware of hidden fat as you prepare foods or eat out. If our studies accurately represent United States children and families, this is an important source of fat. We found that more than 30 percent of the parents used cream cheese, bacon grease, butter and lard when cooking.

Use this guide to determine the fat used in food preparation in your home, at a friend's house or at a restaurant:

Vegetables
- Seasoned with regular margarine or butter—½ teaspoon fat per ½ cup portion
- Stir fried (Chinese style)—½ teaspoon per ½ cup portion
- Breaded and fried—1 teaspoon per ½ cup portion
- French fries—1 teaspoon per 10 small french fries

Eggs
- Fried—1 teaspoon fat per egg
- Scrambled—depends on amount added to pan—all fat is absorbed during cooking (typically 1 teaspoon fat per egg)

Meat, Fish, and Poultry
- Pan fried—½ teaspoon fat per ounce
- Breaded and fried—1 teaspoon fat per ounce
- Basted—½ teaspoon fat per ounce

Salads
- Potato, noodle, tuna, salmon, chicken or egg salad—1 tablespoon fat per ½ cup portion
- Coleslaw—2 teaspoons fat per ½ cup portion
- Tossed salad—1 tablespoon dressing per cup portion

Salt

Before we discuss salt, we need to distinguish between sodium and sodium chloride. Sodium is a trace mineral found naturally in many foods. Your body needs regular, small amounts of sodium. Sodium chloride is a chemically manufactured salt, commonly referred to as table salt.

The average person probably needs no more than a gram of salt a day, yet many Americans eat between eight and fifteen grams of table salt daily. We plaster it on pretzels, popcorn, peanuts, potato chips and French fries. It is sprinkled liberally over mashed potatoes, gravy, meat and vegetables. Some people even sprinkle salt on fresh apples, grapefruit and watermelon.

Table salt may cause hypertension or high blood pressure, if you are salt- or sodium-sensitive. Again, Dr. Berenson's study provides important information. Children who eat a lot of salty foods are more likely to have high blood pressure now and when they are older.[10]

Some cardiologists claim that if we eliminated salt from the American diet, there would be absolutely no high blood pressure in the United States. Other experts claim that the jury is still out. One thing is clear: peoples around the world who eat little salt—Eskimos, Australians, Aborigines, and Panamanian Indians— have very low percentages of high blood pressure. People like the Northern Japanese, who eat thirty-five or more grams of salt a day, have unbelievably high percentages of hypertension—four persons out of ten. When people eat a diet low in salt after having high blood pressure, their high blood pressure usually drops drastically.

Caffeine

Every morning, about 80 percent of America's adult population chugs a mug or two of coffee. By noon, a good share of those 100 million people have had two to five cups.

Laboratory experiments indicate that the caffeine in coffee increases mental alertness, speeds reaction time and helps people think more clearly. In short, caffeine buzzes the brain and nervous sytem, perhaps by increasing the concentration of a hormone stimulator called cyclic AMP, which increases alertness.

Most coffee drinkers notice and want this effect, but they realize they don't get it from a cup or two of coffee. One cup of coffee generally contains only 100 to 150 milligrams of caffeine, a relatively harmless amount. The average coffee drinker goes through two to three cups a day, however, pushing the amount of caffeine to 200 to 450 milligrams. They also may get caffeine from other sources, such as tea, cola drinks or cocoa. Compounding the problem, their bodies develop

TABLE 17
The Caffeine Scorecard
(In amounts usually consumed)

Item	Milligrams of Caffeine (average)	Item	Milligrams of Caffeine (average)
Coffee (5 oz.)		**Soft Drinks (12 oz.)**	
Brewed, drip method	115	Tab	46.8
Brewed, percolator	80	Coca-Cola	45.6
Instant	65	Diet Coke	45.6
Coffee-grain blends	31	Dr. Pepper	39.6
Decaffeinated	2	Pepsi-Cola	38.4
		Diet Pepsi	36
Tea (5 oz.)		**Nonprescription Drugs** (recommended	
Brewed, imported brands	60	dosage)	
Brewed, major U.S. brands	40	Dexatrim	200
Leaf	34	Vivarin	200
Instant	30	Excedrin	65
Iced (12 oz.)	70	Midol, Cope, Easy-Mens	32.4
		Anacin, aspirin, Bromo	
Cocoa (5 oz.)	4	Seltzer	32
		Vanquish	32
Milk Chocolate (1 oz.)	6	Pre-Mens	66
		Dristan Decongestant	16.2

Source: Food and Drug Administration and National Soft Drink Association

an immunity to those boosts in alertness and reaction time. That is why the two-
to three-cups-a-day coffee drinkers easily can increase their consumption to six
to eight cups, which provides close to 1000-milligrams of caffeine. That level can
produce dizziness, restlessness, irritability and tremors.

Children are not immune to caffeine. Your children may not drink coffee, but
they may drink colas, iced tea, cocoa and chocolate milk. They also probably eat
chocolate candy. Two cola drinks and a glass of chocolate milk contain 130 to
170 milligrams of caffeine. For a seven-year-old, that is equivalent to drinking
four to six cups of brewed coffee.

Excessive caffeine consumption has been associated with heart and kidney diseases, skipped heart beats, cancer, gastric upsets, anxiety and insomnia.

Additives

Practically every food you eat contains some type of additive. That doesn't mean
practically everything you eat is bad. Some additives are necessary and do not
adversely affect your health. Other additives may present health hazards. Rather
than cutting from your diet all foods containing additives (it would be almost
impossible), learn more about the kinds of additives in foods and how they can
affect your family's level of wellness.

Additives preserve the freshness of food and enhance its flavor and color. Currently, more then five thousand different kinds of additives are used to process
the food we eat.

The most widely used additives are sugar and salt, which we discussed a few
pages earlier. Some of the other most popular additives are: MSG, mustard, black
pepper, hydrolyzed vegetable protein, sodium caseinate, carbon dioxide, and caramel. Rather than discuss all the additives, I will concentrate on MSG, artificial
colorings, nitrates and nitrites, saccharin, and aspartame.

MSG

Monosodium glutamate, or MSG, is used to improve the flavor of foods. Initially,
MSG was used in oriental cooking, but by the mid-1960s, its use had spread to
the United States. Now it is used widely.

There is no hard evidence that MSG is harmful, but it is directly implicated in
a condition known as "Chinese Restaurant Syndrome." This temporary condition
involves a burning sensation in the back of the neck and forearms, a tight feeling
in the chest, and headaches. Since many Chinese restaurants use copious amounts
of MSG, this condition occurs most often after people eat Chinese food. MSG is
found in other foods, however, such as condiments, soups, candy, baked goods
and pickles.

"Chinese Restaurant Syndrome" is a temporary condition and does not, at first, appear to be serious. Yet, experimental studies found that MSG in the food supply of mice caused deterioration of certain nerve cells. The Food and Drug Administration has concluded that MSG is not hazardous to adults, but they have suggested that manufacturers limit the amount they add to foods.

Artificial Colorings

When foods are processed, they often lose the natural ingredients that made them colorful. Consequently, dyes are used to bring back the lost color. The dyes do not return the natural ingredients, however, and alarming evidence suggests they may create potential health hazards. Red dye No. 40, the most commonly used dye, appears to promote cancer in mice. Yellow dye No. 5 causes allergic reactions in thousands of people. Other dyes are suspected of causing hyperactivity in children.

Avoiding food dyes is recommended, but often difficult. The best way to avoid dyes is to read the label of the foods you eat. That doesn't tell you everything, however, since the dairy industry does not have to list dyes in their labels.

As you read labels, avoid these dyes: oranges No. 1 and No. 2; yellows No. 1, No. 2, No. 3, and No. 4; violet No. 1; reds No. 4 and No. 32; and carbon black. These have been banned in the United States. Only sixteen man-made food dyes have been approved for use, though some scientists feel that even those have not been tested sufficiently.

Since little is known about the approved food dyes, and since approximately 10 percent of America's food is artificially colored, it is best to read labels and try to avoid dyes as much as possible.

Nitrates and Nitrites

Nitrates and nitrites are used to cure meats such as bacon, hotdogs and luncheon meats. Their value, which is to prevent botulism bacteria, is heavily outweighed by the fact that they can combine with digestive juices and other food substances to produce nitrosamines, one of the most powerful carcinogens discovered. Whether or not nitrates and nitrites are directly related to cancer has not been decided. In 1980, the Food and Drug Administration agreed not to ban their use. The United States Department of Agriculture has recognized the possible link, however, and has acted to reduce or eliminate them. Additionally, the USDA has requested meat processors to add vitamin C, which helps retard the formation of cancer-causing nitrosamines.

Saccharin

Although a great deal of controversy surrounds saccharin, the scientific evidence seems to indicate that saccharin increases the risk of cancer. In 1978, the National Academy of Sciences reviewed the saccharin evidence and concluded that the sweetener is a relatively "weak" carcinogen in animals, and probably also causes cancer in humans. Moreover, the National Cancer Institute found that heavy saccharin users have a greater chance of developing bladder cancer.[11]

As with nitrates and nitrites, some experts claim saccharin has no ill effects. The best advice, however, is to try to eliminate saccharin from your diet.

Aspartame

In 1981, the FDA approved the use of aspartame as a substitute for table sugar. In 1983, the artificial sweetener was approved for use in soft drinks. While generally regarded as safe, some researchers are uncomfortable with its current widespread use. They fear that using aspartame-sweetened beverages along with other dietary carbohydrates (cookies, sandwiches, cola) may contribute to headaches or behavior changes in people who suffer from high blood pressure, Parkinson's disease or insomnia.

The Basic Seven Questions

The discussion of sugar, salt, fat, cholesterol, caffeine and additives brings us back to the seven basic food groups. The basic seven, as discussed in chapter 7, leave a lot of unanswered questions. Here are a few:

1. May I eat canned or frozen fruits and vegetables?
2. May I count ice cream as one of the servings of milk? What about whole milk or cream?
3. What kinds of meats should I serve? Are luncheon meats, hotdogs or hamburgers O.K.?
4. Do foods such as white breads, cakes, pies, granola bars and cookies qualify as grain products?
5. How do I cut our fat, cholesterol, sugar, caffeine and salt intake?
6. Are we to eat from the first six food groups before we are permitted to eat from the seventh, which contains soda pop, coffee, candy and alcohol?
7. What about combination foods, such as pizza, macaroni and cheese, TV dinners, meatless bacon, egg substitutes, and so on?

These are important questions. Let me try to answer them.

1. Avoid canned fruits and vegetables. Canning may cause a loss of vitamins. Peas, for example, may lose 38 percent of their vitamins in the canning process. Plus, most cans of vegetables have one-half to one gram of sodium or salt added.
2. Ice cream and ice milk are high in fat and cholesterol. They are also rich in sugar. Therefore, I do not permit ice cream or ice milk as part of the milk

group. They belong in group 7. Whole milk is also not to be included. Only lowfat (2 percent or less) milk products qualify.
3. Lean meats, poultry and fish are acceptable. Luncheon meats are a no-no.
4. Cakes, pie, granola bars, cookies and crackers are unusually high in sugar, fat, possibly cholesterol and salt. White bread is permitted only in a pinch. Whole grain products are recommended.
5. The recommendations made in items 1 to 4 above will allow you to meet the U.S. recommendations on fat, salt, cholesterol, sugar and fiber.
6. Soda pop, coffee and candy are permitted on occasion (one to three times a week).
7. Combination foods, such as pizza, macaroni and cheese, and so on, must be viewed with caution. While they may provide you with vitamins, minerals, protein and other nutrients, they also tend to give you heavy doses of salt, saturated fat, cholesterol and sugar. Furthermore, it has been reported that from the time a frozen TV dinner is prepared at the company until you take it out of your oven and place it on your table, 40 percent of its vitamin A, 100 percent of its vitamin C, 80 percent of its B_{12}-complex vitamins, and 55 percent of its vitamin E have been lost.

The Basic Seven-Modified

Because of all the problems associated with salt, sugar, fat, cholesterol, caffeine and additives, I suggest that my seven basic food groups be modified as follows:

Group 1 Two servings (approximately 1 cup) of fresh or frozen green or leafy vegetables (non-starchy). *No canned vegetables.*

Group 2 One serving (½ cup) of fresh or frozen white or yellow vegetables (starchy). *No canned vegetables.*

Group 3 One serving (½ cup) of fresh or frozen (no sugar added) fruit. No canned fruit.

Group 4 Two servings (2 cups total) of lowfat milk or milk products. Lowfat is 2 percent or less.

Group 5 Two servings of protein foods. These include lean red meat, poultry, fish, beans, lentils and eggs (no yolks). Fish and poultry are not to be breaded.

Group 6 Four servings of whole grain breads, cereals (no added sugars) or grains.

Group 7 One serving of sugar or fat (unsaturated or polyunsaturated oil) per meal.

Now that you know how to modify the basic seven foods, go back to table 13 at the end of chapter 7. Take the test again, without counting canned or high-fat foods, or white bread. How do you and your family fare? If your score is the same as before, congratulations (provided, of course, that you received 100 points). If the modified score is lower (it probably will be), examine the table closely and see where you can make improvements.

Now you know how to eat well. The following strategies will help you and your family do so now and in the future.

"He provides you with plenty of food and fills your hearts with joy" (Acts 14:17).

FAMILY FOOD ACTIVITIES

The activities presented here are designed to: (1) create a more positive environment for good nutrition in your home, (2) increase your family's understanding of what good eating is and (3) help you provide more nutritious meals, menus, and snacks for your family.

The cooking and food preparation ideas are simple to introduce and were formulated and tested to be tasty. But don't rely on just these recipes—use them to spark other ideas. Experiment with ingredients, and expand the quantity as necessary.

The entire family can benefit from these activities, but, as with "Family Fitness Activities," I have suggested ages for which they are especially appropriate.

I. Understanding More About Food

● Shopping (Ages 9–14)

Take your child grocery shopping. Compare products. You may find that one brand of ketchup has more sugar than another brand, or that canned fruit in heavy syrup has more sugar than canned fruit with light syrup, or fruit packed in its own juice. After you compare the processed foods you intend to buy, stroll over to the fresh fruit and vegetable section, and notice that the ingredients are not listed on those products. That's because a head of lettuce has nothing in it but lettuce. A fresh peach is nothing but peach. No sugar or salt added. Explain to your child that usually the more processing the food has been through, the more additives it has accumulated. It is therefore wise to eat as many fresh foods as possible. Also, frozen foods usually have less sugar and other additives than foods in cans or boxes.

● Fats (Ages 9–14)

To demonstrate the differences between saturated, unsaturated and polyunsaturated foods, place the following foods on the dining room table where your child can see them: milk, cheese, butter, shortening, and vegetable oil. Ask your child which foods contain saturated, unsaturated and/or polyunsaturated fats. Usually, polyunsaturated fats are liquid at room temperature, so the vegetable oil qualifies. In-between foods will include milk, which is liquid but quite thick. The items that remain hard at room temperature, such as cheese, butter, shortening and so forth, contain large amounts of saturated fat.

96

After you've completed your object lesson, the child probably will want a snack. If so, pop some popcorn, using vegetable oil rather than lard. Or, better still, use a hot-air popper, which requires no oil at all.

● After Dinner (Ages 8–12)

In the evening, sit down with your child and list everything he ate that day. List what he had for breakfast, snacks, lunch and supper. Don't forget about those goodies he plans to have before bedtime.

Have him identify which of the seven basic groups each food he ate today falls into. Did he get something from each food group today? Did he eat some junk food from group 7? If so, ask him which more nutritious food he could substitute for the junk food next time.

● Read Labels (Ages 9–16)

Go through the various foods in your house and read the labels. Remember, the order of contents indicates the order of concentration of those items. List all foods in which salt (NaCl or Na), sodium or sodium chloride are listed. There may be other compounds that contain sodium, such as monosodium glutamate (MSG). Also list sugars (glucose, galactose, maltose, fructose, sucrose, dextrose and lactose). Notice that these items are added to canned, boxed or bottled products. Review beverages and over-the-counter medications as well.

II. *Improving the Family's Diet*

● Snacks (Ages 10–14)

On one sheet of paper, write the heading "Junk Food Hall of Shame" and on another, "Health Food Hall of Fame." Now go through your refrigerator and cupboards and list on these sheets all the foods you have available for snacking. After you finish, post the Health Food Hall of Fame list in a conspicuous place in the kitchen, as an advertisement for nutritious snacks. You can add to this list from week to week. Also post the Hall of Shame list in the kitchen, but hide it. When family members go a whole week without eating a specific Hall of Shame item, they put their initial by that item. At the end of a month, see who has initialed the most Hall of Shame items. (This means they have eaten the least amount of junk food.) To make it positive, have children initial the Health Food Hall of Fame foods they ate.

• Nutritious Foods (Ages 3–16)

Have each family member select two nutritious foods (one must be a vegetable) they like. Each week, incorporate these favorite nutritious foods into the weekly menu (e.g., Tuesday is Johnny's day, so we're having cauliflower and yogurt). The following week, family members select two different items. This allows everyone to have input into the weekly menu. It also gets them to try different foods.

• Breakfast Menu (Ages 9–14)

Breakfast is the most important meal of the day, yet all too often, children and adults skip it. In an attempt to get your family to eat breakfast, have them plan their own breakfast menus for one week. They can eat whatever they want (no junk food), but it must be more than 500 calories or at least one-fourth of their total calories for the day (i.e., spaghetti, beans, toast, cereal, juice). Keep track of what each person eats. At the end of the week, see who had the most varied menu.

• Snacks (Ages 9–16)

Have each family member fill out the following sheet for one week, recording the snacks they eat.

Pass (This means that you were going to have a snack, but decided against it. Indicate why.)
Snack
Type of Snack
Day
Time
Doing What

The following week, ask them to do the same, but with the following information:

Pass
Snack
Type of Snack
Day
Time
Doing What
Why are you eating a snack?

After the second week, sit down as a family and discuss your records. Did snacking differ from week one to week two? Why do you snack?

● Healthier Eating Away From Home (Parents only)

What do you do when you get your children to eat healthier at home, only to have your efforts sabotaged by snack machines at school or at church and youth functions, where the treats are cakes, chips and sodas?

—*School, Church and Youth Functions*
You speak out, of course. Although you probably won't revolutionize the school lunch program overnight, you can do many things to improve the quality of the foods served at school:

● Lobby for equal time. If only whole and chocolate milk are served, ask for low-fat milk to be *included*. Real wholewheat bread can be served *in addition* to white bread, and fresh fruits frequently can be provided along with standard sweet desserts.

● Ask that the food not be salted. Children can season to taste at the table.

● Make a presentation to the parent-teacher organization, explaining why the lunch program needs revision. Be friendly and flexible—you won't get anywhere by being strident and patronizing. Enlist the aid of other concerned parents in presenting your case to the school board and administration.

● Try to interest your children's teachers in including nutrition units in their curriculum. Volunteer to help with class projects that teach proper nutrition.

● Push for healthy fruit juice and snack machines. If a soda pop machine is installed in the cafeteria, insist that a juice machine be installed next to it.

The point of all this is not to force schools to remove junk food machines, salt and whole milk products, but to demand equal time. This is not threatening. If positively given, these suggestions usually are positively received.

Likewise, suggest alternative, healthier snack ideas to the scoutmaster or church youth leader. Make it as easy for them to serve healthy snacks as it is for your children to eat them at home.

—*Friend's Home*
What if your friends serve them junk food? My advice is to bow out. If your children are eating well at home, their periodic visits to other homes will not ruin their health. In this instance, drawing attention to their eating habits could affect their emotional health, however, and may cause them to be ostracized by their friends. It also probably would make the host uncomfortable.

● TV Advertising (Ages 8–16)

Discuss with your children the advertising techniques used to sell food, soda pop, cereals, candy, and so on. Does the ad tell the entire truth? The ad may say the soda pop has no caffeine, but you are not told that it is high in sugar and sodium and has no nutritional value.

View the ad, then read the ingredients on the label. Talk about hidden messages and facts. Discussing some of the absurdities implied in television ads can make great dinner conservation.

III. *Recipes and Other Eating Strategies*

The following food selection, food preparation and recipe ideas are designed to move you *toward healthier* eating. I could give you a host of recipes without salt, sugar, fat, eggs, and so on. Instead, I have tried to present practical ideas. As your family gets weaned from salt and sugar, you can use more Spartan methods.

My goal is for you to eat a diet of 30 percent fat, 12 percent protein, 48 percent complex carbohydrates and 10 percent simple carbohydrates. These strategies and recipes reflect that purpose.

A few notes about purchasing foods

- Join a food co-op. These offer excellent benefits such as 5–20 percent discounts, bulk food, and foods low in sugar and salt, whole grain products, and foods with few additives or food sprays. Dried fruits, special cheeses and juices are available through food co-ops, as is poultry and beef that is not raised on growth hormones and other unwanted additives. Research your co-op well.
- Buy foods in bulk without sugar. (That way you decide how much sugar to add. Foods bought in bulk can be frozen.)
- Local farmers may sell you selected crops and meats.
- Learn to read labels. Nutrition labels found on commercially prepared food items

SAMPLE NUTRITION LABEL

Nutritional information per serving

Serving Size	one cup
Calories	260
Protein	10 grams
Carbohydrate	49 grams
Fat	3 grams

Ingredient Listing
Lowfat milk, strawberries, sugar, corn sweeteners, nonfat milk solids, pectin, and lemon juice.

The protein, carbohydrate and fat contents are always listed in grams. To convert the grams into calories, remember that Fat = 9 calories per gram, Carbohydrate = 4 calories per gram, and Protein = 4 calories per gram. In the above sample label, there are 27 calories from fat, 196 calories from carbohydrate, and 40 calories from protein. Therefore, this product contains 10 percent fat, 75 percent carbohydrate and 15 percent protein. Also, the ingredients always are listed in descending order of dominance. Lowfat milk is the major ingredient in the above product, then strawberries, sugar, corn sweeteners, etc. In many cases, carbohydrate information also is listed.

help you determine if they are good choices for you and your family. Look beyond the eye-catching caloric content to decipher the meaning of the metric lingo.

• Avoid (or be cautious about) foods that contain the following additives: artificial colorings blue No. 1, blue No. 2, citrus red No. 2, green No. 3, red No. 40 and yellow No. 5; brominated vegetable oil (BVO); caffeine (for children and pregnant women); monosodium glutamate (MSG) (for children); quinine; saccharin; sodium nitrate; and sodium nitrite.

The additives listed above have been poorly tested and serve no essential role. Some studies have been demonstrated that there may be some risk in using products containing them.

You also should be cautious about the following as they, too, have been inadequately researched. Use of these is possibly hazardous, and safer substitutes are available: artificial coloring yellow No. 6; artificial flavorings; butylated hydroxyanisole (BHA); butylated hydroxytoluene (BHT); caffeine (for nonpregnant adults); carrageenan; heptylparaben; mono and diglycerides; monosodium glutamate (MSG) (for adults); phosphoric acid and phosphates; propyl gallate; sodium bisulfite; and sulfur dioxide.

Other points to consider on additives:

1. Dark bread may not be high in fiber. Many brands are simply white bread with caramel coloring. If the label says "caramel," forget it.
2. Words that end in -ose are different forms of sugar.
3. "All natural" means virtually nothing—sugar, cholesterol and sodium are natural.
4. "Organic" foods refers to crops raised without sprays. If you purchase organic foods, know how your farmer raises crops. Otherwise, you may pay up to 40 percent more for the same food you can buy in a regular foodstore.

Additional purchasing strategies:

1. You can buy salt-free potato chips (taste good) and pretzels (taste fair to good).
2. Salt-free soups and vegetables are also available. Most popular brands are pretty weak, but you can season them to your taste.
3. Purchase canned fruit that is packed in its own juice.
4. Purchase fruit juices, rather than fruit drinks. Check labels. Preferred—no sugar added, rather than unsweetened or sweetened.
5. Purchase canned fish (i.e., tuna) packed in water, rather than in oil.
6. Never eat pre-sweetened cereals. The following cereals have 10 percent or less sugar:

Grape Nuts

Shredded Wheat (large biscuit)

Shredded Wheat (spoon size)

Wheat Germ

Cheerios

Puffed Rice

Uncle Sam Cereal

Wheat Chex

Cream of Rice (Hot)

Farina (Hot)

Old Fashioned Quaker Oats (Hot)

Instant Quaker Oatmeal (Hot)

Grape Nut Flakes

Puffed Wheat

Alpen

Wheatina (Hot)

Post Toasties

Product 19

Corn Total

Special K

Wheaties

Cream of Wheat (Hot)

Instant Cream of Wheat (Hot)

Corn Flakes (Kroger)

Peanut Butter

Corn Flakes (Food Club)

Crispy Rice

Corn Chex

Corn Flakes (Kellogg)

Total

Rice Chex

Crisp Rice

Raisin Bran (Skinner)

Concentrate

7. Select vegetable oils that are not hardened, hydrogenated, or partly hardened or hydrogenated.

8. Select soft tub margarines over hard margarine or butter.

9. Select low fat (2 to ½ percent) or skim milk and cheese products.

10. Remember: if it comes in a bag, box or jar, beware. Read all labels carefully.

A few notes about preparing food

● Season food without salt. Here are some sample salt substitutes:[1]

Meat, Fish and Poultry

Beef	Bay leaf, dry mustard powder, green pepper, marjoram, fresh mushrooms, nutmeg, onion, pepper, sage, thyme.
Chicken	Green pepper, lemon juice, marjoram, fresh mushrooms, paprika, parsley, poultry seasoning, sage, thyme.
Fish	Bay leaf, curry powder, dry mustard powder, green pepper, lemon juice, marjoram, fresh mushrooms, paprika.
Lamb	Curry powder, garlic, mint, mint jelly, pineapple, rosemary.
Pork	Apple, applesauce, garlic, onion, sage.
Veal	Apricot, bay leaf, curry powder, ginger, marjoram, oregano.

Vegetables

Asparagus	Garlic, lemon juice, onion, vinegar.
Corn	Green pepper, pimiento, fresh tomato.
Cucumbers	Chives, dill, garlic, vinegar.
Green Beans	Dill, lemon juice, marjoram, nutmeg, pimiento.
Greens	Onion, pepper, vinegar.
Peas	Green pepper, mint, fresh mushrooms, onion, parsley.
Potatoes	Green pepper, mace, onion, paprika, parsley.
Rice	Chive, green pepper, onion, pimiento, saffron.
Squash	Brown sugar, cinnamon, ginger, mace, nutmeg, onion.
Tomatoes	Basil, marjoram, onion, oregano.

Soups

Bean	Pinch of dry mustard powder.
Milk/Chowders	Peppercorns.
Pea	Bay leaf and parsley.
Vegetable	Vinegar, dash of sugar.

- Preparing food for infants: When feeding your baby vegetables and fruit or cereal, *do not* add sugar, syrup, honey or salt. Your baby doesn't know the difference. It may taste bland to you, because you are taste addicted to sugar and salt.
- Learn how to "phase-in" dietary changes. Here are some effective strategies to "wean" your family from highly processed flour, sugar, alcohol, cholesterol, caffeine and salt foods:

Complex Carbohydrates

Phase 1: Start using whole-grain flour in baking. (Be cautious: "whole wheat" may mean nothing more than wheat-refined.) Eat a whole-grain cereal or whole-grain bread daily. Begin eating fruit more often for desserts and snacks. Try whole-grain pastas and crackers. Eat more meatless dishes made with beans and whole-grain products.

Phase 2: Eat whole-grain products most of the time. Eat one meatless meal daily. Regularly eat fruit for snacks and desserts.

Sugar and Alcohol

Phase 1: Avoid alcohol. Begin the habit of not adding sugar to coffee, tea, cereal or fruit. When baking, reduce the sugar to one-half of the amount called for in the recipe. Limit rich desserts to special occasions. Reduce your intake of sweetened soft drinks and candy.

Phase 2: Reduce sugar to 10 percent of total calories each day (on an intake of 2,000 calories per day, no more than 200 calories would come from sugar). If a recipe calls for sugar, use one-third to one-fourth the amount specified.

Cholesterol

Phase 1: Limit your intake of meat, fish and poultry to eight ounces (cooked weight) per day. Limit egg yolks to two per week. Limit organ meats, shrimp and sardines to three ounces per week. If a recipe calls for two eggs, use two whites and only one yolk.

Phase 2: Limit your intake of meat, fish and poultry to three or four ounces (cooked weight) per day. Substitute egg whites for whole eggs in recipes.

Caffeine

Phase 1: Limit coffee to two cups per day. Drink decaffeinated tea and coffee and other beverages.

Phase 2: Limit coffee to one cup per day.

Salt

Phase 1: Avoid adding salt to food at the table. When cooking, use half the amount of salt specified. Begin the habit of buying only fresh, frozen or salt-free canned goods.

Phase 2: Eliminate salt when cooking and at the table. Avoid high-salt foods, such as pickles, sauerkraut and salted crackers. Use only fresh, frozen or salt-free canned foods.

Fat

Phase 1: Substitute low-fat dairy products for high-fat dairy products. Begin the habit of not adding fat to vegetables and breads. Limit fried foods to once a month. Use cooking methods that don't require fat, such as baking, broiling and poaching. Eat only lean cuts of meat. Remove skin from poultry. Eat more fish and poultry, less red meat. Use polyunsaturated oil and soft tub margarine in place of butter and shortening.

Phase 2: Use all fats as sparingly as possible. Count the fat in baked goods as part of your fat intake. Use only low-fat meats and dairy products. Use only polyunsaturated oils and margarines.

Recipes

Vegetables

To get kids to eat vegetables:

1. Use fresh vegetables whenever possible. Be sure to keep them crisp—do *not* overcook.
2. Buy a steamer to fit inside your pans, so vegetables won't sit in the water when cooking.
3. In the beginning, top vegetables with their favorite melted mild cheese.
4. Graduate to using soft tub margarine instead of cheese.
5. Gradually cut back on the cheeses and margarines until you use a very small amount.
6. "Doctor" vegetables with soups—top green beans with mushroom soup with onions.
7. Try fresh vegetables with dips. While dips may not be as healthy, they can get children to eat vegetables. Try kohlrabi (when in season), carrots, radishes, turnips, broccoli and cauliflower.
8. Be cautious with vegetables such as cabbage, sweet potatoes, zucchini, pumpkin and beans (lima, kidney, green). I found that my kids didn't like them as much. Camouflage them by combining them in recipes. Use cabbage in cole slaw; sweet potatoes, zucchini, pumpkin in breads or puddings; beans in casseroles, soups or three-bean salad.
9. Combine vegetables. With frozen vegetables, take a little from several bags and cook together.
10. Try oriental-style frozen vegetables.
11. Be cautious with salt. If a recipe calls for salt, don't use it, or cut the amount in half. The family can season to taste at the table. But be cautious—they may oversalt. The best strategy is to add one half the amount, then one third, then one fourth. Most families tolerate those gradual reductions. Also, see the seasoning ideas already given.

Chunk and Dunk

Try raw carrots, cauliflower, celery, cucumbers, green onions, green peppers, radishes, turnips and zucchini with your favorite homemade Delectable, Delightful, Dynamite Dip:

Blend lowfat cottage cheese with a dab of lowfat or skim milk. Add any one or a combination of: dill weed, garlic powder, finely chopped onion, Beau Monde spice.

Celery Boats

Fill with peanut butter and raisins or soft cheese and pineapple chunks.

Cucumbers, halved, seeds out

Fill with tuna mixed with diced cheese.

Tomato, cored

Fill with lowfat cottage cheese or tuna mixed with a small amount of mayonnaise.

Make 'n' Bake (Baked Slices of Potato)

2 potatoes, washed, unpeeled   margarine

Preheat over to 350°. Slice potatoes into ¼-inch slices. Place on buttered cookie sheet and bake for 30 minutes or until slices are brown. Eat them while they are hot! Taste great dipped in applesauce.

Acorn Squash with Applesauce

Cut acorn squash in half and remove seeds. Microwave on HIGH for 15 minutes or until done. Fill with applesauce and put back in for 2 minutes on HIGH, or until sauce is hot.

Stir Fry Vegetables

3–4 T margarine (can add more if
   sticking occurs)
1 C fresh mushrooms (wash well)
1½ C carrots
2 T water

1 C cauliflower
1 T soysauce, or to taste
   garlic powder to taste
1½ C broccoli
¾ C onions

Rinse vegetables and dice into small pieces. Melt margarine in wok or pan on hot burner. Add each ingredient in the order listed, cooking the harder vegetables about 2–3 minutes each and the softer vegetables about 1½ minutes. Stir vegetables as they cook. Add water, instead of more margarine, to keep from burning. Serves 4–6.

You can start to cut back on the soy sauce (which is high in salt) once your family is hooked on vegetables prepared this way.

Optional: Add or substitute pea pods, turnips, zucchini, celery, walnuts, almonds, chinese cabbage, thin slices of chicken.

Cauliflower Polonaise

1 medium head cauliflower, cut into
   flowerets
1 hard-boiled egg

¼ C dry bread crumbs
1 T margarine
1 T snipped parsley

Boil cauliflower in a covered pan half full of water for about 10 minutes. Drain. Chop the hard-boiled egg (½ yolk). Heat the margarine in a small pan until it is slightly browned. Stir in the bread crumbs, parsley and egg. Spread the mix over the cooked cauliflower.

Cauliflower wtih Lemon Sauce and Almonds

1 medium head cauliflower	⅓ C unsifted flour
water	1 T grated lemon rind
½ t salt	4½ t lemon juice
⅓ C margarine	¼ C sliced almonds

Place cauliflower in a large saucepan with 1-inch of water and salt. Cover and bring to a boil; reduce heat and simmer 12 to 15 minutes, or until tender. Place cauliflower in a warm dish, reserving 1½ cups cooking water.

Melt margarine in a saucepan. Stir in flour and cook 1 to 2 minutes over low heat. Gradually stir in reserved cauliflower water. Cook and stir over low heat until thickened. Mix in lemon rind and juice. Pour prepared sauce over cooked cauliflower and sprinkle with sliced almonds to serve.

Brazil Nut-Mandarin Orange Salad

1 small head romaine lettuce	1 C canned mandarin oranges
1 C green onions, chopped	poppyseed dressing
1 C Brazil nuts	

Tear the romaine lettuce into large pieces. Toss lightly with the onions, nuts and oranges. Add small amount of the dressing.

Stuffed Potatoes

Bake potatoes until done. Slice them open until they stay open (like you would cut a pie). While still hot, fill with:

Crisp-steamed, fresh, hot broccoli
Melted cheese (pour over top)

Options: Add to the cheese a small amount of green onion; add diced ham with all visible fat removed.

Fruits

According to our studies, fruit is children's favorite snack—even more popular than sweets. Children say they don't eat as much fruit as they would like because it isn't readily available to them. A candy bar wrapper is easier to peel off than an orange skin. Make fruit available and you'll be amazed at how quickly it disappears.

Do not add sugar to fruit. You may need to wean your family from sweetened fruit by adding only one half, then one-third, then one-fourth the amount of sugar previously used. Eventually they will enjoy most fruit without sugar.

Filler Ups
Apple, cored

Fill with peanut butter mixed with granola.

Fresh peach, halved, pitted

Fill with plain yogurt mixed with honey and granola.

Nibble Snacks

Fill a plastic bag or container with your favorite mixture of any of these: granola, peanuts and/or other nuts, raisins, dates, sunflower seeds, sesame seeds, dried fruit chunks.

Baked Apples

Core; do not peel. Fill with walnuts, butter, very little cinnamon, and small amount of sugar.

Peanut Butter Roll-Ups

Freeze peeled, ripe bananas. Roll bananas in peanut butter, then roll in chopped peanuts.

Grapefruit with Brown Sugar

Cut grapefruit in half. Sprinkle with brown sugar and top with a grape. Put under broiler for 1½ minutes.

Waldorf Salad

Combine chopped apples, celery and walnuts. Use small amounts of mayonnaise or yogurt for dressing.

Mandarin Oranges with Grapes

Mix a can of mandarin oranges with a handful of fresh green grapes.

Grilled Orange Slices

1 orange	2 t honey
¼ C unsalted margarine, melted	ginger

Slice orange at least one inch thick. Dip slices into melted margarine. Arrange on broiler pan and broil 5 to 7 inches from heat source, turning them once or twice, until they are thoroughly heated. Drizzle with honey and sprinkle with a little ginger. Leave in the broiler until honey and ginger melt and caramelize.

Applesauce

10 cooking apples, pared and cored 1 t cinnamon
½ C water ¼ C brown sugar
   juice of ½ lemon ½ C raisins
¼ C nuts

Slice prepared apples. Combine all ingredients in a crock pot. Cover and cook on low for 8–10 hours or until fruit is tender.

   Alternative: Cook slowly in large, covered pot on top of range until apples are tender but retain some shape. Serve hot or cold.

Apple Crisp

 2 C sliced baking apples ⅜ t cinnamon
⅓ C brown sugar ¼ C margarine
¼ C flour ⅜ t nutmeg
¼ C Rolled oats (uncooked)

Place apples in baking dish. Blend remaining ingredients. Spread over apples. Bake at 350° for 30 to 35 minutes.

Fruit Whip

1 fresh apple, cored only 2 t lemon juice
1 banana, sliced 2 t sugar

Place all in blender. Blend at high speed until very smooth. Serve.

Sherbet

2 C yogurt 2 t vanilla
1 small can frozen concentrated fruit
  juice (orange, grape, apple)

Combine all ingredients, mix well and place in freezer tray to freeze.

Applesauce and Bread

Spread applesauce over toast—leave off margarine or butter.

Dried Fruits

Offer dried fruits for snacks.
   Most preferred: apples, raisins, apricots.
   Least preferred: pears and pineapple.

Fruit Concepts for Children

Have fruit readily available at snack time.

a. Apple, sliced
b. Orange, peeled and sliced
c. Pears, sliced
d. Kiwi, peeled and sliced
e. Peaches, sliced
f. Nectarines, sliced
g. Bananas—as is
h. Grapes, washed (seedless preferred)
i. Tangerines, peeled and sectioned
j. Melons, cut and placed in dish
k. Cherries, washed
l. Blueberries, washed
m. Raspberries, washed

Freeze fruit for the winter. Simply wash, seal in plastic containers or bags, and place in freezer. Not as tasty as fresh, but superior to canned.

Broiled Slices of Orange

2 Oranges
¼ C melted soft tub margarine

Honey
Ginger or cinnamon

Dip orange slices into melted margarine. Place on broiler pan 5 to 7 inches from heat source. Broil, turning slices once, until thoroughly heated. Drizzle with honey and sprinkle with spice. Leave slices in broiler until honey and spice melt and caramelize.

Fruit Juices or Beverages
Frozen Juice

Make fruit juice from concentrate (orange juice, grape, cranberry, crangrape, or cranapple. Place in ice cube freezer trays. Place stick in each individual cube when starting to freeze.

Juice

Grape juice, orange juice and tangerine juice taste more like fruit drinks if ½ to 1 extra can of water is added to concentrate, rather than the normal 3 cans.

Juice Combinations

Experiment with combining various quantities of fruit juice to make novel fruit juices.

Yogosickle

plain yogurt
frozen orange juice concentrate

vanilla

Mix plain yogurt with frozen orange juice concentrate to taste. Add a dash of vanilla. Pour into plastic cups. Freeze to slush stage, insert sticks and freeze. To eat, peel off cup.

Protein Potassium Power

2 C orange juice
1 C apple cider

½ banana
1 egg white

Put all ingredients into blender and mix well.

Peachy Shake

1 C lowfat yogurt	honey to taste
1 C peaches	

Put all ingredients into blender and mix well.

Jogger's Punch

1½ C pineapple juice	1 T honey
½ C lowfat yogurt	6 ice cubes

Put all ingredients into blender and mix well.

Tropical Cooler

2 C cantaloupe	1 T honey
1 C water	1 t lemon juice

Put all ingredients into blender and mix well. Serve over crushed ice.

Strawberry Shake

1 C lowfat milk	½ t vanilla
1 C strawberries	honey to taste

Put all ingredients into blender and mix well.

Orange Drink

½ C orange juice	small piece of orange peel
2 T sugar	1½ C yogurt

Place all ingredients into blender, turn to high speed. Blend thoroughly for few seconds, slightly longer if solid fruit is used.

Strawberry Special

1 C lowfat milk	4 t sugar
2 C fresh strawberries	1 C cracked ice

Place all ingredients into blender. Mix at high speed until contents are thoroughly blended.

Banana Milk Shake

1 C lowfat milk	1 t vanilla
1 medium ripe banana	1 C cracked ice

Place ingredients in the blender. Mix at high speed until thoroughly blended.

Juices

Consider serving all these juices, not just orange juice or apple juice:

—cider
—grape
—crangrape
—cranapple
—cranberry

—pineapple
—tangerine
—white grape juice
—tomato juice (add lemon juice)

Fruit and Milk

Mix 1 cup of fruit (preferably strawberries, bananas, blueberries, and/or raspberries) with 1 cup of lowfat milk in blender. Run at high speed. Sweeten to taste with honey or sugar. Banana does not need sugar.

Bananas & Yogurt Breakfast

2 bananas
2 C plain lowfat yogurt
½ t vanilla or almond extract

½ C + 2 T chopped almonds
¼ C wheat germ
½ C oat bran

Mash 1 banana in medium mixing bowl. Stir in yogurt & vanilla. Mix well. Add ¼ C nuts, wheat germ, oat bran. Stir. Slice other banana. Stir all but 4 slices into mixture. Divide into 2 bowls. Top with banana slices & almonds. Two servings.

Meat

Select meats which are lean, such as chicken and turkey. Before cooking, cut all visible fat from meat. With fowl, remove skin. Broil and bake your meats. Let all the drippings collect away from the meat. Always put a lift under the meat. After cooking foods, wrap them in paper towels.

Start thinking of the following transition: from ham, to red meats, to fowl (chicken and turkey), to fish. If preparing fish, fresh is infinitely superior to frozen. In fact, they taste like two different kinds of food. Purchase mild fish, such as cod, scrod, monk, and white fish.

Poor Man's Lobster

Use fresh or frozen cod (or white fish). In a large pan, bring to a boil enough water to reach the bottom of your steamer. If you do not have a steamer, boil the fish directly in the water. Add a tablespoon of vinegar to the water to reduce the odor. Steam the fish until it breaks apart in chunks and is very white. Fish can be dunked in melted butter (in time, soft tub margarine). Or add cheese and slivered almonds and heat in your microwave until the cheese melts.

Bran Parmesan Chicken

1½ C 40% Bran Flakes
  1 egg
  ¼ C lowfat milk
  ¼ C all purpose flour
    dash of pepper

⅛ t ground sage
3 T grated Parmesan cheese
4 chicken pieces, washed and
  patted dry (1 to 1½ lbs.)
1 T margarine, melted

Crush 40% Bran Flakes cereal to measure ¾ cup. In shallow dish, beat egg and milk slightly. Add flour, pepper, sage and cheese, stirring until smooth. Dip chicken pieces in egg mixture. Coat with cereal. Place in a single layer, skin side up, in greased or foil-lined shallow baking pan. Drizzle with margarine.

Bake at 350° about 45 minutes or until tender. Do not cover pan or turn chicken while baking. Makes 4 servings.

Crispy Chicken

1 frying chicken (2½ to 3 pounds),
  cut into serving pieces.
1 C corn flake crumbs

1 C skim milk
seasoning, if desired.

Preheat oven to 400°. Remove all skin from the chicken, rinse and dry thoroughly. Season. Dip each piece in milk, shake to remove excess, and roll in the crumbs. Let stand briefly so coating will adhere. Place chicken in an oiled baking pan. (Line pan with foil for easy clean-up.) Pieces should not touch. Bake 45 minutes. Crumbs will make a crisp "skin." Makes about 4 servings.

Chicken Supreme

2 C cooked chicken, cut into bite-
  size pieces
¼ C slivered almonds, toasted
½ can mushrooms (6 oz.)

½ jar chopped pimientos (4 oz.)
1 C cold water
1 C dry instant nonfat milk
2 T whole-wheat pastry flour

Mix milk and flour in top of double boiler. Add cold water and stir until smooth. Place over hot water in bottom of double boiler. Cook, stirring constantly, until thickened. Add chicken, almonds, mushroom and pimientos. Mix well. May be served over cooked brown rice. Makes 4 servings.

Fresh Fruit and Chicken Salad

watermelon
cantaloupe
banana
pineapple chunks
seedless grapes

peaches
chicken
dill pickle
salad dressing
lettuce

Use these fruits or any combinations you wish. Cut into bite-size pieces and toss together. Chop the dill pickle and add to the chicken. Mix with enough salad dressing to hold salad together. Serve by placing lettuce leaves around the edge of individual salad bowls. Put chicken in the center; place fruit around the chicken. Garnish with parsley, if desired. Turkey, or tuna packed in water may be used in place of chicken.

Ham Banana Rolls with Broccoli

1 T margarine	1–2 t prepared mustard
1 T flour	4 firm bananas, peeled
¾ C lowfat milk	2–4 t melted margarine
1½ C grated sharp cheddar cheese	4 servings crisp-cooked broccoli
4 thin slices of boiled ham	paprika
	pepper to taste

Melt margarine in small saucepan. Stir in flour and slowly add milk, cooking and stirring until mixture boils and is thickened. Remove from heat. Add cheese and stir until melted. Season to taste with pepper.

Spread one side of each slice of boiled ham with mustard. Brush bananas with melted margarine; wrap each one in a ham slice, with mustard side next to banana. In large flat casserole or baking dish, alternate banana-ham rolls with servings of broccoli. Pour hot cheese sauce over banana rolls and broccoli in casserole. Sprinkle with paprika. Bake in 350° oven 30 minutes. Makes 4 servings.

Burgers with Yogurt

1 lb ground beef	½ C wheat germ
½ t salt	1 C yogurt
pepper	¾ C fine dry bread crumbs
1 onion, finely chopped	

Mix beef, salt, pepper, onion and wheat germ together in large bowl. Add yogurt gradually, beating constantly. Add bread crumbs and mix thoroughly. Shape into patties and place in shallow baking pan. Bake in 375° oven until done. Makes 6 patties.

P'Nut Butter

2 C roasted peanuts, shelled	¼ C peanut, soy or safflower oil
¼ t salt	

Remove peanut skins and put peanuts in the blender. Blend for one minute. Add the oil gradually, one tablespoon at a time, blending from time to time. Add the salt and blend until the peanuts are partly or all chopped up.

Put your peanut butter in a container with a tight-fitting cover. Refrigerate for several hours before using.

Breads and Grains

Homemade granolas are easy to make and can be tailor-made to suit family tastes.

Use whole-grain flour in rolls and bread recipes. Just remember that whole-grain flour will not raise as high as regular white flour. You may wish to use half white flour and half whole-grain.

Chewy Treat

½ C honey
½ C peanut butter
½ C dry milk

4 C Rice Krispies
1 t vanilla

Heat honey. Remove from heat, add powdered milk, peanut butter and vanilla. Mix and pour over Rice Krispies. Form into small balls.

Homemade Granola

3 C rolled oats (uncooked)
1 C chopped walnuts
¼ C honey
½ C almonds

⅔ C raisins
¼ C margarine, melted
½ t cinnamon

Combine all ingredients except raisins in 13″ × 9″ pan. Mix well. Bake at 350° for 20 to 25 minutes or until golden brown, stirring occasionally. Remove from oven and add raisins. Store in tightly covered container in dry place.

Toasted, Roasted Cheese Sticks

4 slices of bread, toasted
  margarine

Parmesan cheese

Spread toast with margarine and sprinkle with cheese. Cut into thin strips. Place on cookie sheet in 250° oven for 15 minutes. Cool and store in covered container.

P'Nut Butter Banana Bite

1 slice bread
  peanut butter

1 banana
chopped peanuts

Spread peanut butter on bread. Slice banana on top. Sprinkle with peanuts.

Honey-Nut Spread

1½ C walnut pieces
  3 T corn oil

2 T honey

Put all ingredients into blender. Blend until smooth and creamy.

Oat Granola

3 C rolled oats (quick or old
   fashioned, uncooked)
1 C shredded or flaked coconut
1 C coarsely chopped nuts
¼ C honey

¼ C margarine, melted
1½ t cinnamon
½ t salt
⅔ C raisins

Combine all ingredients except raisins in ungreased 13″ × 9″ baking pan; mix well. Bake in preheated moderate oven (350°) for 5 to 30 minutes or until golden brown, stirring occasionally. Stir in raisins. Cool thoroughly; store in tightly covered container in cool dry place or in refrigerator. Serve as cereal with lowfat milk or as a snack. Makes about 6 cups granola.

Microwave Oven Directions: Combine all ingredients except raisins; mix well. Cook in ungreased 11″ × 7″ baking dish in microwave oven at HIGH 8 to 10 minutes or until light golden brown, stirring after every 2 minutes of cooking; stir in raisins.

Fruit/Nut Granola

3 C rolled oats
1 C wheat flakes
½ C wheat germ
1 C bran (wheat, corn or oat)
½ C sunflower seeds

1 C chopped nuts
1 6-oz. can frozen apple juice
   concentrate, thawed
¼ C mild vegetable oil
1½ C dried fruits (raisins, apricots,
   etc.)

Put oats, wheat flakes, wheat germ, bran, seeds, nuts in roaster. Stir in oil, juice. Bake 30 minutes at 300°. Stir once or twice. Remove from oven. Stir in fruit. Cool, cover, store. Serve with milk. Yields 8 cups.

Whole-Grain Muffins

¾ C lowfat milk
¾ C bran cereal
1 egg
¼ C vegetable oil
¼ C honey
¼ C firmly packed brown sugar

1 C rolled oats (quick or old
   fashioned, uncooked)
½ C raisins
⅔ C all purpose flour
1 T baking powder

Combine milk and bran cereal in medium-sized bowl. Add egg, oil and brown sugar; mix well. Add remaining ingredients, mixing until dry ingredients are moistened. Fill 12 greased or paper-lined medium-sized muffin cups ⅔ full. Bake in preheated hot oven (400°) about 15 minutes. Makes 1 dozen muffins.

100% Whole-Wheat Bread

7½ C whole-wheat flour	1 T salt
2 T dry yeast (2 packages)	1 C bran
5 C warm water	½ C wheat germ
4 T honey	½ wheat flakes
4 T molasses	½ C skim milk powder

Place whole-wheat flour in large mixing bowl and set in the oven for 20 minutes at the lowest temperature. Stir once so it is all warmed.

While flour is warming, dissolve the yeast in 5 cups warm water; add the honey and molasses to the mixture and set aside. Use a big enough bowl as it really grows.

Add the yeast mixture to the flour, along with the salt, bran, wheat germ, wheat cereal and powdered milk. Add flour to proper texture and let rise. Knead in whole-wheat flour to form loaves.

Oil bread pans. Place loaves into pans, so about half full. Let rise 1 hour— covered—avoiding drafts.

Bake in preheated oven at 350° for 1 hour. Remove from oven, but allow to cool in pans about 20 minutes. Loosen by running knife around edges of pans.

This recipe makes 2 large or 4 small loaves.

Applesauce Bread

2½ to 3 C all purpose flour	¾ C unsweetened applesauce
½ C 100% Bran cereal	¼ C lowfat milk
¼ C firmly packed brown sugar	3 T margarine
½ t salt	1 egg, room temperature
1 pkg active dry yeast	

Stir together ½ cup of the flour, the 100% Bran cereal, sugar, salt and yeast in a large mixing bowl. Set aside.

Combine applesauce, milk and margarine in small saucepan. Heat until warm (120–130°). Margarine does not need to melt. Gradually add to cereal mixture and beat 2 minutes at medium speed of electric mixer, scraping bowl occasionally. Add egg and ½ cup flour. Beat 2 minutes at high speed, scraping bowl. Stir in enough additional flour (1½ to 2 cups) to make a stiff, sticky dough. Cover with towel. Let rise in warm place until double in volume.

Stir down dough. Spoon into well-greased 1-quart round casserole. Cover and let rise in warm place until double in volume.

Bake at 375° about 35 minutes. To prevent over-browning, cover loosely with foil during last few minutes of baking time. Remove from casserole. Cool on wire rack. Makes 1 loaf (15 slices).

Desserts

Desserts are a way of life for Americans. Many of the "Fruit Recipes" can fit in this category. If you are determined to bake desserts, use fruit-based desserts such as apple cobbler or blueberry buckle. Or serve tapioca, bread and rice puddings. Custards also can be used, but use one-half the egg yolks called for.

Store-bought or homemade yogurts with fruit mixed throughout can be frozen and then served with chopped macadamia or pistachio nuts.

Here are some more dessert ideas:

Eggnog

Blend together:

1 egg white	½ t almond extract
1 C lowfat milk	½ t nutmeg
½ t vanilla	1 T nonfat dry milk powder

Banana Fruit Shake

Place a banana and chilled fruit juice in blender. (Orange, pineapple, cranberry and apple juices all make delicious combinations with bananas.) Mix only until smooth and creamy. Serve in a chilled glass. For a colder drink, add a teaspoon of cracked ice while blending.

Yogurt Pie

pie shell	1 T honey
fruit	1 t vanilla
1 C yogurt	
½ lb cottage cheese (small curd or country style)	

Bake an 8-inch pie shell. Line bottom of pie with fresh strawberries, raspberries, blackberries or sliced bananas. Sprinkle with small amount of sugar. Whip together the remaining ingredients and fill the pie with the yogurt mixture. The pie should be refrigerated for several hours before serving.

Apple Tapioca

3 C sliced tart apples	½ t salt
2 T margarine	2½ C water
¼ t cinnamon	1 to 2 T lemon juice
⅓ C Minute Tapioca	
1 C firmly packed light brown sugar	

Place apples in greased baking dish. Dot with margarine and sprinkle wtih cinnamon. Combine remaining ingredients in saucepan. Let stand 5 minutes. Cook and stir over medium heat until mixture comes to a full boil (6–8 minutes). Pour over apples in baking dish. Cover and bake in moderate oven (375°F) 25 minutes, or until apples are tender. Remove from oven and stir. Serve warm with lowfat milk. Makes 6 to 8 servings.

Fruit Juice Tapioca Pudding

¼ C Minute Tapioca	2½ C apple or grape juice
¼ C sugar	1 T lemon juice (optional)

Combine tapioca, salt, sugar, fruit and lemon juice in a saucepan. Let stand 5 minutes. Bring to a boil over medium heat, stirring occasionally. Remove from heat; stir after about 20 minutes. Serve warm or chilled. Makes 4 to 6 servings.

Bread Pudding

Mix together:

3 to 4 egg whites (beaten)	2½ C skim milk
¼ C sugar	½ t cinnamon

Add and mix:

6 to 8 slices whole-wheat bread (torn into cubes)	½ C raisins

In microwave: 25 minutes at medium temperature or 20 minutes at bake temperature

IV. *Optional Activities*

• Family Garden

Plant a family garden—good exercise and nutrition, and fun. Here are some handy suggestions:[2]
1. Plant just enough for your family—avoid being overwhelmed the first year. Later, you can expand.
2. Plant crops that are easy to tend, taste good (and are hard to get—or expensive in stores), such as:
   —leaf lettuce
   —spinach
   —sugar snap peas
   —tomatoes
   —cucumbers
   —herbs (to use fresh)
   —Alpine strawberries

—blueberries
—raspberries

Eating Out

Restaurants and chefs differ in preparing food. Here's how food prepared by six different ethnic restaurants or chefs varied regarding calories from fat, carbohydrates and protein:[3]

	Fat	Protein	Carbohydrate
American	1	3	6
French	2	4	5
Mediterranean	3	1	2
Mexican	4	2	1
Italian	5	5	4
Chinese	6	6	3

Key: 1 = Highest percent of calories
     6 = Lowest percent of calories
For Example: American has the highest percentage of fat, lowest percentage of carbohydrates and middle percentage of protein.
Conclusion: Eat Chinese or Italian; don't eat American or French.

● Eating in Flight

If you are on a special diet and must fly a lot, here's what selected airlines are willing to do for you:

Type of Meal	Airline					
	American	Eastern	Pan Am	TWA	United	US Air
Low-calorie	X	X	X	X	X	X
Low-sodium	X	X	X	X	X	X
Low-fat		X	X		X	X
Low-cholesterol	X	X	X	X	X	X
Vegetarian	X*	X	X	X	X	X
Diabetic	X	X	X	X	X	X
Hypoglycemic		X			X	
High-protein			X			
Low-carbohydrate	X	X		X	X	
Gluten-free		X	X			
Bland/soft	X	X	X		X	

*Can specify if strict or lacto-ovo.

• Water Purity

Some families are concerned about water purity. Here is some information on selected companies' water filters:

	Percent of chlorine removed	Percent of chemical pollutants removed	Taste	Initial cost*	Replace-ment filter cost*	Rated filter life (# of gallons)*
Ametek CSI-GAC10 Ametek, Inc. Plymouth Products Div. Sheboygan, Wisconsin	94	63	Worse than tap water	$ 27.95	$ 8.50	1,200
Amway Water Treatment System Amway Corporation Ada, Michigan	100	99	Better than tap water	$250.00	$80.00	750
Aqua-Guard Universal Water Systems Milwaukee, Wisconsin	58	39	Not distin-guishable from tap water	$ 30.00	$ 3.50	400
Astro-Pure Astro Pure, Inc. Margate, Florida	97	52	Not distin-guishable from tap water	$240.00	$60.00	2,000
Clean Water Machine Norelco North American Philips Corp. Stamford, Connecticut	87	0	Better than tap water	$ 49.95	$ 4.95	250
Ecologizer Rush Hampton Industries Sanford, Florida	68	41	Not distin-guishable from tap water	$ 30.00	$ 9.95	1,000
Filter Flask Filtercold Corp. Phoenix, Arizona	98	51	Worse than tap water	$ 30.00	N/A	600
Filterite CF-10 Brunswick Technetics Timonium, Missouri	94	66	Worse than tap water	$ 70.00	$11.95	750
Pure Water 99 Pollenex Associated Mills, Inc. Chicago, Illinois	62	46	Not distin-guishable from tap water	$ 25.00	$ 6.00	200

Seagull IV General Ecology, Inc. Lionville, Pennsylvania	99	66	Better than tap water	$320.00	$39.95	1,000
Water Dome Neo-Life Hayward, California	98	73	Better than both bottled spring and tap water	$119.95	$24.95	500

*Information supplied by companies.

Chapter 9:
Fatness—America's Heartbreak

" 'Everything is permissible for me'—but not everything is beneficial. 'Everything is permissible for me'—but I will not be mastered by anything." (1 Corinthians 6:12).

Paul stated flatly that he would not be mastered by anything but Jesus Christ. Even though he was free to do as he wanted, all things were not beneficial to him. In time, these things could control him.

From a health point of view, Paul is telling me that my desires for food, easy living and lack of responsibility are O.K., but not healthy or wise. They are not healthy or wise because in time they may master me. They may become my god.

Food is good. So is fat. Are you controlled by your drive to eat more or less food? Are you allowing too much or too little body fat to master your thoughts and actions.

Fatness has been with us for a long time. The Egyptians, Babylonians, Romans and Greeks talked about gluttony and overeating. Greek and Roman physicians called chest pain and obesity "the rich man's diseases." In the Old and New Testaments, the Bible speaks disparingly of guttony.[1]

In the past 2,000 years, the problems of fat and weight control have continued to expand so that today at least 34 million Americans are obese. Some estimate the count at 70 million. Either way, the numbers are alarming, as is the effect on these individuals' health.

Remember the last time you backpacked, climbed a mountain or carried a suitcase through an airport terminal? After a short time, you wanted to rest. The first thing you did when you stopped was take the pack off your back or put down the suitcase. Why? Your muscles ached. They were screaming for rest and more oxygen. Now imagine carrying a twenty- to thirty-pound backpack each day. Your different body systems—muscular, skeletal, circulatory and hormonal—would be under a greater strain to support the additional load. Your body would soon rebel.

It's no different with fat. Excess fat is considered a "pack on the back." Your bones and muscles strain to support the additional load. Your heart and lungs work harder to assist your muscles in moving all the fat around. For example, the extra fat raises your resting and working heart rates, often 10 to 30 beats for any task—anything from sweeping the floors to climbing stairs. That means your heart may beat 14,000 to 42,000 times more per day. Even your breathing rate increases. Scientists tell us that a person who carries too much fat generally takes 2 to 3 more breaths per minute, even when sleeping. This is 2,800 to 4,400 more breaths per day.

The extra fat problem goes beyond extra breaths and heart beats, and tired muscles and bones. A committee convened by the National Institutes of Health says anyone 20 percent overweight, as determined by life insurance height/weight tables, needs medical help because obesity is a disease. Dr. Jules Hirsch, the committee chairman, says, "It is a disease, and it carries with it the risk for increased mortality."[2]

Obesity, according to the committee, is clearly associated with high blood pressure, abnormally high levels of cholesterol in the blood, adult diabetes, and increased risk of cancers of the colon, rectum and prostate in men, and cancers of the gall bladder, bile passages, breast, cervix, uterus and ovaries in women.

Fatness goes beyond these physical problems. It causes emotional problems. Self-concepts and relationships have been destroyed by unwanted bulges and

---

PLAGUE #5

Diabetes

Diabetes affects one out of twenty people in the world. Diabetes mellitus is a disorder of the process in which the hormones insulin and glucagon regulate sugar concentrations in the blood. When the body doesn't produce or use insulin properly, hyperglycemia results. If the body produces enough insulin, but the tissues don't utilize the insulin properly, the concentration of glucagon increases. When that happens, the extra glucagon causes the liver to burn up protein and fats from tissues throughout the body. The results: persistent hyperglycemia or diabetes mellitus.

There are two types of diabetes: maturity- and juvenile-onset. Juvenile-onset diabetes is probably caused, in people who have a genetic defect of some type, by viral infections such as mumps, measles, hepatitis and upper respiratory infection. Juvenile-onset diabetes is treated with insulin, diet, the use of selected hormones, exercise and even pancreas transplants.

Maturity-onset diabetes is relatively simple to control, although it is a more complicated disease. The disease can be caused by a change in insulin production, or by the tissues being resistant to accept insulin. Whatever the reason, the tendency to get this disease seems to be inherited. Members of families with a history of maturity-onset diabetes should:

● keep their weight and body fat low
● eat a diet low in simple sugars
● exercise regularly
● avoid too much stress

Excess use of drugs and alcohol can exaggerate the problems of diabetes. Diabetics also should keep their cholesterol level and saturated fat intake low. Their chances of having a stroke or heart attack are two to three times greater, and their chances of developing gangrene, vision and kidney problems, emphysema and other lung problems are fifty times greater than the average American. All these problems are related to blood vessel damage.

bumps. It seems the fatter people get, the sadder they get. But more on this near the end of the chapter.

Before we get into any further discussion, let's understand a little more about weight management.

Weight Management: A Simple Model

The word *calorie* represents a unit of energy. The unit can be used to express either the amount of energy stored in food (one apple has 75 calories) or the amount of energy required to sustain life's activities (sleeping uses 1 calorie per minute, walking uses 5 calories per minute, for example). Energy stored in food is consumed as "fuel," and in order to provide the energy required to sustain life, your body tries to keep a fine balance between the number of calories you eat and the number of calories you "burn" through daily activities. For example, if you eat 2,000 calories in food each day and use 2,000 calories through activity, you are in a caloric balance and your weight will remain constant.

On the other hand, if you eat 2,000 calories and burn only 1,900, you are in trouble. You have an extra 100 calories. What happens to the 100 calories? The liver converts them into fat. The blood then carries this fat to the various fat cells of your body, where it is stored. While 100 calories doesn't sound like much, if you follow this pattern for thirty-five days, it will amount to 3,500 calories, which is one pound of fat. If you gain one pound of fat every thirty-five days, you will gain approximately ten pounds by the end of one year!

Weight management, then, is simply understanding three important points: 1) Your weight remains the same when you balance calories expended through sleep, work and play with the calories you eat. 2) Your weight increases when the calories you expend are less than the calories you eat. 3) Your weight decreases when the calories you expend are greater than the calories you eat.

Weight, Fat or What?

In addition to these three points, you must look at your weight, body and fat from another perspective. Divide the ingredients of your body into two categories: fat and lean body tissue.

> Fat = storage fat and essential fat
> Lean body tissue = muscles, bones and other (organs, nerves, blood, etc.)

Dividing the body into fat and lean body tissue allows researchers such as Dr. Albert Behnke, a retired scientist for the United States Navy, to talk about the concept of a "reference" man and woman.[3] This concept will help you understand if you have a weight problem and what you can do about it.

While men and women are similar in many ways, they are vastly different when it comes to body fat and lean body tissue. God, in His ultimate wisdom, knew and planned for that. Look at table 16. You'll see the reference man is four inches taller and twenty-nine pounds heavier than the reference woman. His bones weigh eight pounds more and his muscles weigh twenty-four pounds more than the woman's. The reference female, however, has about ten pounds more fat.

Notice that men and women differ most in muscle tissue and essential fat. Essential fat is stored in the marrow of your bones, as well as in your heart, lungs, liver, spleen, kidneys, intestines, muscles and parts of your nervous system. You need this fat to be healthy. In women, the breasts and hips also contain essential fat. This sex-specific fat increases the female essential fat to four times that of the male (12 percent versus 3 percent).

The other major sites of storage fat are around internal organs and directly beneath the skin. The storage fat around the organs (hearts, lungs, intestines) protects these organs and guards against starvation. The fat under the skin, subcutaneous fat, serves as storage and insulation against the heat and cold. The difference between the male and females in storage fat should not be very large (12 percent in men, 15 percent in women). (Throughout this book the terms *fat* and *body fat* refer to storage fat.)

While everyone is concerned about too much fat, too little fat also can cause health problems. "Minimum weight" is a person's actual weight minus his or her storage fat. For the reference man, that would be 136 pounds; for the reference woman, 107 pounds. On rare occasions, you will find healthy men and women who are functioning well at less than the minimal weight, but most people should never drop below their minimum level. Don't lose too much weight or fat!

People often think of fat as a sort of punishment, or something God gave us to ruin our good looks or lower our self-esteem. Actually, fat is nothing less than a miracle. It is a masterpiece of design and the best energy storage system known

TABLE 16
Reference Man and Woman

	Men	Women
Age	20–24	20–24
Height	5'8½"	5'4½"
Weight	154 lbs	125 lbs
Total fat	23.1 lbs (15%)	33.8 lbs (27%)
Stored	18.5 lbs (12%)	18.8 lbs (15%)
Essential	4.6 lbs (3%)	15.0 lbs (12%)
Lean body tissue	131 lbs	91 lbs
Muscle	69 lbs (44.8%)	45 lbs (36%)
Bone	23 lbs (14.9%)	15 lbs (12%)
Other	38.9 lbs (25.3%)	31.2 lbs (25%)
Minimum weight	136 lbs	107 lbs

to humans. It helps keep us warm, provides us with energy, and equips us for survival during real famine. That is why your body probably has a natural affinity toward getting fat. Isn't it interesting that Eskimos living in very cold climates tend to be short and stout? And African warriors living in sweltering tropical regions often are built like radiators—tall and lean to keep cool. The problem with fat has cropped up in modern-day America, not because fat is bad, but because our civilization has eliminated the human body's original need for it. We have air-conditioners, heaters, and clever food storage arrangements, so food is always handy. That's why nowadays some fat is good, but too much fat is bad.

In the early part of this century, before World War I, fat was considered a status symbol. Only people who had servants and lots of money could afford to be fat. If you wanted to align yourself with the successful, you put on weight.

People back then also were convinced that fatness meant good health, and doctors encouraged parents to fatten their children. Before the discovery of antibiotics, a child's only defense against sickness was his or her body. The doctors reasoned that extra fat helped keep the child from starving while the natural immunity system fought disease. As a consequence, parents were pleased to see their children put on fat. This attitude was unfortunate, as underexercising and overfeeding children are two major reasons for adult obesity and heart attacks.

Anorexia and Bulimia

With all this discussion on weight and fat, I would be remiss not to mention two new health concerns that have entered the family picture. These concerns are anorexia nervosa and bulimia. Ninety percent of anorexics and bulimics are women, particularly teenage or young women.

Anorexia nervosa is self-starving. The woman (or, rarely, the man) gradually starts to eat less and exercise more. Her behavior becomes so compulsive that she may exercise two to eight hours a day and eat or drink nothing but diet pop and water. Soon her weight drops—weights of eighty pounds or less on a five-foot-five-inch frame are not uncommon. Anorexia is a big league problem and not to be treated lightly.

Most anorexics are perfectionists and compulsive. They are "good little girls" with a straight A average in school. For several reasons, they feel that they don't measure up to society's demands for slimness. Consequently, they get caught in a passion to lose weight. They are driven by an obsessive fear of being fat, and they have wildly distorted views of their bodies—picturing themselves as fat, even though they are extremely thin.

Bulimics, on the other hand, gorge on food. They may consume more than 30,000 calories in a day, or even at a sitting, and then purge themselves by inducing vomiting or taking diuretics and laxatives.

Bulimics' eating patterns are bizarre. Some have eaten all the food in the refrigerator at a sitting, eaten the food out of the cat's or dog's dish, rummaged through garbage cans to find food, and eaten the cardboard box the food came in. Then they move to the bathroom and vomit or excrete all that was eaten. Some bulimics are exceptionally thin, some are quite heavy, and some yoyo in their weight. Some people suffer from anorexia and bulimia. They rarely eat (anorexia) and if they do, they quickly vomit the food (bulimia).

Eating disorders such as anorexia or bulimia stem from a society that equates success with thinness. And they take root as early as seven years of age. We conducted a study regarding self-esteem and body fat and found that many young girls based their self-esteem or slimness. Not so with young boys; their self-esteem was affected negatively only if they were grossly obese. Research in other parts of the country substantiated our findings. According to Dr. Nancy Rigott of Massachusetts General Hospital, 80 percent of adolescent girls have been on a diet by the age of eighteen.[4]

Why do some children have extreme eating habits while others do not? Some researchers think the disorders are especially likely to develop when parents set too high standards or achievement levels for their children. Or the parents try to exert too much control over their children's lives. This seems true, since many anorexics express delight in their ability to control their eating. They feel as though their weight and eating are the only things in their lives that they control. Therefore, they like to demonstrate to themselves (and to others) their incredible self-control. It is not uncommon for an anorexic to sit with an empty plate while others are eating, despite the fact that she has not eaten for a week or longer.

Extreme weight loss and eating disorders also may be cries for help in a troubled family, or withdrawal from adult sexuality and responsibilities. I repeat: Eating disorders are a heavy issue and require professional help—not self-care.

Not all women were meant to be thin. It is necessary, but difficult, for the bulimic or anorexic to recognize and internalize this truth. They also must learn not to base their self-worth on how they look, nor establish their self-esteem by comparing themselves to someone else—movie stars, models, etc. They must become comfortable with their self-image.

Josh McDowell, in his book *His Image—My Image,* explains, "A healthy self-image is seeing yourself as God sees you—no more and no less. . . . In other words, a healthy self-image means having a realistic view of ourselves from God's perspective, as we are portrayed in His Word. I add to the phrase 'no more and no less' because some people have an inflated view of themselves (pride), while others have a self-deprecating view of themselves (false humility)."[5]

And how does God view us?

- We are the peak of God's creation (Genesis 1:26,27).
- We were created a little lower than the angels (Hebrews 2:7).

- We are objects of God's redemptive purposes in the world (John 3:16).
- As redeemed people, we have angels watching over us (Hebrews 1:14; Psalm 91:11,12).
- Jesus is preparing a place for us for eternity (John 14:1-3).
- God has been made rich because we who are Christ's have been given to Him (Ephesians 1:18).
- God sent His Son to die for us (Mark 10:45).

We are special. We are loved. If only these young people would understand and internalize this. As parents, we must reinforce our children with the fact that God loves them dearly. God does not evaluate them on how they look. Neither should they.

Of course, parents also have problems with self-esteem. Most of us speak disparagingly of ourselves because we have put on forty pounds since we said "I do." We don't like the way we look or feel, and get caught in the same trap as the anorexics and bulimics. We base our self-worth on our looks. We have unrealistic expectations of ourselves. Secretly or openly we want to look like the magazine model or the athlete. We want to be more than God expects us to be. We allow ourselves to worship slimness and muscles. But God loves us. Alleluia! So we need to get over the glumness and accept our bodies. We should take care of our bodies, but not worship them.

The issue of weight, slimness and body worship is one of the most perplexing problems I deal with. Perplexing because obesity is dangerous, and people should lose weight. Yet we seem to take leanness to an extreme. We allow it to get out of hand. We worship thinness, and soon this muddled thinking gets tied into personal will and self-control (see pages 169–171).

As parents, you probably are rightly concerned. How do you strike a balance—not too fat, not too thin? It may take Solomon's wisdom to achieve that, but you can't go wrong by emphasizing how God loves us all, reinforcing the child's self-esteem, and recognizing that everyone is different.

Dr. Simeon Margolis, professor of medicine at Johns Hopkins Medical School, says it clearly: "As long as someone is getting adequate exercise and not overeating, his weight should not be a problem as long as it is within 15 percent of the recommended Height/Weight Table. An exception to this rule would be anyone suffering from conditions such as diabetes, hypertension and high triglyceride levels, in which weight control is particularly important."[6]

Some of us must learn to let go of leanness.

"Such regulations [not eating, tasting or touching food] indeed have an appearance of wisdom, with their self-imposed worship, their
false humility and their harsh treatment of the
body, but they lack any value. . . ." (Colossians 2:23).

Chapter 10
Losing Fat: Eating Less or Moving More

"Don't you know that you yourselves are God's temple and that God's Spirit lives in you? If anyone destroys God's temple, God will destroy him; for God's temple is sacred, and you are that temple" (1 Corinthians 3:16, 17).

The human body is magnificent! It is "fearfully and wonderfully made"[1] by a wonderful Creator, who seeks to dwell within it. "Don't you know that you yourselves are God's temple and that God's spirit lives in you?" Wow! That's chilling, but to me, also very thrilling.

God's temple—the believer's body—is sacred. It deserves and requires special care, which will keep it strong and useful. Carelessness, lack of understanding, or misuse can destroy it.

One way to maintain God's temple is by taking proper care of excess body fat, which, left unattended, can be destructive.

If you wish to lose fat and weight, you have three choices: eat less; move more; or eat less and move more. All three will put you into a calorie deficit, so you will lose weight. But not all three are equal. Take a look at each.

Eating Less

Dieting is the most common way people try to lose fat. While most dieters do lose weight, the experts report that only 5 to 10 percent of the obese are able to lose the appropriate fat weight and keep it off through dieting. The great percentage of dieters regain the lost pounds quickly, usually within a few weeks.[2]

Why don't diets work? There are five basic reasons. First, dieting is no fun. It requires Spartan will power. Judging by the 5 to 10 percent success rate of dieters, most people don't have the will that their highly-restrictive diet regimen requires.

Second, some people are emotionally addicted to food. When under stress, they eat excessive amounts of food, and they gain weight. Then they diet, which increases their stress. When the stress becomes acute, they go back on their eating binge, which causes them to be more upset. They are caught in a tragic cycle of stress, eating, depression, guilt, dieting, stress and more eating.

A third reason for the lack of dieting success is social pressure. Eating is a fundamental aspect of nearly every American social gathering. At parties we enjoy cheese, snacks, nuts, pretzels; at sporting events, hot dogs and soft drinks; at weddings, cake and punch; and birthdays, cake and ice cream. How can any dieter hope to be successful when, at every turn, society strongly reinforces that we are expected to eat—and to eat too much?

A fourth and major problem with dieting involves new trends in nutritional and physiological research. It has been known for several years that reducing caloric intake (dieting) decreases the basal metabolic rate, or BMR—the underlying rate at which we burn calories to sustain life. This phenomenon once helped our ancestors conserve body fat through periods of famine. It now helps many people sustain a flabby midsection throughout their attempts to trim up by dieting. The body also can increase the basal metabolic rate when excessive amounts of food are eaten, hence the thin person's futile attempt to gain weight by overeating.

The new setpoint theory expands upon these two principles in explaining the dieter's plight. According to this theory, the body operates on a type of internal standard, or setpoint, which dictates the percentage of fat that should be maintained. Obese individuals have high setpoints and their lean counterparts have low setpoints.[3]

Regardless of your setpoint, when your fat content falls below it, your body responds by increasing your appetite. If you do not eat additional food, your BMR decreases to conserve fat stores. Conversely, when your fat content rises above the setpoint, your body responds with a decrease in appetite and an increase in BMR. Hence, whether predestined as obese or lean, your body fights to maintain its fat content within pre-set limits.

These problems notwithstanding, some people can't keep excess weight off because of a fifth and more basic reason: Dieting does not attack the real cause of obesity. While most of the population attributes obesity to overeating, there is clear evidence to the contrary. In an article on successful weight-loss programs, Dr. Peter Wood indicates that Americans have become fatter in the past sixty years while per-capita food consumption has *decreased*. Even on an individual basis, several research studies (e.g., survey of 1,485 London civil servants) have shown that food intake decreases with increasing fatness. In one particular investigation of lean women tennis players, the average diet contained 2,400 calories as compared to 1,500 calories for similar sedentary individuals.

Thus, it appears that overeating cannot be the cause of obesity, nor can dieting be the correct remedy. What then?

Plague #6

Obesity

Government reports show that each decade we are getting fatter. In fact, height/weight charts have been adjusted to accommodate the gradual increase in weight, so today the average person is told he or she can weigh seven or nine pounds more than the person of just one decade ago. Americans gain an average of one to two pounds a year from age twenty to age fifty. Consider these facts:[6]

— 20 percent of the children six to nine years of age have excess body fat.
— More than 10 million children up to age eighteen carry too much fat.
— Before the age of eighteen, 80 percent of girls have been on a diet.
— The average parent gains one to two pounds each year.

— Over $50 million is spent each year on diet and exercise books.
— Over $6 million is spent on diet drinks.
— Over $200 million is spent on diet pills.
— Over $1 million is spent on cosmetic surgery.
— Billions are spent on diet foods, weight loss programs, doctors and hospital costs.

Obesity seems to stay with people. An obese child usually becomes an obese teenager and adult. Dr. William Clarke, a researcher from the University of Iowa, has investigated cardiovascular disease risk factors among children in Muscatine, Iowa. He says, "Well over half of our kids who were overweight in the first grade are overweight when they reach high school."[7]

Normal Weights for Children

Normal weight range (girls will be expected to be at the low end and boys at the high end of the scale after age 14).

Age	Weight in Lbs	Age	Weight in Lbs
6 months	15–18	10 years	68–73
1 year	21–23	11 years	72–84
2 years	25–28	12 years	84–92
3 years	31–33	13 years	90–105
4 years	35–37	14 years	100–110
5 years	38–45	15 years	105–120
6 years	46–49	16 years	105–135
7 years	48–55	17 years	110–147
8 years	54–62	18 years	115–152
9 years	60–70		

Source: National Center for Health Statistics

Obesity is prevented by:
- Exercising vigorously at least four times a week
- Changing eating habits gradually, as well as moderately reducing calories (200 per day)
- Consuming less alcohol
- Dealing positively with stress
- Minimizing television watching

Moving More

As you may have guessed already, fat accumulates not so much from overeating as from underdoing. For example, obese people have been found to spend up to four times as many hours watching television as do thin people. And fat people walk an average of 2.2 miles a day, whereas a normal-weight person walks about 4.8 miles a day.[5]

My wife, Beth, and I have five children, in all shapes and sizes. It is interesting to watch them grow and mature. It is especially interesting to notice their basic activity levels and predispositions to gain or maintain weight. Some of the children have been very quiet from birth on (in fact, even in their mother's womb). Others have been extremely active. The placid children always have enjoyed sedentary activities—reading, riding in the car, table games, sit-down type of work. The active children have been in perpetual motion from day one. Our quiet children seem to struggle with their weight. Our active children never weigh themselves. They don't stand still long enough to step on a scale.

To discover your children's activity levels, you might try something I did when our children were five or six years old. I tried to follow them for a day. I did whatever they did—rode a bike, painted, read, climbed trees—you name it. I stayed with one of my sedentary children for the entire day. One of my active ones exhausted me by 9 A.M.

Why is an increase in physical activity so much more effective than dieting for weight loss? There are four possible reasons. First, an increased number of calories are burned during the activity. While some people argue that it takes a great deal of effort (e.g., walking thirty-five miles) to lose one pound of fat, they completely ignore the cumulative effects of activities. (One half hour of daily walking produces a fat loss of fifteen to twenty pounds per year.) Second, after vigorous activity, the metabolic rate usually remains elevated for several hours, thereby burning even more calories than at normal, sedentary levels. Third, participation in regular exercise often is accompanied by an increase in the basal metabolic rate, again cumulatively burning more calories than at sedentary levels. This increase in BMR may result from, among other factors, the significant increase in muscle mass that generally accompanies an exercise program. A fourth and final influence of physical activity upon fat content involves the setpoint theory. Exercise appears to be the only effective and healthy way to lower the pre-set level of fat that the body strives to maintain.

Thus, the overall effect of this increase in physical activity is a significant increase in energy production (calorie-burning), a significant increase in lean body tissue (better shape and tone), and a significant decrease in fat content. By comparison, dieting sadly promises decreased levels of energy production, no change or a decrease in lean body tissue, and no permanent change in fat content.

In chapter 6, I suggested ways to improve your physical fitness. I discussed the importance of intensity (how hard), duration (how long) and frequency (how often) in cardiovascular exercise. I also covered the importance of training heart rate exercise. That same information applies here, I encourage you to re-read that section.

Walking, God's Perfect Exercise

If you have a weight or fat problem, the best exercise to help you control your body weight is walking. It is pleasurable, safe and convenient. In addition, walking is for anyone, it's aerobic, which means it's good for your heart, and it fits your lifestyle. It's also a great family activity.

To get started on walking, do the following:

Week 1: Walk 10 to 15 minutes—nonstop. Don't worry about speed; walk at a pace that feels good to you. Do this four times this week.

Week 2: Walk 15 to 20 minutes four times this week. Follow the same guidelines as for week 1.

Week 3: Walk 20 to 25 minutes four times this week. Follow the same guidelines as for weeks 1 and 2.

Week 4: Walk 25 to 30 minutes four times this week. Follow the above guidelines.

Week 5 & 6: Walk 30 minutes four times each week. Follow the same guidelines.

Follow the guidelines I gave you on page 58–66. Once you have your exercise heart rate, look at Table 17.

Locate your percentage of maximum heart rate in the left hand column. Then look to the right hand column for the number of minutes you are to walk. If you had walked at 55 percent of your maximum heart rate, you would be expected to walk for 42:31 to 50:00 minutes four times a week. That becomes your exercise level. Walking the number of minutes at the designated heart rate on table 17 will cause you to use about 300 calories.

Follow this walking regimen for at least four weeks. Then take the ten-minute walk test again. Repeat the same procedure. You may find you need to walk farther because you are getting in better shape, or you may find that you are walking faster, so your heart rate has increased.

TABLE 17
Number of Minutes of Recommended
Walking at Different Training Heart Rates

Percentage of Maximum Heart Rate	Number of Minutes to Walk
40%	65:01–72:00
45%	57:31–65:00
50%	50:01–57:30
55%	42:31–50:00
60%	35:01–42:30
65%	30:01–35:00
70%	20:01–30:00

When your body and head call out for more or different exercise, read chapter 6 again and consider these exercises:

Aerobics

Advantages: A fun activity for all ages and both sexes.

Disadvantages: You cannot know if you improve from week to week, other than by subjective feelings. Also, aerobics has a fairly high injury rate, especially among older women who try to do too much too soon.

Calories: Uses 4 to 10 calories a minute.

Bicycling and Stationary Bicycling

Advantages: Bicycling is an excellent fat-control activity for practically all ages. It can provide you with a vigorous workout. It not only strengthens the leg muscles, but it also subjects the body to very little wear and tear.

Disadvantages: Most people pedal too slowly to derive the full fat-burning benefit. Cycling at eight miles per hour will not, as a rule, burn a significant number of calories. If you are relying on bicycling as a primary fat-burning exercise, pedal fast, ride up hills, and/or use a gear that offers substantial resistance.

Calories: Uses 3 to 10 calories a minute.

Cross-country Skiing

Advantages: It burns more calories than any other fat-burning exercise.

Disadvantages: You can't ski year-round. In some parts of the country, you can't ski at all.

Calories: Uses 4 to 12 calories a minute.

Running

Advantages: Running is an excellent activity for reducing body fat.

Disadvantages: Running is not for everyone. It can shorten the muscles in the back of your legs, reduce flexibility and make you prone to injury and leg pain. Obese people may find it too hard on their legs, knees and ankles.

Calories: Use 5 to 10 calories a minute.

Running-in-Place and Rope-Jumping

Advantages: These activities are good rainy-day replacements for outdoor activities.

Disadvantages: Most people who rope-jump or run-in-place find that motivation is the basic problem. These activities tend to cause knee and ankle pain. It also is difficult to measure progress.

Calories: Both use 4 to 10 calories a minute.

Stair Climbing

Advantages: This activity burns a lot of calories.

Disadvantages: Extremely boring. It may be too demanding for most people and is suggested only as a supplement to another activity.

Calories: Uses 7 to 15 calories a minute.

Swimming

Advantages: An extremely effective activity for the obese. The water provides support, so swimmers have fewer problems with their ankles, knees and hips.

Disadvantages: You need a pool and the ability to swim. You also may find it hard to keep going for an extended period of time. When you become an extremely efficient swimmer, you may have difficulty burning enough calories.

Uses 5 to 10 calories a minute.

In addition to the walking program and other exercises, it's good simply to move more. Learn to do things the hard way:

- Park your car in the farthest parking spot.
- Walk to the store when possible.
- Get off public transportation two or three blocks from your destination.
- Use the stairs, rather than the escalator or elevator.
- Move as much as possible.

These kinds of activities can help you burn off an extra 25 to 100 calories a day—or 2.5 to 10 pounds a year.

Eating Less and Moving More

The best way to lose weight and fat is to exercise, but this method may be too slow for some people. As a result, I propose a slight reduction in calories and an increase in activity. Most people can cut 100 to 200 calories a day without excessive hunger—but don't cut more than that. Here are the foods to eat less of. They are high-calorie low-nutrition. The foods are listed with the calories per item and the amount that gives you 200 calories. Each day eliminate one or several of these foods to reduce your calorie intake by 200 calories.

Therefore, to lose weight I encourage you to take the following steps:

1) Exercise aerobically for at least 30 minutes, 4 times a week. See table 17.
2) Cut 200 calories a day out of your diet. Select the foods from table 18.
3) Follow the behavior change activities for eating and physical activity, which follow this chapter.

I think you will find this regimen—200 calories out of the diet and 300 calories burned in physical activity—palatable and safe. You also will find it fairly rapid, as you will lose about a pound a week. And the weight you lose will be fat, not lean body tissue.

Now you know how to lose weight. This type of approach—eating less and moving more—has several advantages:

1. You'll lose fat and weight.
2. It is not difficult; most of us can part with 200 calories a day.
3. Since you're exercising, you'll get fit as you lose weight.

Table 18
High-Calorie/Low-Nutrient Foods

Food	Calories Per Item	200-Calorie Amount
Vegetables		
French fries	17 each	12 average
Olives	8 each	24 small
Pickles, dill or sour	15 each	13 large
Pickles, sweet	25 each	8 small
Canned vegetable mix	41/1½ cup	1½ cups
Canned, salted vegetable juices	13/ounce	16 ounces
Fruit		
Canned peaches in syrup	125 each	1½
Dried apricot	32 each	6
Fruit drinks	19/ounce	10 ounces
Avocado, small	425	½
Sweetened fruit	250/cup	¾
Meat, Fish, Lentils, Nuts and Eggs		
Visible fat, any meat	50/tsp.	4 tsp.
Bacon	33/strip	6 strips
Corned beef	62/ounce	3 ounces
Hot dogs	125 each	1½
Salami	125/ounce	1½ ounces
Luncheon meats	62/ounce	3 ounces
Duck	300/avg. serv.	⅔ serving
Goose	300/avg. serv.	⅔ serving
Sausages	250 each	¾
Patés	50/Tbsp.	¼ cup
Oily fish, such as:		
Herring, fresh	225/avg. serv.	9/10 serving
Mackerel, fresh	150/avg. serv.	1⅓ serving
Sardines, canned	25 each	8
Tuna, oil-pack	500/cup	⅜ cup
Deep-fried fish	225/avg. serv.	9/10 serving
Deep-fried poultry	325/avg. serv.	⅗ serving
Spareribs	41 each	5 avg. ribs
Egg yolks	60 each	3⅓ average
Nuts	15 each	13
Beans, kidney/navy	200/cup	1 cup
Peanut butter	100/Tbsp.	2 Tbsp.
Shellfish:		
Crab, unshelled	30/ounce	6⅔ ounces
Shrimp, fresh	10 each	20 average
Thick stews	250/cup	¾ cup

Food	Calories Per Item	200-Calorie Amount
Grains, Breads, Cereals		
Pre-sweetened cereals	130/ounce	1½ ounce
Sweetened granola	130/ounce	1½ ounce
Packaged cereals	110/ounce	1¾ ounce
Crackers, white	15/2" square	13 2" square
White bread	65/slice	3 slices
Muffins	125 each	1½
Oils and Fats		
Lard	125/Tbsp.	1½ Tbsp.
Butter	100/Tbsp.	2 Tbsp.
Margarine (regular)	100/Tbsp.	2 Tbsp.
Mayonnaise	100/Tbsp.	2 Tbsp.
Milk and Milk Products		
Cream, 20%	33/Tbsp.	6 Tbsp.
Ice Cream	150/scoop	1⅓ scoops
Ice milk	125/scoop	1½ scoops
Cream cheese	50/Tbsp.	4 Tbsp.
Sour cream	400/cup	½ cup
Cheeses (hard)	100/ounce	2 ounces
Whole milk	167/cup	1¼ cups
Whole milk yogurt	165/cup	1¼ cups
Snack Foods and Other		
Thick gravies	50/Tbsp.	4 Tbsp.
Cake	125/1" slice	1½ slices
Pie	2800 each	⅛
Chocolate	50/Tbsp.	4 Tbsp.
Coconut, dried	25/Tbsp.	8 Tbsp.
Donuts, plain	150/avg. size	1⅓ average
Potato chips	200/cup	1 cup
Pretzels	16/avg. size	12½ avg.
Cookies	125/ounce	1½ ounces
Syrups	60/Tbsp.	3⅓ Tbsp.
Soda pop	12.5/ounce	17 ounces
Alcohol beverages	100/shot	2 shots
Beer	12.5/ounce	17 ounces
Candy, small	50/bite/size	4 bites
Animal crackers	8 each	25
Fig bars	50 each	4
Popcorn with butter & salt	65/cup	3 cups
Sherbet	100/scoop	2 scoops
Jam	50/Tbsp.	4 Tbsp.
Jelly	50/Tbsp.	4 Tbsp.
Pizza, mushroom	1200/medium	⅙ medium
Puddings	400/cup	½ cup

4. The lifestyle adjustments you need to make are small. That's the best way to make changes. Mark Twain said, "Habit is habit and not to be flung out the window by any man [or woman], but coaxed down the stairs one step at a time." That's good advice on eating and exercise habits.
5. The weight-loss rate is reasonable—not too slow, not too fast. You lose about a pound a week.

The following pages contain fun, wholesome and effective strategies your family members can use to take weight off and keep it off. Enjoy the activities, and the results.

"Do you not know that your bodies are members of Christ Himself?" (1 Corinthians 6:15).

FAMILY WEIGHT CONTROL ACTIVITIES

Here are ways to motivate your family and improve attitudes about weight, fat, eating and exercise. On these pages, you will find trigger stories, self-perception activities, fat tests, and suggestions for exercise and cutting calories. You should supplement these ideas with those found in the "Family Fitness Activities" and "Family Food Activities" sections. Also apply the information from chapter 15, "Managing Time, Setting Goals and Getting Started."

I. *Understanding the Problems of Too Much Weight and Fat*

● **Twenty Pounds Overweight** (Ages 9–16)

Children have vivid imaginations, but most can't imagine what it would be like to be even twenty or thirty pounds overweight. To illustrate to them the effect of extra pounds, fill a backpack, handbag or other container with heavy objects, such as books. Now take a walk together or do another kind of physical activity. You'll both quickly notice that your child has much less endurance and energy. Discuss that if this extra weight were in the form of fat, he or she always would have to carry it around.

   In addition to causing constant exhaustion, excess weight negatively affects self-concept, and can keep a person from enjoying physical activity and good health.

● **Dangers of Fatness** (Ages 5–16)

On a large piece of paper, have family members list all the dangers of too much body fat. On another, have them list why people don't try to lose weight. Then play a game. Count your reasons why people don't try to lose weight. Get out enough dice to cover that list (for twenty reasons, use four dice). Number the reasons, beginning with the number of dice (four if there are four dice). Each person throws the dice and reads the reason that corresponds with the number rolled. He or she explains why it is not a good reason.

● **Trigger Stories**

The purpose of these stories is to help children and adults understand the feelings of an overweight person. Present them after a meal, when driving in a car, or during family devotions.

a. **Bill, the New Boy** (Ages 5–14)

   Bill is new on the block. He is heavy and cannot play sports well. Your friends decide to stand in front of his window and call him "fatty." What could you do? What might happen?

b. **Jim and the Date** (Ages 14–16)

Jim, a new tenth grader, is very heavy. All the other kids make fun of him behind his back and to his face. That irritates you. You have felt sorry for him and tried your best to make him feel welcome.

Two weeks ago, Jim thanked you for befriending him and said you prevented him from dropping out of school. You felt very good about that compliment. But last night he asked you to go to the school social (the biggest event of the year). What could you do? What might happen?

c. **Shopping** (Ages 12–16)

You're shopping for school clothes with your sister. Nothing you try on fits. Your mother says, "It's too bad you gained so much weight. Look at your sister—Everything fits her perfectly." How do you feel? What can you say?

d. **Chocolate Chip Cookies** (Ages 9–16)

Your father comes into your room just as you polish off a bag of chocolate chip cookies. He says, "For the last time, cut it out. You have to make up your mind to stop overeating. Have some willpower. It's just a matter of disciplining yourself. If you don't, you'll end up fat like all your friends." How do you feel? What can you say?

e. **Grandma** (Ages 10–16)

Your family thinks you should lose weight. Grandma, however, insists that you're just right and look "healthy." She offers you lots of food and says, "Just a little bit more won't hurt you. It's good to eat well." She bakes all the time and has candy everywhere. What can you say? How will she feel?

f. **Pressure** (Ages 8–16)

There is a lot of pressure today to be thin. Some people think you can't be popular or even happy unless you're thin. Some make fun of those who are fat. How would you feel about someone who was overweight? Could that person still be your friend?

g. **Mary** (Ages 10–16)

Mary, a teenager, has about ten pounds to lose and worries about the extra weight. One evening she was at a party and overate. Later that night, she was so mad at herself for eating so much, she went outside and forced herself to vomit. She felt better because she knew the food was out of her system. How do you feel about Mary's behavior?

h. **Tummy Flattener** (Ages 8–16)

Businessman John Smith looks very important in his suit. He is careful to buy clothes that fit him well and make him look trim. He also makes sure he always is tan. If John gains extra weight, he starves himself until he loses it. Lately, he's had trouble keeping his weight down, so he is wearing a tummy flattener under his shirt. As long as he looks good, he feels good. What do you think?

i. **Sensitive Joan** (Ages 8–16)

Joan is quite overweight. So are her parents and all of her grandparents. Joan watches what she eats, plays sports and is quite active, but still struggles with her weight. She gets teased a lot because she is so heavy, and the boys don't ask her out on dates. Joan is very nice though. She is sensitive, caring and loyal to her friends. How do you think you could help Joan feel better about herself?

j. **John and Bill** (Ages 8–16)

John is very popular with everyone at work. He's funny and always tells jokes. He also smokes a lot, and he eats a lot of junk food, but he is proud that he manages to stay thin. One day John made fun of his friend, Bill, who is overweight. He said some very mean things, but everyone got a good laugh out of it. What would you have done if Bill was your friend and you were in the room when John was telling the joke?

● My Friends and Me (Ages 12–16)

Have each family member fill out the questionnaire below, or answer these questions in a group. Circle *T* if the statement is true about you, *F* if it is false.

T F a. I feel it's better to be slightly overweight than slightly underweight.

T F b. If my friends or I do well, I think of dining out, rather than rewarding the accomplishment with physical activity.

T F c. Most of my friends are always on, thinking of going on, or going off a diet.

T F d. My friends and I feel that physical education is a waste.

T F e. Whenever depressed, my friends and I tend to eat, sleep, or watch more television than usual.

T F f. When someone else is on a diet, my friends and I might suggest that they "break the diet once in a while," or say "You don't look so good—you need to eat more" or "Why don't you put on more weight?"

T F g. None of my close friends are into sports.

T F h. Most of my friends are very inactive. We prefer to do sitting activities rather than physical activities, such as skating or swimming.

T F i. My friends and I find eating contests amusing. In fact, the ability to chug a beverage quickly is a macho sign.

T F j. Most of my friends are more concerned about what they are going to eat or have for dessert than how active or physically fit they are.

Review your answers carefully. If you circled three or more *T*s, you can conclude that your environment and friends are food-oriented and sedentary. If that is the case, plan some ways to become more activity-oriented. Record your observations and explain them to the rest of the family.

● You and Your Friends' Eating Habits (Ages 12–16)

If you agree with the statement below, circle the letter *T*. If not, circle the letter *F*.

T F a. My friends and I rarely eat breakfast.

T F b. When we do eat breakfast, it tends to be coffee, sweet rolls or donuts, rather than a blend of cereal, milk, fruit and toast.

T F c. My friends and I tend to eat quite a bit of low-nutrition/high-calorie convenience foods.

T F d. Between meals most of us eat high-calorie/high-sugar snacks, rather than fruits and vegetables.

T F e. My friends and I drink two or more colas or sodas a day.

T F f. My friends and I tend to be very casual about the types of food we eat.

T F g. Our place of employment or school does not serve nutritious meals. When it does, the foods generally are extremely high in calories.

T F h. My friends and I are meat and potato eaters. We eat few fruits, vegetables and salads, but a lot of animal protein.

T F i. My friends and I tend to select restaurants based on the quantity, rather than quality, of food. (Quality refers to a wide selection of foods, prepared nutritiously and relatively low in fat, salt, sugar and caffeine.)

After taking this brief test, review your answers carefully. If you circled three or more *T*s, you can conclude that your environment and friends encourage you to eat the wrong kinds of food. If that is the case, plan some ways to change this today. Record your observations and explain them to the rest of the family.

● Memory Game (Ages 8–12)

See who can memorize Dr. Henry Jordan's Eating Rules quickest. You are allowed to read the sheet of rules for thirty seconds. Then see how many rules you can remember. Take turns until everyone has memorized all the rules. You do not get credit for rules you remembered the last time—you must recite all ten rules together, not necessarily in order:[1]

a. Try to eat with others.

b. Eat slowly and never on the run.

c. Choose foods that must be eaten slowly.

d. Take smaller portions than you feel you can eat.

e. Wait five minutes before taking seconds.

f. Don't use food as a reward or for relief.

g. Enjoy what you eat.

h. Don't save the best for last.

i. Don't clean your plate.

j. Eat only when you are hungry.

● Low-Calorie/High-Calorie (Ages 5–14)

Divide the family into two teams. Show a picture of an activity to team 1. That team guesses the number of calories the physical activity uses per hour. If the answer is correct, the team scores one point. If it is incorrect, the other team guesses.

Variation: Show pictures of foods and have the teams guess the caloric content.

II. *Ways to Measure Fat and Your Percentage of Fat*

Measuring Body Fat:

● The Pinch Test (Ages 5 and up)

To find out if you or any member of your family carries too much body fat, take the pinch test. This will tell you whether your weight is composed of muscle or too much fat. Pinch your upper arm just above the outside of your elbow. Mom, if you can grab more than one inch, you may be carrying too much fat. Dad, ¾ inch is your upper limit. Kids, ½ inch is plenty.

● Tests for Mom, Dad, and Children (Ages 16 and up)

a. **Chest/Waist Test.** Stand with your shoulders pulled back and your chest at maximum expansion. Measure the circumference of your chest just below the armpits. Be certain your tape measure is flat and level. Then measure your waist (at the navel), with your stomach relaxed—not sucked in or forced out. For men, the chest should be at least five inches greater in circumference than the waist; for women, the difference should be ten inches. A smaller difference indicates that you are too fat.

b. **Weight Gain Test.** Recall what you weighed when you were eighteen if you are a woman, or twenty-one if you are a man. If memory fails, dig out old medical records. You can assume that each pound gained since that time represents an accumulation of fat.

c. **Mirror Test.** The quickest, easiest way to discern if you are too fat is to get undressed and stand in front of a full-length mirror. Do you like what you see? Have your body contours changed? If you look fat, you can reasonably conclude that you are fat. If you sag where you don't want to sag, or your waist protrudes, you're probably moving into obesity. Ask yourself these questions:

	YES	NO
1. Does my stomach protrude?		
2. Are my hips too big?		
3. Do I have saddlebags on the tops of my thighs?		
4. Do my breast or chest muscles sag?		
5. Do I have handlebars above my hips?		
6. Do the backs of my arms seem flabby?		
7. Do my legs seem to have the cottage cheese look?		
8. Are my ankles too big?		

If you answer "Yes" to any of these questions, you are probably too fat. On the other hand, don't be too hard on yourself. Younger women are especially apt to want to measure up to a fashion model's figure, which—unless you are built along long, lean, ectomorphic lines—is not possible or even desirable.

● All About You (Ages 5 to 10)

Show your children the following six drawings. Ask them these questions:

a. Which drawing looks like you?
b. Which picture do you like best? Why?

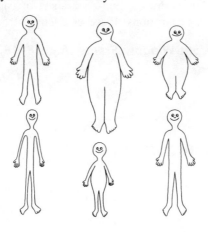

● May, Bill, and You (Ages 5 to 8)

Show your children these pictures and questions. Ask them to answer the questions and draw the appropriate pictures.

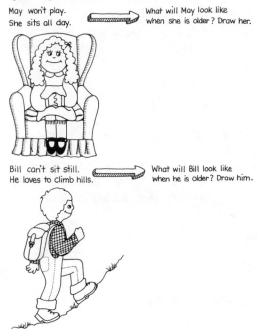

May won't play.
She sits all day.

What will May look like when she is older? Draw her.

Bill can't sit still.
He loves to climb hills.

What will Bill look like when he is older? Draw him.

● Window Frames (Ages 8–16)

Window frame continuums can help you see how you and your children feel about their weight.

Tell them: "I'm going to draw a line on a sheet of paper. Between the two ends of the line are lots of positions. Place yourself where you think you are."

a. Exercise and Weight Window Frame (Ages 8–16)

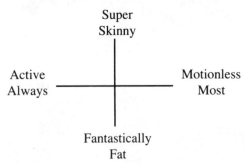

Super
Skinny

Active
Always

Motionless
Most

Fantastically
Fat

This is a good self-image activity. Have your children mark their points on the vertical and horizontal lines, avoiding marking right at the center.

After the children place themselves on the lines, talk together about how other people see them. Have family members place each other on the lines. Other people's perceptions usually differ greatly from our own, as we tend to be harder on ourselves.

Note: Most females (children and adults) picture themselves as fatter and more motionless than males. Most males tend to see themselves as thinner and more active than females.

b. Weight and Food Window Frame (Ages 8–16)

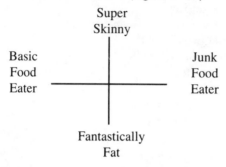

As before, have the children mark their positions on the vertical and horizontal lines, avoiding marking at the center.

After they place themselves on the line, talk together about how other people see them. Have family members place each other on the lines. Other people's perceptions usually differ greatly from our own, as we tend to be harder on ourselves.

NOTE: Females tend to see themselves as heavier and better eaters than males. Males tend to see themselves as thinner and poorer eaters than females.

• Questions on Weight, Activity, and Foods (Ages 10–16)

Ask your children to answer these questions. Discuss their answers with them.

a. Is your present weight too light, just right or too heavy?

b. Is it easy or hard for you to lose weight?

c. Is it easy or hard for you to gain weight?

d. Do you think that anyone in our family is overweight or underweight? Why do you think they are?

e. What do you think is the best way to lose weight?

f. Do you consider yourself very active, active, moderately active or sedentary?

g. Do you think foods cause people to gain weight? If so, which foods?

h. How often do you eat meals? Snacks?

i. Do you think we have a lot of junk food (candy, cookie, cake, soda pop, and/or ice cream) in our house?
j. When watching television, do you eat?
k. Do you eat more when you are angry, bored, depressed, lonely, sad or unhappy?

III. *How People Feel About Fat and Weight*

● **Pick an Ad** (Ages 5–16)

Select a magazine ad that shows an attractive male or female doing something physical or eating. Show the ad to your children and ask them these questions. Discuss with them their answers.
a. What does the ad tell you about people in our society?
b. What is the ad trying to sell you?
c. What else is the ad trying to sell?
d. Does this ad make you feel that you aren't as good as other people?
e. Does this ad encourage you to be healthier?
f. Do you feel a person could get what he or she wanted by following the advice of this ad?
g. Do ads encourage people to change their appearance?
h. Do you think men or women generally are more dissatisfied or satisfied with their appearance?

● **Time Marches On** (Ages 8–16)

The ideals of beauty change from time to time. Ask the children to do and discuss the following:
a. Ask people at church, school or home what makes a person handsome or beautiful.
b. List these characteristics.
c. Ask grandparents or older people what was considered beautiful or handsome twenty to fifty or more years ago.
d. Find pictures from old magazines. How have people's ideas of looks and appearance changed?
e. What does the Bible say about beauty?
f. What did this lesson teach you?

IV. *Weight Control Activities (Food and Activity)*

● **The 200-Calorie Food Solution** (Ages 12 and up)

On page 138 in chapter 10 are foods that are high in calories and relatively low in nutrients. If you want to lose weight, make a plan to cut one of these foods out of your diet for the next fourteen days.

After fourteen days: What did this exercise teach you?

● **The 300-Calorie Activity Solution** (Ages 8 and up)

Here are some activities you can use to burn an extra 300 calories a day. If you want to lose weight, make a plan to add one of these activities for the next fourteen days.

300-Calorie Activities

Activity	Duration	Distance (Optional)
Aerobics	30 minutes	
Badminton	40 minutes	
Basketball	30–40 minutes	
Boxing	15–20 minutes	Non-stop
Bicycling	25–30 minutes	9 miles
Calisthenics	30 minutes	Non-stop
Cross-country skiing	20–25 minutes	2¼ miles
Curling	1 hour	
Fencing	40–45 minutes	
Football	40–45 minutes	
Golf	2–2.5 hours	12–15 holes
Handball	30–40 minutes	
Hockey	30–40 minutes	
Lacrosse	30–40 minutes	
Racquetball	30–40 minutes	
Rope skipping	30 minutes	
Rowing	30 minutes	
Running	25–30 minutes	3 miles
Skating	1 hour	
Skiing downhill	30 minutes	Continuous
Soccer	30–40 minues	
Stair climbing	20 minutes	
Stationary cycling	30 minutes	9 miles
Stationary running	30 minutes	
Squash	30–40 minutes	
Swimming	25–30 minutes	¾ mile
Tennis	45 minutes	
Volleyball	40–45 minutes	
Walking	45–50 minutes	3.5 miles
Wrestling	15–20 minutes	Non-stop

After fourteen days: What did this exercise teach you?

● **Fast-Food Mania** (Ages 3–16)

Fast-foods are a way of life in America. You and your children probably will eat at fast-food restaurants frequently during the next year. To help you survive in fast-food restaurants without gaining weight, select lower-calorie foods. Here are serving sizes and calories of selected fast-foods:

fast-food restaurants without gaining weight, select lower-calorie foods. Here are serving sizes and calories of selected fast-foods:

Fast-Foods and Calories

Item	Serving size (oz)	Calories	Item	Serving size (oz)	Calories
Cheeseburger			**French Fries**		
Arby's	5½	492	Arby's	2¼	195
Burger King Whopper	9	663	Burger King	1¾	158
Hardee's Big Deluxe	8¼	557	Hardee's	2¼	202
Jack-in-the-Box Jumbo Jack	7¾	544	Jack-in-the-Box	2¼	217
McDonald's Big Mac	7	587	Kentucky Fried Chicken	3½	221
Roy Rogers ¼-lb	6	416	Long John Silver's	3½	282
Wendy's Single	7¼	547	McDonald's	3	268
			Roy Rogers	3	230
Chicken			Wendy's	3½	317
Jack-in-the-Box Supreme	7¾	572			
Kentucky Fried			**Roast Beef Sandwich**		
Fillet Sandwich	5½	399	Arby's	5½	416
Kentucky Fried Original			Hardee's	4¾	294
2-piece Dinner	7¼	720	Roy Roger's	5¼	298
McDonald's McNuggets	3¾	284			
Roy Rogers Fillet			**Other**		
Sandwich	6	526	Domino's Cheese Pizza	¼ of 12″	340
Wendy's Fillet			Hardee's Chili Dog	4¾	329
Sandwich	6	441	Hardee's Ham & Cheese	4½	326
			Jack-in-the-Box Taco	2½	174
Chocolate Shake			Jack-in-the-Box Super Taco	4¼	311
Arby's	11	365	Pizza Hut Pizza	¼ of 12″	400
Burger King	9¾	367	Roy Rogers Ham/Swiss	6	416
Hardee's	8½	273	Taco Bell Taco	2¾	194
Jack-in-the-Box	11¼	324	Taco Bell Taco Light	4¾	375
McDonald's	10¼	377	Wendy's Chili (small)	10½	310
Roy Rogers	13¼	518			
Wendy's	8½	367			
Fish					
Burger King Whaler	6½	502			
Hardee's Big Fish	6¼	515			
Long John Silver's					
Fish Sandwich	7¼	560			
McDonald's Filet-O-Fish	5	373			

In addition to watching calories, remember that most of these fast-food items are high in salt, sugar, saturated fat and cholesterol.

● Foods I Say "No" To (Ages 8–16)

Quite often, we eat foods we know are fattening. Then we feel guilty. Have your children list ten foods they like but they think are high in calories and low in nutrition. Then they list five to ten foods they think they could substitute. These foods should be relatively low-calorie/high-nutritional foods. Have them check off how many times they ate each during a week. The junk foods are worth -1; the good foods are worth $+1$. They should try to get a score of at least $+10$ for the week.

Sample Week for Good E. Twoshoes

Junk Foods	M	T	W	T	F	S	S	Score	Good Foods	M	T	W	T	F	S	S	Score
Potato chips	1		1					−2	Banana	1	1	1		1	1	1	+6
Pop		1			1			−2	Apple		1	1	1		1		+4
Snickers								0	Orange			1		1			+2
French fries								0	Carrots		1					1	+2
Donuts					1			−1	Broccoli				1				+1
Candy	1				1			−2	Oatmeal		1			1			+2
Twinky		1						−1	Grapes	1			1			1	+3
									Whole-wheat Bread	1	1	1	1	1	1	1	+6
								−8									+26

TOTAL SCORE: 26 − 8 = 18

• Junk Food Challenge (Ages 9–14)

Have family members list their ten favorite junk foods. Each week, they must cut out one of the ten. When they do, they receive one point. The next week, they cut out another. If they continue to cut out the junk food from the first week, they receive two points. The minimum total of points a person could receive would be 10; the maximum would be 55 ($1+2+3+4+5+6+7+8+9+10$). The winner at the end of ten weeks selects an activity for the whole family to do together.

• My Ten Most-Favorite Foods[2] (Ages 5–14)

Have all your children list their ten favorite foods on a piece of paper. Read aloud these instructions:

a. Circle the food you could most easily do without for one year.
b. Mark a plus next to each food that's relatively high in nutrients.
c. Indicate with a dash those items high in calories and low in nutrients.
d. Star those foods low in calories.
e. Use a checkmark to code those foods you eat too much of or too often.
f. Put a 5 by the items that would not have been on your list five years ago.
g. Put an *X* next to junk foods.

After they have coded and reviewed their lists, ask them to write answers to the following three questions on the back of their paper:

a. What did the "Ten Most-Favorite Foods" exercise tell you about your food selection?
b. Are all of the food groups represented? In balanced amounts?
c. What, if anything, do you plan to do as a result of the exercise?

● Snack Smorgasbord Night (Ages 5–14)

Select one night as a snack smorgasbord night. On that evening, each family member prepares a nutritious snack, which everyone samples. Younger family members may receive help from an older brother or sister or parent. All snacks must be low in salt and sugar. This activity can help family members discover nutritious snacks to replace junk food.

● Save Fat Food Money (Ages 8–16)

Have family members keep track of the amount of money they spend on junk food in one week (pop, candy bars, and so on). Then inform them that you will match every penny they do not spend on junk food. All the money is put into a special fund for fitness purchases, such as a new exercise bike or jogging shoes. Every family member's contributions are recorded. Run the contest for one month.

● Block Fitness (Ages 3–16)

Get together with a few other families on your block and organize a Feelin' Good party in the spring or at the end of the school year. Have each family bring nutritious food and beverages to the party. Also ask each family to plan two activities that are fun and promote physical activity. They do not have to be competitive. In fact, one of the two should not be competitive. For example, have a treasure hunt, bicycle rally or walk rally. Encourage the children to organize some of the activities.

An alternative: Invite neighbors for a walk, bicycle ride or swim. Tie it in with a holiday weekend and make it an annual affair. Follow it with a nutritious potluck lunch.

● Contract Writing (Ages 8–16)

Have family members write down one or two goals for the next month in each of the following categories. Have them indicate where they are now and where they want to be. Examples:

Exercise:
a. I want to be able to run two miles. Presently, I can run ¼ mile.

b. I want to be able to touch my toes. Now I can touch my knees.

Weight Control:
a. I want to lose 4 pounds. Presently, I weigh 115.
b. I want to lose one inch off my waist, which is now twenty-six inches.

Nutrition:
a. I want to stop eating candy bars. Presently, I eat one a day.
b. I want to eat a good breakfast every morning. Now all I have is a piece of toast.

Have each family member date the contract and indicate when it will expire. Example:

Starting Date January 1   Ending Date February 1

Also have each person find two witnesses who will sign the contract and agree to help. Example:

Witness Agreement
"I agree to check on _____(Lisa)_____ at least twice every week for the next month and make sure she is sticking to her contract. If she fails on one of her goals, I will encourage her to keep trying and to not give up. At the end of one month, I will help her test herself to see if she has achieved her goals. I have read the above contract and am willing to help _____(Lisa)_____ achieve her goals."

First Witness's Name _____(Becky Kuntzleman)_____ Date _____12/25/84_____

Second Witness's Name _____(Beth Kuntzleman)_____ Date _____12/31/84_____

Each person should choose a reward and include it in the contract. Example:

Reward
"When I achieve my goals, I will reward myself by taking Dad cross-country skiing."

Signed _____(Lisa)_____

Contract writing has two rules: 1) You may not set a goal of losing more than one pound per week. 2) You may not reward yourself with food.

• Diary (Ages 8–16)

If you or your child want to change or add a behavior, keep track of it by making a diary. Fill a small notebook with pages like those on page 155 and 156 of this book, or adapt these charts for your chosen behavior. Carry your diary with you at all times.

If you want to control the food that you eat, record in your diary everything you put into your mouth—water, pie, cake, bean sprouts, carrots, cake batter, pencils—everything. Include the time, place, your feelings and, if possible, the calories, or at least the portion size. Or use your diary to monitor your feelings of stress (when you experience it, when you don't); your exercise level (everything from sleeping to running); drug usage; or any other behavior.

Why is a diary useful? (1) It shows you problem patterns and habits. You will be amazed at what you will learn about yourself. (2) Keeping a diary probably will change your habits. You will be more conscious of what you are doing, so you probably will tend to do some things less and others more. You might hesitate to reach for a bag of M & M's or a Pop Tart, or be more prone to go for a walk. (3) It allows you to compare your current behavior with what you did several weeks ago. (4) It acts as an incentive.

At the end of each week, you may want to plot changes that you've noticed. This might include, "I'm eating less food between meals, I'm drinking fewer soda pops, I'm eating fewer desserts." Your evaluation can be subjective and objective.

Instructions for Using Your Food Diary

1. Complete the diary right after eating.
2. Note the time when you started eating.
3. Note where you were eating.
4. Note what you were doing while eating (e.g., reading, cooking, watching television, etc.).
5. Fill in the food and the amount.
6. Look up and enter the number of calories in each food.

Food Diary

Day: _____ Date: _____

Time	Where You Were	Activity	Your Feelings	Food and Amount	Calories
6:00 A.M.– 11:00 A.M.					
11:00 A.M.– 4:00 P.M.					
4:00 P.M.– 9:00 P.M.					
9:00 P.M.– 6:00 A.M.					

Instructions for Using Your Exercise Diary

1. On a scale from 1 to 5, record your pre-exercise attitude level (1 being minimal stress, 5 being highly stressed).
2. Record pre-exercise heart rate, range of heart rate during exercise, and post-exercise recovery heart rate (taken one minute following exercise).
3. On a scale from 1 to 5, record your attitude regarding the outcome of your workout (1 being poor, 5 being great).

Exercise Diary

Date: _____

	M	T	W	Th	F	S	S
Number of Hours of Sleep Night Before							
Pre-Exercise Attitude							
Activity							
Time of Day							
Length of Workout							
Heart Rates Pre- During Post-							
Post-Exercise Attitude							

Weight: _____

Chapter 11:
Addiction—Cola to Coke

"No matter which way I turn I can't make myself do right. I want to but I can't. When I want to do good, I don't; and when I try not to do wrong, I do it anyway. Now if I am doing what I don't want to, it is plain where the trouble is: sin still has me in its evil grasp" (Romans 7:18–20, LB).

A long, sticky, molasses-colored streamer hung from the ceiling in the summertime. Any fly, boldly buzzing near enough to investigate the sweet, yummy-looking paper, was caught and held fast.

As a child, I watched the flypaper to see how many it caught. For the flies, it was a losing battle. One touch and the fly was trapped. No amount of struggling could bring freedom. Some flies died from tasting the sweet-smelling poison on the streamer; others, from struggling to be free. The flies didn't want to get caught, but they did. They wanted to get free, but they couldn't.

Likewise, in Romans 7, Paul says he was caught in a lifestyle of sin. Hard as he tried, he could not free himself. But be not dismayed—Paul found hope and victory. He wrote, "Oh what a terrible predicament I'm in! Who will free me from my slavery [addiction] to this deadly lower nature? Thank God! It has been done by Jesus Christ our Lord. He has set me free."[1]

Our society is filled with enslaved people. Many of us are addicted to, or overuse, food, drugs, tobacco, alcohol, caffeine, television, work, exercise, our bodies, our minds and even our families. But we can find the same hope and victory that Paul did by putting our trust in the Lord Jesus Christ.

We know that addictions are bad for us. Smoking causes lung cancer; heart disease; cancer of the throat, larynx and lips; emphysema; chronic bronchitis; and higher susceptibility to other infections.

Alcohol ruins relationships, livers, hearts, marriages and jobs.

Drugs blow our minds, jobs, wallets, stomachs and families.

Television immobilizes us, robs us of conversation and dulls our senses.

Plague #7

Cirrhosis

Cirrhosis of the liver, a disease in which many cells are killed and replaced by scar tissue, is a leading cause of death among middle-aged Americans. One form of this disease is caused by chronic alcoholism. From 10 to 20 percent of all alcoholics have cirrhosis to some extent. Cirrhosis also can be caused by toxic drugs or chemicals, such as pesticide residues, food additives and industrial materials, including benzene and lead. Or, the disease sometimes develops after a bout of viral hepatitis.

As a preventive measure, people who drink heavily, have had hepatitis or jaundice, take large amounts of legal or illegal drugs, or work around toxic industrial chemicals should have liver function tests done yearly. Fortunately, the liver is able to regenerate itself. There is some evidence that an unusually nutritious diet high in protein, B-complex vitamins (especially choline) and vitamin E can help repair a damaged liver. Food rich in vitamins C and A also are believed to promote healing.

Caffeine contributes to heart disease, cancer, digestive disorders, breast disease, birth defects, kidney problems, headaches and anxiety.

Overwork may build up the economy, but it destroys families, bodies, minds and motivation.

Overeating adds fat to our bodies, ruins self-concepts, contributes to heart disease and high blood pressure, and makes us tired.

Why Do We Abuse Ourselves?

People are aware of these harmful effects. Why, then, do they continue to abuse themselves? Why do they get caught in the flypaper? Why do they struggle with things and lifestyles they know are wrong?

In the past, doctors thought that each person who was addicted to eating, gambling, alcohol, tobacco, drug, work, or sexual addiction had unique characteristics. Experts now realize that isn't so. An addict is an addict. And people overindulge in activities (from alcohol to Zen), for three basic reasons: 1) to relieve pain, 2) to reward or give pleasure, and 3) to support low self-perceptions.

Addictions for Relief of Pain. To relieve pain, a person may turn to the effect of addictions. Many kinds of activities (running, smoking, drinking, overeating) change the amount of natural opiates produced at the nerve endings of the pain system. Or they produce chemical cousins of these opiates, which act like the natural ones. Either way, the activity provides relief from physiological pain. Also, to escape or mask psychological pain from the loss of loved ones or from feeling unloved or unwanted, some people indulge in drugs or alcohol.

Addictions for Pleasure or Reward. Pleasure is a powerful motivator. Addictions such as gambling, taking drugs or daydreaming provide relaxation and give a physiological and psychological lift. The lift can be seductive, as it makes us feel good. So we reward ourselves with another cigarette, a piece of cake, or more sex.

Addictions to Cause Pain. Some addicts strive for pleasure; others strive for pain. A person may be addicted to cigarettes because he feels unworthy to have good health or to live long. Another eats large amounts of food because she wants to justify that her body is not beautiful. Some people develop relationships with partners who make them feel lousy. Dr. Stephen B. Bank, Professor of Psychology at Wesleyan University in Connecticut, summarizes this point nicely: "Many people involved in hurtful relationships are often atoning for an abortion or a failed marriage or career. Feeling unworthy of happiness, they look to others for the punishment they feel they deserve."[2]

Let's look at a few addictions to get a clearer picture of how they are developed and fostered.

Smoking

Most smokers lit their first cigarette in response to peer pressure. As youngsters, they and their friends thought it was the adult thing to do. In time, they found that they needed to smoke. They needed the stimulus of smoking to get started in the morning. They also needed cigarettes to relax. Ask smokers why they light up first thing in the morning, and they'll say, "It wakes me up." Ask them why they smoke after supper and they'll say, "It relaxes me."

As incongruous as this may seem, some people are convinced that the only way to get a lift, or to mellow out, is to smoke. They feel they need to smoke, and they enjoy it, so simply telling them to stop is not an adequate solution.

Alcohol

Alcohol addiction isn't much different from smoking. Most drinkers enjoy the supposed stimulation they get from alcohol. They notice that after a few drinks at the ballpark, they cheer louder and laugh more than the teetotalers. They think that when they have a couple of cocktails at lunch, they impress everyone with their witty and urbane conversation. People are convinced that everything from hobbies to parties are more enjoyable with a can or glass in one of their hands.

Drinking also may relieve pain, since certain properties in alcohol have qualities similar to morphine or opiates. Again, trying to tell people to stop drinking, when they are getting a lift or pain erasure, is ineffective.

Pills

Never before have Americans of all ages consumed so many sleeping pills, pep pills, diet pills, sedatives and tranquilizers as they do today. And all in this age of health awareness. We have pills—prescribed and over-the-counter—for every purpose and many with no real purpose at all. People, with help from advertising, think they have discovered the easy way out of problems. They are convinced there is nothing that cannot be cured by the right pharmaceutical concoction. Some people take a pill every morning to clear the cobwebs. Every evening they take another to help them sleep. Others take pills to lose weight or reduce anxiety. Drugs have become a way of life. We turn to them for assistance instead of learning to handle our problems in a mature, self-reliant way.

Our society has become extremely casual about drugs. On the evening I wrote this page, a friend of mine went to a local pharmacy with a prescription for benadryl for her sixteen-year-old daughter, who had chickenpox. The pharmacist started to count out thirty benadryl tablets. My friend, a nurse, said, "Oh my goodness, I don't need that much. My daughter only needs about ten pills to get her through the next day or two." The pharmacist said, "Well, take the other twenty. Your daughter can then take the benadryl to get her to sleep." Talk about casual attitudes!

Just like alcohol and tobacco, pills offer stimulation. They give a lift, a rise, to overcome fatigue, or relaxation to overcome the pain of anxiety, frustration or pain itself. People look to pills when they experience the blahs and burnout, or when they want energy. People have more confidence in chemicals than in their own God-given capacity to enhance their health and well-being.

Tobacco, alcohol or illegal drugs are no-nos to many Christians. They know their bodies are temples of the Holy Spirit. Yet, many clear-headed Christians take over-the-counter drugs or prescribed medications at the drop of a hat—aspirin for a headache or PMS, cough medicine for a cough (and to go to sleep), anti-histamines for allergies. Nothing is basically wrong with using these drugs, but, we must remember, the headache may dissipate with rest, relaxation and recreation. We may know that it is a result of pushing ourselves too hard at work, but we don't want to slow down. Our PMS may be aggravated and heightened by the stress of overwork, but we opt for aspirin instead of rest and relaxation. Maybe we could have relieved our allergies by avoiding certain foods, or a cough by drinking plenty of fluids and resting more, but we prefer to take medication.

We also abuse prescribed drugs. Some of us literally demand pills from our doctors. If they don't give us what we want, we "shop" elsewhere. I call this passion for medication an addiction.

Coffee and Caffeine

Americans enjoy coffee. We drink hundreds of gallons a year. We enjoy its full aroma and taste. Nothing may smell better than coffee perking on the stove, but why do you drink it? Simply because you enjoy it, or because it gives you a lift? Or why do you drink a cola beverage in the afternoon? For its liberal dose of caffeine?

The died-in-the-wool coffee addict swears he can't get started without that first cup of coffee in the morning. Research supports the claim that the caffeine in a cup of coffee or a cola produces a notable stimulus to the nervous system. Laboratory experiments indicate that coffee increases mental alertness, speeds reaction time and helps people think more clearly. So, again, trying to tell a person to stop drinking coffee is not a solution.

Overeating

People love to eat. It provides pleasure and good feelings. Many times food is associated with family and friends, or connected with pain erasure and reward.

Vast numbers of children are encouraged to overeat (or at least to eat when they don't desire to eat), in order to avoid negative consequences: "If you don't finish your dinner, dear, you can't watch television tonight." Or to get what they want: "If you finish your soup, I'll take you to the park after lunch." Or to win adult love and approval: "You're such a good girl—you ate all your mashed potatoes."

All this is bad enough, but in addition, children often are rewarded with food when they have been "good," successful or submissive. Think of the number of Little League coaches who take their winning teams to the ice cream shop; the doctors who hand out lollipops to young patients who don't cry; and the parents who give their children special treats when they bring home good report cards. Therefore, children equate rewards with food.

Kids also are soothed and comforted with food. I've seen parents use cookies to divert a child's attention from a badly scraped knee (which I've even been tempted to do myself). When adults psychologically manipulate with food, is it any wonder that their children invest eating with emotional connotations?

Very often a child's first exposure to "forced feeding" occurs within the first months of life. Many times a baby cries because of a desire for cuddling, companionship, a change of diapers, a change of scene. But the mother (or father) tends to interpret any crying as a demand for food and immediately attempts to appease the child with breast or bottle. Thus, very early in life the child associates gratification of all emotional and physical needs with eating. Placating a baby with food, when he or she wants attention or stimulation, also can discourage the child's budding interest in actively exploring the outside world.

Established in babyhood, strengthened during childhood and confirmed during the teenage years, the pattern of eating for gratification or to relieve tension and frustration carries over into adulthood. Stressful situations not only cause adults (who are thus conditioned) to overeat; stress also encourages them to refrain from physical activity. People who are depressed or overstressed manifest a strong desire to sleep. So a vicious cycle is set up. The more stress, the stronger the craving for food, the less active the person becomes—and the more weight is gained. In time, anxiety over an individual's own obesity reaches a point where the obesity itself causes stress, and the cycle is complete.

Television

In the 1950s, television began to have an impact on the American way of life. Evening meals were scheduled around "Howdy Doodie" and "Frontier Playhouse." By the 1960s, 90 percent of American homes had a television; televisions that showed Vietnam battles, "Captain Kangaroo" and "Peyton Place." Ninety-eight percent of our households had at least one television by 1970.[3] During this time, it was estimated that the average child watched 3.5 hours of television each day and saw more than 250,000 commercials by the time he or she graduated from high school. More recently, it has been estimated that the average television is turned on for more than 7 hours per day. Preschoolers average 33 hours per week. The typical 6-year-old entering first grade today already has seen approximately 10,000 hours of television.

And television's reach is becoming more pervasive. Cable is wired into about 40 percent of all United States homes, bringing with it as many as eighty programming options. It is estimated that at least 1 million U.S. homes have satellite antennas that can grab signals from space. In 1984, consumers purchased 8 million videocassette recorders.

Television, through no fault of its own, occupies an extremely important part of our lives and homes. It has affected our lifestyles. It even has spawned a holiday—Super Bowl Sunday.

Why do we watch television? It gives us pleasure, enjoyment, entertainment and thrills. We also use it to relieve pain. With a flip of a switch, we escape into the fantasy world of network and cable television. And, as with other addictions, we develop an insatiable desire for more—more sex, more violence, more realism, more news, more cartoons, more entertainment, more escape.

Nothing is inherently wrong with watching television (or as I should say, watching programs). Something is drastically wrong, however, when a show becomes a fix, mainlining a quick kick to us to get us through the day, week or weekend.

Consider your television habits. Do you plan your day or evening around certain programs? If so, you may be addicted.

Sports Addiction

The needs to be stimulated, relieve pain and find pleasure also are manifest in the high attendance at spectator sports. And again, people seem to cry out for more. Race car promoters say that the best way to assure a packed grandstand is to have an occasional spectacular crash. People seem to be repelled by the sight of blood at a boxing match, but after the increased number of deaths in the ring in recent years, tickets are selling better than ever. During last year's baseball season, fans set attendance records, while players appeared to break records for the number of bench-clearing brawls. Rodney Dangerfield provided a rather sad commentary on our society when he said, "I went to the fights the other night and a hockey game broke out."

As with television, nothing is inherently wrong with sports. I derive a great deal of pleasure from watching and participating in sports. But we each must ask ourselves: Has it become such a focus in my life that it controls my day, my thinking and my joy?

Running and Exercise

In 1983, researchers at the University of Arizona presented data which was disconcerting to exercisers. These investigators said that obligatory runners (those who hate to miss workouts and feel guilty when they do) suffer from the same psychological problems that people with anorexia nervosa (self-starving) do. That is, runners have extraordinarily high self-expectations and a tendency toward depression.[5]

This finding sent ripples of furor through the running community. As you would expect, runners faulted the study. So, researchers at Duke University Medical Center in Durham, North Carolina, decided to evaluate this thesis. They compared a group of male and female runners (who had scored high on a questionnaire that measured compulsiveness about exercise) with a group of anorexics. The runners and anorexics were given a standard personality test, which evaluated psychological traits such as hypochondria, depression, paranoia and anxiety. The researchers found that the anorexics suffered much more from depression, hostility and anxious feelings, while the runners were evidently well-adjusted and coped with stress effectively.[6]

The Duke investigators said that runners do not have the personality characteristics of anorexics. They did not say, however, whether or not running was addictive. It is entirely possible for runners to go to extremes, to become addicted to a good thing. Signs of this are exercising when injured or sick, feeling a strong compulsion to exercise even though they already exercised that day, planning their entire day's activities around exercising, and allowing exercise to negatively affect relationships and jobs.

A word of caution—many people use the above rationale as an excuse not to exercise. Nonsense. A moderate amount of exercise is healthful—more so than eight or more hours of pressured work, seven hours of television, and other compulsive habits such as gambling.

The point of all of this talk about addictions is not to offer my bleak judgment on the human race. Rather, I'm trying to show that some of us criticize the overuse of alcohol, drugs and tobacco, while we overuse or are addicted to television, sports, coffee, and food. We feel we need them to get through our days, indicating that we're worshiping things, not God.

I'm not pointing a finger just at you—I, too, have had my share of addictions. As a teenager, I had a low opinion of myself, so I wanted to prove my worth to myself and to others. Consequently, I threw myself into my first job. I tried to do many things to succeed. But every time I reached a new goal, I was disappointed. I never felt satisfied. Eventually I became addicted to work. It gave me a "rush," a buzz—a temporary sense of worth. But it was destroying my zest for living, my family and my true self-esteem.

My addiction was socially acceptable and people congratulated me on being very industrious. But overworking was as dangerous as tobacco, gambling or alcohol. It had become my god. Work didn't ruin me and my family financially, as other addictions might, but it almost ruined me emotionally and spiritually. I had to learn to put work in perspective, to save my family and myself.

More recently, I needed to deal with another addiction: running. I had started to run at age thirteen. During my teenage years and early twenties, I ran to keep in shape for sports. As I pursued a masters degree and later a doctorate in exercise physiology, I became convinced of the value of exercise. So I biked, swam and, primarily, ran to keep fit and healthy. I ran four to five times a week, from one to six miles at a crack. Over the years, however, I noticed that my running took on a different meaning. From my early thirties on, I ran because my head called for it. I really enjoyed it. I liked the good feeling that I received from running forty-five to fifty minutes six days a week.

Then two things happened that made me evaluate my running. To celebrate my fortieth birthday, I decided to run forty miles. I also decided to use my run to solicit contributions for the Jackson-Hillsdale County Youth for Christ organization. We planned many festivities, including a 10K run, a blister buster with 500 people running and walking with me to help raise money. It was to be a gala birthday event.

In preparation, I ran fifteen to twenty miles every other day for three months. That took two to three hours, three to four days a week. Running that much required planning. My entire day focused on how, where and when I would run. All of my behavior—time with my family, my job, sleep—were dictated by my training. I realized that running was running my life.

Ten months later, as my daughter's high school graduation present, I took Deb to Colorado to climb Long's Peak. The day of our climb, we were on the trail by 6 A.M. We climbed all morning and reached the peak at about noon. After enjoying the view and the excitement of scaling the mountain, we started our descent. We returned to our base camp at around 4 P.M., joyous that we had scaled the 14,141-foot mountain and returned in ten hours. We had a grand time. After resting for about an hour, I thought, *You know, Charlie, you haven't had your run today. You'd better hit the roads.* I suddenly checked myself. *Why do I need to run? I have just exercised the equivalent of more than a marathon.* Slowly, I began to see that running had become the major focus of my life.

Over the next two years, I still found that I was planning my day's events around my running. My work, sleep and relationship schedules all centered on my 4:30 P.M. run. It had become my number one priority. I was hooked. I liked the immediate feeling from running that was caused by the chemical changes in my brain (pain erasure), and the good feelings that resulted from a sense of accomplishment and from the control I had over one area of my life (pleasure). But, running had become my god. This realization and several other factors led me to make God number one. I established a policy that for each hour I spent exercising, I would spend one hour in the Word. I've done this for more than a year and have found it extremely rewarding. What a difference in my life!

Again, my addiction was not harmful in the ways that alcohol, tobacco, overeating or television are. It didn't ruin my health—it improved it. Running was (and is) a positive force in my life. In addition to helping me physically, it helped me emotionally, and even spiritually, since the long quiet runs gave me time for reflection. It increased my energy. I was more attentive. In some ways, it made me a better father and husband. But I was worshiping my daily run. I needed a balance.

In the next chapter, we'll discuss how to find a balance—how to control an addiction, whether it be smoking, crocheting, watching television, or going on buying sprees. But first, we'll look at the characteristics of an addicted personality.

"Those who let themselves be controlled by their lower natures live only to please themselves, but those who follow after the Holy Spirit find doing those things that please God" (Romans 8:5, LB).

Chapter 12:
The Addictive Personality

"Walk by the Spirit, and you will not carry out the desire of the flesh" (Galatians 5:16, NAS).

The desire of the flesh is what got humans into trouble in the first place. Our desire to be godlike. Our desire to control our own lives also spawned the technological society. Tragically, technology is out of control. We feel like a number—unwanted and unloved. We think, *If I'd die tomorrow, who would care?* To cope with this anguish and need to rise above it all, we use drugs, alcohol, work, television, food and tobacco.

In the previous chapter, I discussed addictions and why people get tied up in work, alcohol, food, tobacco, drugs, overeating, caffeine and television. Now I want to talk about the addictive personality—the common characteristics of those who put something or someone ahead of God.

First, addictive persons exhibit, occasionally or consistently, patterns of behavior that others deem clearly abnormal and sometimes self-destructive. For example, alcoholics have "just one drink," despite a history of a lack of control once alcohol is in their systems. Overeaters "reward" or "comfort" themselves with binges of food—often of the junk variety—while always claiming they are going to lose weight or go on a diet.

Second, when this abnormal behavior is pointed out, addicts deny that any problem exists. They offer the most fantastic rationalizations, generally based on their belief that "this time it will be different." The delusion that they can control their compulsive behavior is the common characteristic of all addicts. Thus a woman addicted to destructive relationships says of a new companion, "This guy is different from all the others"; the chocoholic maintains "I've got the problem licked now." Addicts continue to show the same pattern of behavior, while convincing themselves that the results will be different than before.

Additional behavior characteristics of addiction vary from person to person. A great deal of the addiction's influence on a person depends upon his or her personality, social perceptions, value systems, motivations and interests. The environment also is important. A permissive, free environment makes the formation

167

of some habits easier and the breaking of those habits more difficult. On the other hand, an environment that strongly preaches and teaches against an addiction, such as smoking, gambling and drinking, can produce tremendous guilt and trauma for a person who adopts those behaviors.

Depending upon your upbringing, you may view addictions as sin, depravity, disease, bad habits and/or demonic. You may even argue which addictions are worse. Some people put alcohol addiction far above television abuse or overeating. What about gambling? Overwork? Overexercising? Undereating? Compulsive sleep and daydreaming? Where do the love of money, chocolate, sweets, caffeine, valium, librium and aspirin fit in?

Whatever the substance or activity, if it controls your activity, you are hooked. The question is: How do you get your addiction under control?

Plague #8

Lung Diseases

Today, we must contend with lung diseases that slowly kill more than 30,000 Americans a year and contribute to 60,000 additional deaths. These chronic diseases deprive the brain and body of oxygen and force the heart to work overtime. These lung problems are linked to heredity, to factors such as smoking and air pollution, and to occupational exposure to selected hazardous substances. The major cause of respiratory ailments, however, is smoking. Smokers run a three-to-twenty-times-greater risk of chronic lung disease than nonsmokers. Common lung problems are chronic bronchitis and emphysema.

Chronic Bronchitis

The all-too-common "smoker's cough" is the first stage of bronchitis, a disease in which the minute hairlike projections lining the respiratory tract lose their ability to function and then are destroyed. When this happens, the harmful particles in smoke and polluted air no longer are intercepted by the nose or diverted into the throat where they can be safely swallowed. They move into the windpipe and gain entry to the lungs. These particles encourage sputum to be formed. Bronchitis increases the likelihood of respiratory infections and moderately increases the risk of death from infuenza or pneumonia.

Chronic bronchitis is prevented by:
- Not smoking
- Avoiding a polluted environment (chemicals or small dust particles)

Emphysema

In emphysema, the many air sacs in the lungs are damaged. Because of the damaged sacs, the waste product, carbon dioxide, accumulates in these sacs instead of being exhaled readily. Since chronic bronchitis, a precursor to emphysema, has narrowed or blocked the bronchial tubes and blood vessels, little life-giving oxygen can enter the air sacs. Eventually, the stressed air sacs tear, the capacity for delivering oxygen to the blood is further limited, and the lungs become permanently expanded. Although there is no cure for emphysema, bicycle riding, walking or gradual exercise designed to increase breathing capacity can provide relief. Drugs also are used.

Emphysema is prevented just as chronic bronchitis is—by not smoking and by avoiding a polluted environment.

Asthma

A third lung disease is bronchial asthma. It is caused by an allergic reaction to dust, pollen or some other allergen, by a respiratory infection, or by stress. Smoking exaggerates the condition.

In the past, everybody thought that if you educated people about the dangers of smoking, drinking alcohol, overeating and overworking, they would stop. Today, we know that awareness is only one small aspect of helping addicts. For, despite a tremendous surge of knowledge in the dangers of addictions, more and more people seem to be addicted. Facts are not enough. People need to understand the nature of the addiction and specifically what they can do about it.

If you want to bring something under control, you must first admit that you are addicted and that you cannot control it with will power. You may get "psyched up" and be effective for a short time, but unfortunately, over the long term, will power doesn't work. Your physiological and psychological needs and the memory of the experience remain. So when you break your habit, you experience a powerful craving. It becomes irresistible. You cannot muster all your energies to stop when you feel the urge to do it. When you attempt the will-power approach, you become unbearable because you direct so much attention toward your addiction. In time, you again are planning your daily activities around your addiction, or planning another activity to get your mind off of it. So it does not matter if you are a racehorse junky, television soap opera freak, or coffee-holic. You must "fess up" that your habit is your god—your reason to exist—and that you need help to control it.

Your second, and most important step, is taking your problem to God. As I said, you cannot solve your addiction by putting more of yourself into stopping. After all, that has been the problem all along—you have been too "me-centered." Your ego has been in control. Now you must surrender yourself to God; you need to humble yourself before Him.[1] You can't save yourself, only God can.

The Bible tells us that three forces cause us to want our addictions—the world, the flesh and the devil. It addresses the dangers of the world: "Stop loving this evil world and all that it offers you, for when you love these things you show that you do not really love God; for all these worldly things, these evil desires— the craze for sex, the ambition to buy everything that appeals to you, and the pride that comes from wealth and importance—these are not from God. They are from this evil world itself." The things of the world, such as money, food, tobacco, alcohol, running, television or work, are neutral. But when we put the phrase "love of" in front of any of these, we place God in the back seat and our addiction in the front.

The Bible also warns us about the flesh. Paul writes, "For the flesh (the old sin nature) sets its desire against the Spirit, and the Spirit against the flesh; for these are in opposition to one another, so that you may not do the things that you please."[3] External forces (drugs, alcohol and so forth) and internal forces (the desire to use them) are constantly fighting to win control over us. We are never free from this pressure; the conflict will continue as long as we are on this earth. We will never be free from temptation, but we need not sin.

What is the difference between temptation and sin? Temptation is that which causes us to think about doing something contrary to God's will. Everyone is tempted. Even our Lord was. Temptation becomes sin when we start to focus on our desire, which becomes lust and often is followed by the actual act.

The third force that works against us in the area of addictions is the devil. We're told to let God have our worries and cares. After all, He is always thinking about us and watching everything that concerns or worries us. We also are told to be careful of Satan's attacks. He will try to destroy and defeat us, using all kinds of cunning and subtle ways, such as addictions. We don't want pain, we want pleasure. Some of us don't think we are worth God's help, so we look to the external forces of drugs, alcohol, television, food, chocolate and coffee for relief.

Of course, placing your addiction before the Lord and living by God's grace does not eliminate your own responsibility. Instead, God's grace gives you the freedom you need for victory. You can count on the resources He has given you to help you say "no" to your addictions. These resources include:

- The gift of His love, which tells you that as a child of God, you are loved and forgiven. (See the summary of God's love on page 167 in chapter 9 of this book.)
- The gift of other people who have the capacity and ability to help you through difficult times and provide necessary support.
- The gift of self-help groups, which also can provide encouragement and direction. Such groups include Alcoholics Anonymous, Gamblers Anonymous and Overeaters Anonymous.
- The gift of resources that have been developed and proven successful at helping people with their addictions. Many of these are in the following section—Family Addiction Control Strategies.

Before you try these family ideas, ask yourself these questions. First, how committed am I to changing my behavior? There are subtle but important differences between saying, "I wish I could stop overeating" and "I am going to quit overeating and get my weight under control today." The degree of commitment obviously varies.

Second, are you convinced that you can accomplish your goal? Telling yourself you want to lose 100 pounds may be unrealistic because of your physiology. It is not unrealistic, however, to say you are going to cut 200 calories a day out of your diet and step up your activity to burn off 300 more calories. Make behavior goals—not physiological goals.

Third, do you clearly have in mind the advantages and disadvantages of breaking your habit? It may involve dropping old friends. Are you ready for that kind of commitment? Will the environment in which you live provide the support you need? Will your spouse, family, co-workers, and friends support your decision to give up overeating, drinking coffee or watching three hours of television a day?

Last, but not least, recognize that you will do this one day at a time. Do not think in terms of dropping the habit for the rest of your life. Instead, assume that you will break the habit for today. Pray that God's grace and God's help will be sufficient to get you through the day. Focus on today. There is no reason to worry about tomorrow.

"Do not worry about tomorrow, for tomorrow will worry about itself. Each day has enough trouble of its own" (Matthew 6:34).

FAMILY ADDICTION CONTROL ACTIVITIES

This section summarizes addiction control activities for the family. Since addictions range from A to Z, I have tried to provide a variety of activities, which may be adapted as you wish.

The purpose is to teach children what addictions are, how to help others who have addictions, and how to be sensitive to their problems. I hope that these activities will provide constructive ideas to build a child's assertiveness to not participate in harmful habits.

As in the other sections, these games are best used in the age range indicated. Optimally, parents are to do the activities with the children.

I. *Attitudes and Pressures Toward Addictions*

Have your children imagine and respond to the following situations:

● Parents and Drugs (Ages 9–16)

Have the children role play: You are a parent and you find out that your kids are taking drugs. You found out one day when you were cleaning their room and discovered some strange pills and marijuana. After role playing, discuss conversation. What are your conclusions?

● Alcohol and a Party (Ages 10–16)

You are at a party and several of your friends are drinking alcohol (or using drugs). They start to tease you because you don't want to drink. They call you "chicken" and tell you you're afraid to act adult. What would you do?

● Dance and Alcohol (Ages 14–16)

You go out one night, and your date is driving. You go to his school dance, and while you are there, your date sneaks some alcohol. You tell your date that you don't think he should drive in his condition, but he rejects your idea and demands to drive anyway. What do you do?

● Different Crowd (Ages 9–16)

One of your friends at school starts to hang around with a different crowd. You like this person, but don't like her new friends. Your friend wants you to hang around with her new friends, but you refuse. Your friend starts to drink and take drugs. You see a lot of changes in her behavior. Her grades drop, and she begins to skip classes. You really care about your friend. What can you do to help her?

● Pills and the Stranger (Ages 7–14)

One day, you and your friends are playing at the park. A stranger comes by and asks you if you'd like to have some fun. One of your friends says, "Sure." The stranger then offers everyone some pills that he says will make you feel good. He says they are free, if you want to try them. What do you do?

● Smoking and Work (Ages 14–16)

You always had told yourself you would not smoke. You didn't like the smell, and you knew cigarettes were bad for your health. One summer you get a job, and two of the people you work with smoke. They keep offering you cigarettes, and one day you accept. You start to smoke because you want to be accepted. You tell yourself you'll only smoke a few cigarettes a day, but by the end of the summer you are hooked. What should you do?

● A Friend and a Cigarette (Ages 9–16)

You are invited to a friend's home after school. When you arrive, you find that his parents aren't home. Your friend wants you to try a cigarette with him. He tells you his dad smokes three packs a day, and it won't hurt you. He says, "If you don't smoke, you are a chicken, and I'm going to tell all your friends." What could you do?

● Dieting Mom (Ages 9–16)

Tony's mom is a little overweight. She says she's tried every diet and still can't lose weight. She's heard about some pills that she can take to help her get rid of the fat. The pills are not legal, however, and Tony's mom knows they have dangerous side effects and are addictive. She takes them anyway. Tony notices that after she's taken them for a few days, she seems cranky and irritable. She also seems nervous. What could Tony do to help his mom?

● Four Packs a Day (Ages 9–16)

Dad is a heavy smoker—four packs a day. You have read that secondhand smoke also can hurt *your* lungs and heart. No other family members smoke, and they all are upset about Dad's habit. He cannot smoke at work, except at selected times, but when at home he chain-smokes. You want him to stop, but you don't know how to ask him. He is very touchy about it. What could you do? What are some potential outcomes?

● Room Polllution (Ages 9–16)

You are sitting in a closed room. Two adults (close friends of your parents) are smoking. Your eyes start to water, and you have difficulty swallowing, but you are not permitted to leave the room. What could you do?

● Arcade Fever (Ages 9–14)

Joey is a video game enthusiast. He loves to play video games. At first, he just had a lot of fun. But soon Joey had to play five or six times, then ten. He began to skip classes to play more. He even stole money from his mom's purse to help pay for the games. Now, when Joey plays, he has to get the highest score. If someone beats him, he gets very mad. Do you know anybody like Joey? Do you think this is good for Joey? What could you do to help him?

● Missing Church (Ages 12–16)

Joshua is one of the best runners at his school. He loves to run. He loves to compete. During cross-country season, he won every race he entered. The more he ran, the more he thought about running and the more he trained. Sometimes, when he was in church, he dreamed about running a race, rather than listening and thinking about the meaning of the service. One Sunday, Joshua wanted to run a very important race, so he skipped church. He told himself he would do something special that week to make up for missing church, but he never did. Pretty soon, Josh started to miss a lot of Sunday services in order to race. Then he missed one so he could go on a long training run with some other good runners. Is Joshua addicted to running? Do you think this is good?

● What Will Happen? (Ages 5–9)

Show your children these two pictures. Ask them what will happen, what they will do, what their friends would do, and what the parent should do?

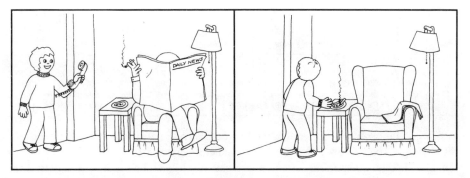

What will happen?

● Addicted, Who Me? (Ages 9–16)

Talk with your family about how people can become addicted to many things by letting things interfere with what is truly important in life. Then have family members spend ten minutes going through the house finding things that can lead to addictive behavior. (Examples: coffee, headphones, television, candy, books, and so on.) Pile the objects in one room and discuss them.

● Doing Drugs (Ages 9–16)

On a large piece of paper, have family members list all the reasons people do drugs. On another piece, have them list why people don't do drugs. Then play a game. Count the reasons people do drugs and get out enough dice to cover every excuse (twenty excuses = four dice). Number the excuses (begin with 4 if you're using four dice). Each person throws the dice and explains why the corresponding reason for doing drugs is poor.

● Retire a Millionaire (Ages 10–16)

Have your children figure how much money they would save by age sixty-five if, instead of smoking one pack of cigarettes a day from now until then, they put the same amount of money in the bank. Assume they will receive 10 percent compounded interest, and that the cost of cigarettes will increase 10 percent annually due to inflation. Example:

Age	Infla-tion	Cost Per Day	Yearly Savings	Interest	Total
14	–0–	$0.75	365 × .75 = $273.75	–0–	$273.75
15	.07	0.82	365 × .82 = 299.30	273 × 10% = $ 27	273 + 27 + 299 = $ 600
16	.08	0.90	365 × .90 = 328.50	600 × 10% = 60	600 + 60 + 328 = 988
17	.09	0.99	365 × .99 = 361.35	988 × 10% = 99	988 + 99 + 361 = 1448
18	.10	1.09	365 × 1.09 = 397.85	1448 × 10% = 145	1448 + 145 + 398 = 1991

By age eighteen, a fourteen-year-old would save $1,991. How much would that be by age sixty-five? Discuss other financial savings to nonsmokers, such as cheaper life insurance and less sickness and disability. This is not to mention the fact that at sixty-five they will be more likely to be healthy enough to enjoy the million dollars.

● Vegas Values (Ages 8–14)

Try this fun approach to discussing personal values. List, in pairs, those values that you would like the family to discuss. Put one comfortable topic with one that requires more openness and is more revealing. Put a number beside each pair. Members of the family take turns throwing the dice. Whatever number comes up, they voice their view on the corresponding value topic. (They may choose one or the other.) Examples:

a. 1) Someone lights up a cigarette during a movie, and the theater has a "No Smoking" rule. What would you do?
   2) Your best friend decides to start smoking. What would you do?
b. 1) You promised yourself and your family not to drink pop. You are at a friend's house and are offered a pop.
   2) Drinking coffee the first thing in the morning is O.K.
c. 1) Nothing is wrong with drinking four to five cups of coffee a day. Agree or disagree. Why?
   2) Watching television all the time isn't the same as being addicted to coffee.
d. 1) Candy bars and chocolate are addictive and never should be eaten.
   2) A candy bar at 3 P.M. gives me a lift.
e. 1) The amount of time you spend with your family is not really important, as long as your time together is quality.
   2) Working overtime three to four times a week is O.K.

● Advertising (Ages 8–14)

Collect a bunch of old magazines. Sit at a table and ask half the family members to go through the magazines and cut out all those advertisements that encourage the readers to do unhealthy things (such as smoke, drink). Have the other family members cut out advertisements that encourage people to be active and healthy (active pictures with alcohol or cigarettes associated do not count). Who had the easiest time finding pictures? Have both groups make a collage. What does this exercise tell you about advertising? Discuss.

● Addictions and You (Ages 8–14)

Ask family members to rate each of the following in terms of their potential to become addictions for them. Have them rate them on a scale of 1 to 10 (1 being not likely, 10 being very likely). That is, how addictive do you feel running could become for you?

If they like to do something that is not bad for their health, ask them what they could do to ensure they do not become addicted.

Ice cream	Coffee	Sports	Candy bars
Television	Work	Alcohol	Potato chips
Cigarettes	Betting	Pop	Other (your choice)

If any item is rated 7 or higher, see if the person can go two weeks without it in order to re-establish control.

II. *The Effects of Smoking on Your Body*

● The Lung Junk Test (Ages 7–14)

Have your child administer this test: Ask an adult smoker to light a cigarette and inhale. When the smoker exhales, he or she is to hold a white handkerchief over his or her nose and mouth.

a. Have the person repeat this several times.
b. Examine the handkerchief. What do you see?
c. Why do you think this is so?
d. What do you feel is happening to the lungs?

● The Non-smoker's Pulse Test (Ages 9–16)

You or your child do this one, if you are a nonsmoker. Simply record your pulse rate while you are sitting in a well-ventilated room. Then enter a small, smoke-filled room. After sitting there for at least ten minutes, take your pulse.

a. What happened to your pulse rate?
b. Why?
c. Should nonsmokers be concerned about having to breathe other people's smoke?

• The Smoker's Pulse Test (Ages 9–16)

Have your child record the pulse rate of an adult smoker who has not smoked for two hours. Then ask the smoker to light up and begin to smoke a cigarette.

a. What is the smoker's pulse rate after smoking half the cigarette?
b. What is the pulse rate after he or she has smoked the whole cigarette?
c. Why did the pulse rate change?

NOTE: In the previous two questions, I suggested you use an adult smoker. Do you know why?

In most states, it is unlawful for a minor to purchase cigarettes. It is also unlawful for minors to possess or use tobacco on public property (like your school). That raises two questions:

a. When was the last time you heard of someone getting arrested for using tobacco?
b. If this is a law, why is it never enforced?

• Stinko (Ages 8–12)

Perform the following experiment. Have two family members volunteer to take part in the stinko contest. Both must shower, wash their hair, brush their teeth and put on clean clothes. Then have one of the participants sit in a smoke-free room or go for a walk in the fresh air. Have the other sit in a room in which there are several lit cigarettes. After ten minutes, bring the two together and have other family members rate them on a scale of 1 to 10 for a) freshness of breath, b) clothing freshness, c) hair odor, d) general impression. Discuss what smoke does to clothing, breath and hair, and how it affects attractiveness.

III. *Putting Thoughts into Action*

• Television Addiction (Ages 7–16)

Have each family member vote for one favorite show and then limit television watching times to those programs. Learn to watch television programs, not television. Dream up new activities to fill the extra hours you'll have when the television set is off. Try playing games together, listening to the radio, writing, reading, enjoying outdoor activities, conversing. You'll be amazed at how productive you can be when the television is not demanding your attention.

● Community Action (Ages 12–16)

As a family, discuss community health concerns related to addictions. What could be done to help stop addictions? Consider doing the following:

a. Write a letter
   1) Write a letter to the editor of your local newspaper a) about alcohol advertising on television, b) about smoking in public, or c) congratulating someone who quit smoking.
   2) Write a letter to your congressmen or senators about upgrading your state's school lunch program.
b. Attend a meeting
   1) Write to the local heart and lung association or similar organization, and ask to be put on its mailing list.
   2) Attend local chapter meetings of various groups, including Alcoholics Anonymous, and find out what kind of educational programs on heart health and/or addictions they offer for children and adults.
   3) Ask your church group, club or school to have a meeting or invite a speaker on health.
c. Volunteer, visit, subscribe
   1) Volunteer to hand out information on alcohol and drug abuse.
   2) Visit hospitals and see the consequences of drug abuse.
   3) Subscribe to a magazine that focuses on education regarding alcohol and drug abuse.

● Review (Ages 8–16)

Have family members review their habits for a week and record an estimate of their usage, being as accurate as possible.

			Quantity Per Day						
Item		*Portion*	*Mon*	*Tues*	*Wed*	*Thurs*	*Fri*	*Sat*	*Sun*
a.	Coffee	cups							
b.	Tea	cups							
c.	Chocolate candy/drinks	each/cups							
d.	Cola beverages	12 oz.							
e.	Beer	12 oz.							
f.	Wine	4 oz.							
g.	Hard liquor	1½ oz.							
h.	Tranquilizers	tablets							
i.	Sleeping pills	tablets							
j.	Barbiturates	tablets							
k.	Amphetamines	tablets							
l.	Tobacco/marijuana: cigarette/pipe/cigar	each							
m.	Food	calories							
n.	Television	hours							
o.	Exercise/sports	hours							
p.	Work	hours							
q.	Gambling	hours							
r.	Other, be specific								

From this review, try to determine if any habits are controlling your lives.

• Analyzing Your Behavior (Ages 12–16)

This activity will help you and your family better understand why you indulge in your favorite habits and will help you choose the best way to quit.

Here are some statements people made to describe what they get out of over-doing something. How often do you feel this way? Circle one number for each statement. Important: *Answer every question.*

Doing My Habit

		Always	Frequently	Occasionally	Seldom	Never
a.	I do my habit to keep myself from slowing down.	5	4	3	2	1
b.	Doing my habit is pleasant and relaxing.	5	4	3	2	1
c.	I do my habit when I feel angry about something.	5	4	3	2	1
d.	When I can't do my habit, I find life almost unbearable until I can.	5	4	3	2	1
e.	I do my habit automatically, without even being aware of it.	5	4	3	2	1
f.	I do my habit to stimulate me, to perk up.	5	4	3	2	1
g.	I find my habit pleasurable.	5	4	3	2	1
h.	When I feel uncomfortable or upset about something, I do my habit.	5	4	3	2	1
i.	I am very much aware when I am not doing my habit.	5	4	3	2	1
j.	I do my habit without realizing I just did it moments before.	5	4	3	2	1
k.	I do my habit to give me a lift.	5	4	3	2	1
l.	I want to do my habit most when I am comfortable and relaxed.	5	4	3	2	1
m.	When I feel blue or want to take my mind off cares and worries, I do my habit.	5	4	3	2	1
n.	I get a real gnawing hunger to do my habit when I haven't done it in a while.	5	4	3	2	1
o.	I've found myself doing my habit, but didn't remember starting it.	5	4	3	2	1

How to Score

1. In the spaces below, enter the numbers you circled. Put the number you circled for question A over line A, for question B over line B, and so on.

2. Add the three scores on each line to get your totals. For example, the sum of your scores over lines A, F and K give you your score on Stimulation; over lines B, G and L give you your score on Pleasurable Relaxation.

____ + ____ + ____ =			_____
A	F	K	Stimulation
____ + ____ + ____ =			_____
B	G	L	Pleasurable Relaxation
____ + ____ + ____ =			_____
C	H	M	Crutch: Tension Reduction
____ + ____ + ____ =			_____
D	I	N	Craving: Psychological Addiction
____ + ____ + ____ =			_____
E	J	O	Habit

Scores can vary from 3 to 15. Scores 11 and above are high; scores 7 and below are low.

This test provides you with a score on each of five factors that describe many people's behavior. Your habit may be characterized by one or a combination of these factors. In any event, this test will help you identify why you use your habit and what kind of satisfaction you feel you get from it.

The factors are five different ways of experiencing or managing certain feelings. The first two feeling-states represent the positive feelings people get from their habits: a sense of increased energy or stimulation; and the enhancing of pleasurable feelings accompanying a state of well-being. The third is the decreasing of negative feelings by reducing a state of tension or feelings of anxiety, anger, shame and so on. The fourth factor is a complex pattern of increasing and decreasing cravings for your habit, representing a psychological addiction to your habit. The fifth is habit, which takes place in an absence of feeling—purely automatic.

A score of 11 or above on any factor indicates that this factor is an important motivation for you. The higher your score (15 is the highest), the more important a particular factor is in your habit. In your efforts to quit, it will be useful to discuss that factor with others.

● Drugs in the Home (Ages 10–16)

a. Have family members list all the drugs you have in your house—legal included.
b. For each drug, write the following:
  ● Who bought it.
  ● Why it was bought—because of advertising, friends, price, parents, doctors, or other reasons.
c. Decide if:
  ● The item was picked by examining several alternatives.

- The item was chosen after carefully considering the pros and cons of the alternatives.
- The item was a free choice.
d. Answer these questions. Will you:
  - Keep buying it?
  - Stop buying it?
  - Change to another brand?
  - Pass (not answer at this time)?

• Alternatives to Addictions (Ages 9–16)

Have family members share alternative activities for addictions. Then pick an activity that someone feels he or she may be addicted to and plan to do a new activity in its place.

The other "Family Activities" sections offer many ways to divert family members from selected addictions and to help them handle stress positively. Also, Chapter 15 provides strategies and values to help addicts break unwanted or undesirable habits.

Chapter 13:
The Stress of Life

"I have worked harder, been put in jail . . .
been whipped times without number. . . . Five
different times the Jews gave me the terrible
thirty-nine lashes. Three times I was beaten
with rods. Once I was stoned. Three times I
was shipwrecked. Once I was in the open sea
all night and the whole next day. I have trav-
eled many weary miles and have been often in
great danger from flooded rivers, and from robbers. . . . I have faced grave dangers from
mobs in the cities and from death in the de-
serts. . . . I have lived with weariness and pain
and sleepless nights. Often I have been hungry
and been thirsty. . . . I have shivered with
cold. Then, besides, all this, I have the constant worry of how the churches are getting
along" (2 Corinthians 11:23–28, LB).

If ever anyone lived a stressful life, Paul did. As I recall his experiences, I wonder,
Who am I to complain? Yet I still do. My pressures may not compare to his, but
I often feel stressed.

The Stressed American

I have plenty of company—70 to 90 percent of all Americans experience stress.
The "rat race" is no longer a joke. By necessity or by chance, many of us are
falling into the trap of trying to cram twenty-five hours into an already crowded
twenty-four-hour day. We seem to take on more and more responsibility with less
and less time.

In the 1950s our homes were characterized as harmonious and a haven from
the world. Since then, they have changed drastically. Family dinners are a thing
of the past. Now we graze. We pick up food on the run, snack here and there,

go to the local chicken or hamburger fast-food restaurant for the evening meal. Some of us skip dinner and catch a bedtime snack of pizza and pop. If we eat in the morning, our menu is two breakfast bars, a cup of coffee and a swig of O.J.

Homes have become dispatch centers. Kids are transported to little league games, day-care centers, scout meetings, dance classes and church. Stereos and televisions blare many hours a day, leaving little opportunity for conversation, rest and solitude. Parents wrestle with two jobs, "latchkey" kids and incredible travel schedules.

Even our churches, in campaigning for family stability and order, vie for our time by offering week-night activities and weekend seminars on "Life and Family Enrichment."

Early in our nation's history, people enjoyed the comfort of a large house surrounded by a few acres of a quiet countryside, an environment that changed little, if at all. Home was where people held similar values and beliefs. People had a sense of security and stability.

Today, things have changed dramatically. In my lifetime, I have gone from watching *Flash Gordon* at the Saturday matinee in the 1940s to watching people actually walk on the moon. My dad used to take me to the airport to see the first Lockheeds, which could cross the continent in twelve hours. I was impressed. It took three days by train. Now, I have to cope with breakfast on the plane from Chicago, only to get off the plane in Los Angeles and be taken out to breakfast. When I was seven, someone gave me a toy from Japan. I thought it was cheap. Today, Japan probably leads the world in craftsmanship. As a child, I went from door to door on Halloween and my neighbors guessed who I was. Now kids come to the door by the hundreds (204, to be exact, in 1984), and I give them a little treat (a toothbrush, pencil or running shoelaces, of course). I haven't the foggiest idea who 95 percent of them are.

Years ago, my best friend's dad took me for a ride in his car. We stopped for gas. He ordered ten gallons, paid less than $2.00 and got a roadmap free. Today, two dollars would fill 1/20th of my tank. I'd pay $1.95 for a roadmap. I remember getting three channels on our black-and-white television in 1950 (one was kind of fuzzy). We were lucky, we lived near Philadelphia. Today, my color television picks up seventeen channels.

In our town of eighteen hundred people, my dad was one of maybe twenty who had a college education. Today, I live in another town of eighteen hundred people. Many have a college education, and twenty have doctorates. My mother was one of the few women in town who worked. Today, four out of ten workers are women. My dad's salary as a pastor was all of $1,200 in 1932. When I was ten, it was $4,000. Today, the average pastor makes $25,000.

Change and Stress

The rapid rate at which our society has and is changing is one of the primary reasons our levels of stress are so high. Things are moving so fast that we can't keep up with them. In today's world, we simply cannot escape change. We are in the midst of what Alvin Toffler, in 1970, called "future shock."[1] Future shock occurs because we are unsure—unsure about what will happen tomorrow, next year, in ten years. We can't be sure, because we're right in the midst of rapid change. And we adapt poorly.

While working with more than five thousand patients, researchers discovered that changes in a person's life often were accompanied by changes in health. Major life changes, such as death of a spouse, divorce, separation or a jail term, had the greatest impact. Even pleasant changes, including marriage, retirement or an outstanding personal achievement, created stress for many people. Minor variations in daily routine, such as a vacation, Christmas or a change in sleeping habits, also were found to affect health.

Discussing this long-term study at a conference in New York, Dr. Thomas H. Holmes said that 93 percent of the major health changes in the group studied were associated with a cluster of life changes that amounted to a "life crisis." According to Holmes, "The greater the life change or adaptive requirement, the greater the vulnerability or lowering of resistance to disease, and the more serious the disease that does develop."[2] In short, change—dramatic or subtle—can create tremendous stressors.

And stress can kill. Researchers know that unrelenting stress can cause ulcers, heart disease, high blood pressure, cancer, auto-immune disease, greater susceptibility to the flu, and on and on. Consider that in 1984:[3]

—30 million Americans had some form of heart or blood vessel disease
—25 million Americans had high blood pressure
—8 million Americans had ulcers
—12 million Americans were alcoholics
—5 billion doses of tranquilizers were prescribed
—3 billion doses of amphetamines were prescribed
—5 billion doses of barbiturates were prescribed

Contributing to the problem, our changing culture causes us to suffer from an identity crisis. There was a time when everyone knew his or her place. Either you were a peasant or a prince; a lowly dirt farmer or a land baron; a chimney sweep or a scholar. And it was easy to tell who was what. (I am not advocating a return to this type of life; I'm simply pointing out that people knew their places and stayed put.) Today, millionaires' kids run around in frazzled blue-jeans, daughters of paupers primp for proms, and "shop rats" cruise the town in sports cars. Merely looking in the mirror doesn't tell you who you are.

Neither does looking to the church necessarily tell you how to live. Yet, at one time, churches had a tremendous influence and literally dictated how their members were to act. If someone stepped out of line, he was told about it. Now, church members and leaders can't agree on the order of worship, let alone abortion, war, gay rights and birth control. Additionally, in the past, people in the same community tended to hold similar values and beliefs. More often than not, they were from the same ethnic background—Jewish, Polish, Slavic, and the like. So their political, social, educational and religious values were the same. Today, society's mobility, television, and the intermarrying of ethnic groups have helped produce confusion—true future shock.

Because of these changes, people are constantly off-guard, uncomfortable and unsure. Values and beliefs are ill-defined. To survive, people must continually adapt to change. It's pervasive and inescapable, which, of course, means that the accompanying stress is impossible to avoid. In fact, efforts to avoid stress often produce more stress.

Stress and Life

According to the late Dr. Hans Selye, of McGill University in Montreal, the absence of stress is death.[4] Stress is essential for life. It allows you to enjoy life—to feel, think, smile, pray, care and love. Stress gives you an opportunity to participate in the life God has given to you. What is necessary is a balance and an understanding that stress should be a positive, rather than a negative, force.

Even people who seem to have it made experience stress. Nursing home directors say that one of the biggest problems they face is helping their residents cope with stress, even though all of their needs apparently are met. The reason for this is change. The nursing home represents an entirely different lifestyle from that to which the residents have been accustomed. Think how disoriented you would be if you lived somewhere for eighty years and suddenly were transplanted to new surroundings and friends, with little to do and virtually no opportunity to solve life's problems and concerns. You'd feel that you had dropped out of life, with all its joys, frustrations, sorrows, memories and excitement.

Also, people who try to get away from it all often find their stress follows them to that remote cabin or island retreat. As long as you live, wherever you are, you will have stress. And chances are, tomorrow will bring more stress than you had today.

Initially, this may sound pretty bleak. The usual approach to a problem is to try to eliminate it, but I just said that stress cannot and should not be eliminated. It is the spice of life. So what do you do? Develop a grin-and-bear-it attitude? Hold on and hope for the best? A far better solution is to take a closer look at stress and then learn how to deal with it best.

In reality, stress is neutral. It is neither good nor bad in itself. What makes stress good or bad is how we handle it, or more importantly, how we *react* to stress or stressors. We can turn our stress into good stress, which Selye calls eustress (positive stress). Or we can turn it into negative stress, which Selye refers to as distress. We can deal with stress efficiently, or we can be governed by it and allow it to destroy us. The first response enhances and helps us enjoy life. The second wreaks havoc with our bodies. It's almost that simple.

Let's take a closer look at how we can allow stress to kill, harm and maim our bodies.

General Adaptation Syndrome

In the 1930s, Selye coined a phrase, "the general adaptation syndrome,"[5] to describe how stress affects the human body. This syndrome identifies three responses to stress: alarm, resistance and exhaustion. The alarm stage is the sense of excitement, anxiety or anger you feel when you get into a disagreement with another person. If it becomes a heated argument, your nervous and endocrine systems move into action. You get a surge of adrenalin, which increases your pulse rate and, perhaps, causes some perspiration under your arms. Blood pressure rises; muscles tense. This response is rather short and quite normal, and it may save your life. If you are driving and a truck suddenly pulls into your lane, the increase in adrenalin and nervous sytem activity allows you to swerve instinctively and miss the truck. Afterward, you may be amazed at how clearly and accurately you reacted.

If an argument continues, the alarm stage changes to resistance. Rather than reacting, your body decides to fight. The pituitary gland begins to produce hormones that equip your body for a longer contest. One hormones raises your blood pressure, another stimulates your metabolism. Another hormone increases your blood sugar levels and alters your immunity system. These changes provide you with the wherewithal to keep going.

Under normal circumstances, the second stage gives way to exhaustion, which allows your body to rest and recover. This is the tired feeling that follows a long, heated discussion. The resistance phase provided the necessary stimulus to get you through the argument. Now you need time to unwind, put the disagreement in perspective and relax. In a matter of hours (or even minutes) you are back in the swing of things.

If everyone quickly completed this neat pattern of disagreement (alarm), heated debate (resistance), and resolution (exhaustion), I would have little need to write this chapter. But, everyone doesn't—Christians included. When I give seminars on health and well-being for secular or Christian groups, my stress talks are always the most popular, people are the most attentive, and they ask the most thought-provoking questions.

Why are people so interested in stress? Because it is pervasive, and most of us don't know how to deal with it positively. We allow stress to become so overwhelming (alarm) and to continue for days, weeks, months or even years in the resistance stage, without ever reaching the exhaustion phase. So our bodies eventually exhaust themselves with disease (ulcer, heart attck, auto-immune disease) or physical and emotional exhaustion.

If we don't respond properly, stress at the office, insufficient finances, deteriorating relationships or nagging doubts about our self-worth result in the following cycle: stress, mental exhaustion, more stress, insomnia, chronic fatigue and more stress.

Fatigue

One phase of this cycle is chronic fatigue, which can be physical, mental or emotional. Eighty percent of fatigue is emotional, and it causes much of our physical and mental fatigue. It also robs us of the abundant life.

Emotional fatigue is radically different from physical and mental fatigue. Its causes are insidious; its cure is complex. Emotional fatigue is associated with hurrying, worrying, emotional stress, a fast-paced society, ill-defined goals, obstacles that seem insurmountable, change, and a feeling that you can solve all your personal and family problems by yourself.

Plague #9

Emotional Fatigue

Emotional fatigue can set you up for a host of mental disorders, which are summarized in this chapter. But perhaps the most disconcerting thing about emotional fatigue is the tired feeling it produces for most of us. When we finish a long day at the office or at home, we generally feel physical fatigue, but it is produced by emotional overload. Our lack of interest in running, attending a church meeting, going shopping, or even eating out with family or friends is due to the emotional fatigue that manifests itself as physical fatigue. How?

Scientists use an electromyograph (EMG), which measures the strength of muscle contractions, to demonstrate the emotional fatigue-physical fatigue relationship. When you perform a physical activity, such as opening a window, your brain tells the muscles involved how and when to contract so that you can perform the task automatically. The EMG records these contractions.

Interestingly, the EMG also has shown that even the suggestion of opening the window causes your muscles to contract. Likewise, the sound of the alarm clock in the morning and the subsequent thought of going to work can produce measurable contractions in your muscles, even before you move. Worrying about paying bills, making a speech or firing an employee can cause neck and similar muscles to contract. In other words, involuntary mental activity can elicit a physical response. Consequently, you can feel physically exhausted at the end of the day, even though you spent most of your time sitting.

Emotional fatigue can be caused by boredom, depression, anger, anxiety or burn-out.

Boredom

You may experience boredom when your day-in and day-out routine do provide adequate stimulation to your brian, nerves and hormonal systems. For physiological and psychological reasons, this lack of stimulation reduces your feelings of energy. While sameness can cause boredom, change can produce depression, anger, anxiety or burn-out.

Depression

Depression can be a downward spiral. When you feel depressed, you experience inertia. You don't want to do anything—physically, mentally or emotionally. Soon, you're not satisfied with how you're handling life's problems. You become more depressed, so you sleep more. This produces less fitness and more depression. Then, you focus on your depressed or decreased self-concept. Your poor self-concept can cause even lower levels of energy and turn you inward. Your behavior becomes erratic, and you soon experience total inertia—a point at which you can't seem to get anything together.

This problem is not new, and religious leaders are not immune to it. Martin Luther suffered through tremendous bouts of depression. So did John Wesley. J. B. Phillips, the Bible translator, experienced four years of the dark night of the soul. David, Moses and Job, expressed despair.

Anger

Anger also can produce fatigue. Anger stimulates your nervous system. Your blood pressure rises, your heart rate increases, and hormones are secreted. You explode! Or you fume.

The good news about exploding is, you probably dissipate your emotions and relax your muscle tension. The bad news is, the recipient of your outburst may lash back at you, heightening your anger and creating a greater nervous response on your part. While arguing, you may be full of energy, but afterward you feel whipped. Also, the recipient of your outburst is hurt. As a result, you feel guilty, which adds to your stress. "An angry man stirs up dissension, and a hot-tempered one commits many sins."[6]

Repression of your anger doesn't work either. Repressed anger produces seething, which is dangerous psychologically, physically and spiritually.

If you keep other emotions such as guilt and jealousy inside, they produce a similar response. The guilt and jealousy also can cause you to be angry, and the cycle starts again.

Anxiety

Another source of fatigue is anxiety, which is closely allied with depression. Psychologists refer to a continuum with depression at one end and anxiety at the other. Often a person is anxious first, and as the anxiety builds and heightens, it progresses into depression, which is the circuit breaker for anxiety.

Anxiety-producing situations cause people to get more and more whipped up. Their fear, anticipation of something stressful, and worry increase. They become more and more apprehensive. Soon, the anxiety interferes with their ability to concentrate. That is followed by psychosomatic symptoms, which produce more anxiety. Hormone levels skyrocket. Soon their body is caught in an overload. To protect the body, various systems shut down and they become depressed. More anxiety follows.

The result of this circle is decreasing energy, and possibly increasing disease.

Burn-out

Picture a building that has just burned. The outside structure still stands, but the inside has been gutted—all that remains is an empty shell. That's burn-out. You feel as though everything inside of you has been ripped, burned and thrown out.

Burn-out does not result from stress. It occurs because people enter a job or task with high expectations. They want to save the world, revolutionize society or change people's lives. They work hard. In time, they feel that people don't change. Society wants to stay like it is. Soon people realize that their goals are thwarted. Consciously or unconsciously, they sense that they are not making progress. In time they become bitter, cynical and angry. They are burned out.

Emotional Fatigue

Often these factors—boredom, depression, anger, anxiety, and burn-out—lead to emotional fatigue, which takes your mind, body and emotions beyond your ability to cope. So you become more bored, depressed, angry, anxious or burned out. It is a vicious circle.

Modern day emotional fatigue also is caused by:

—Your desire to solve all your problems by yourself. "Cast all your anxiety on Him because He cares for you."[7]
—Placing your will in front of God's will.
—Setting unrealistic goals or having an idealistic view of the world.
—Pushing yourself to your emotional limits (we usually know our physical, but not our emotional, limitations).
—A lack of sound health habits, particularly good physical fitness and eating habits, proper weight maintenance, addiction avoidance, and good stress management skills.

Type A Behavior

No discussion on stress would be complete without a discussion on the Type A personality. Cardiologists Meyer Friedman and Ray Rosenman, from San Francisco, used this label to describe the coronary heart disease person.[8] The Type A person tries to squeeze twenty-five hours into twenty-four, takes on more responsibilities but has less time, tries to do two or more things at once (such as shaving and driving a car), has difficulty saying no, is very punctual, and does not take time to enjoy God's good world. They are the classical workaholics. They are hostile, impatient, aggressive and angry.

At the other end of the spectrum are Type B people, who take a more relaxed approach to life. They are productive but tackle one task at a time, are less impatient, accept themselves and are less angry. Some people are basically Type A or Type B; most people have tendencies toward one extreme or the other.

If a Type A person is comfortable with himself, don't try to change him. As Selye explains, some people are born to be race horses and others to be turtles. If you force a race horse to be a turtle or vice versa, you create stress.[9] Everyone must learn to live at his own pace, and we must learn to accept others, whatever their pace.

The real issue is not Type A versus Type B. It's the traits that Rosenman and Friedman tack on at the end of the definition—Type A people are more angry, hostile, impatient and aggressive. Those feelings, which seem to be the culprits in disease, indicate that they are not dealing positively with life. But those traits are not exclusive to Type A. Slower, more deliberate people who respond negatively also can be angry, hostile and impatient. Conversely, fast-paced people who handle stress appropriately can be happy, outgoing and fun-loving, and can enjoy the life God has given them.

Anger, frustration, hostility and impatience, in any person, are reactive behaviors—the killers of life, health and spirit. They stem from an inflated view of self and what is expected (or, more importantly, was expected) out of life. Many angry people feel gypped—they think life passed them by. Even some Christians feel this way; they think God should have had bigger plans for them. In time, these people (Christians and non-Christians alike) slip into bitterness. They become disenchanted with life, God and others.

Several years ago I experienced some bitterness and felt myself slipping into depression, despair and "feeling sorry for myself." As I did, I looked at older people. I noticed some were bitter, angry and hostile. Others had a serene presence, despite hardships, frustrations and disappointments. When I asked about their feelings, the former showed only anger. The serene expressed that God was in control of their lives. They said they didn't understand the reasons for the disappointments and reversals, but they knew that God saw the big picture of life.

They were not so presumptuous as to tell God what was best. Like Paul, they had "learned to be content whatever the circumstances."[10]

No matter what your personality, you can learn to be content in all circumstances—even stressful ones. You can learn how to better deal with stress and to understand the place God has given you in this world.

Remember, you cannot, and should not, avoid stress. It would be impossible to enjoy sex, love, football games, a breath of fresh air, a good book, music, an exciting church service or an inspiring preacher without the actions of your hormonal and nervous systems. Stress can add tremendous zest to your life, or it can be debilitating. You must find the proper balance, which permits a certain amount of stimulation and a certain degree of relaxation. Of course, that sounds easy, but we both know that it's not. The next chapter offers more help.

"Be content with what you have, because God has said, 'Never will I leave you; never will I forsake you' " (Hebrews 13:5).

Chapter 14:
Developing the Hardy Personality

"We can rejoice, too, when we run into problems and trials for we know that they are good
for us" (Romans 5:3, LB).

How can problems and trials be good for us? Paul explains, "They help us learn
to be patient. And patience develops strength of character in us and helps us trust
God more each time we use it until finally our hope and faith are strong and
steady. Then, when that happens, we are able to hold our heads high no matter
what happens and know that all is well, for we know how dearly God loves us."[1]
Today:

—We wear water-resistant watches.
—We plant germ-resistant seed corn.
—We grow disease-resistant lawns.
—We build earthquake-resistant buildings.

We also have stress-resistant people. We admire them, praise them and wish
we could be like them. Perhaps we can, if we want it enough to work at it. For,
as the watches, seed corn, lawns and buildings resulted from long hours of research, study, trial and error, and development, it also takes a lot of doing to
develop a hardy personality.

Notice what the beautiful verses from Romans say is involved in this process:
problems, trials, patience, strength, character, hope, faith, steadiness and trust in
God. The result? You can hold your head high "no matter what happens."

Two psychologists at the University of Chicago, Drs. Susan J. Kobasa and
Salvatore Maddi, discovered that some people have stress-resistant personalities;
they are not stress-reactors. For these people, stress is a positive force. Why?
Kobasa and Maddi learned that stress-resistant people have a specific set of attitudes toward life that make up their hardy personality. These attitudes are the
three Cs: commitment, challenge and control.

The first attitude of the hardy personality is commitment. The stress-resistant
person has a strong purpose in life: to save lives, teach children, build the best
car in America, do God's will. According to these psychologists, they "find it

easy to be interested in whatever they are doing and can involve themselves in it wholeheartedly. They are rarely at a loss for things to do. They always seem to make the maximum effort cheerfully and zestfully."[2]

Their second attitude is a sense of control over life's events. They are actively involved in their own lives. They state their feelings, express their wishes, and do something about situations in their lives. They "believe and act as if they can influence the events taking place around them. They always reflect on how to turn situations to advantage and never take things at face value."[3]

Their third attitude is that life is a challenge. To these people, there are no problems, only possibilities. Dr. Robert Schuller of Garden Grove, California, personifies this attitude. His *Tough Times Don't Last but Tough People Do* book and talk are a case in point. Stress-resistant people are action-oriented and daily ask themselves, "What is my biggest obstacle and what have I done about it today?" In other words, "They see life as strenuous but exciting."[4]

One of Kobasa and Maddi's studies showed that people who rated high on these attitudes had fewer stress-related illnesses than others. Those who rated low in hardiness were ill far more frequently and were characterized as:[5]

1) People who find tasks boring or meaningless and therefore hold back from getting involved. Surprisingly, they appear taxed or stressed.
2) People who feel powerless and act as if they are passive victims of forces beyond their control. Instead of using resources or initiative, they prepare themselves for the worst.
3) People who feel threatened by change because they think it is natural for things to remain stable. They fear change because it seems to disrupt comfort and security.

The three Cs that Drs. Kobasa and Maddi discovered do not surprise those familiar with Scripture.

1. Commitment. Christians are to be committed. We are to have a purpose in life. We know that God sent Jesus to save us from sin and that it is our responsibility to tell all people this good news. We are to be earnestly and wholeheartedly committed to helping, loving and giving to other people. The Bible warns us against being lukewarm.[6] Paul, as committed a Christian as ever lived, challenged the church in Rome, "Never be lacking in zeal, but keep your spiritual fervor, serving the Lord."[7]

2. Control. The feeling that you have control over life's events or can influence the events around you has a different twist for the Spirit-filled Christian. Paul tells us, "In all things God works for the good of those who love Him, who have been called according to His purpose."[8] In other words, as Christians, we know that history is going some place with God in charge. Although we may not understand events, we are assured that we are all part of God's plan. We may not

be controlling world and personal circumstances, but God, in His infinite wisdom, is. We have great comfort in that knowledge.

As Christians, we also know we can influence life's events through prayer. And prayer can move mountains, change lives and transform situations, if that is part of God's plan—not just our selfish wishes. Knowing we have the most powerful ally in prayer gives us assurance of control over life's events.

3. Challenge. Christians should find life a challenge—strenuous, perhaps, but rewarding and fulfilling. "Let us run with perseverance the race marked out for us. . . . Consider Him (Jesus) who endured such opposition from sinful men, so that you will not grow weary and lose heart."[9] William Barclay, world-renowned Scottish New Testament interpreter, noted that this passage provides a near perfect summary of the Christian life—a life with, among other things, a goal, an inspiration and an example.[10]

Life is filled with opportunity. That doesn't mean it won't be hard and stressful, that it won't have its frustrations. But life and all the challenges will help you grow and flesh out your philosophy. Challenge gets us back to the purpose of this book. "We confidently and joyfully look forward to actually becoming all that God has had in mind for us to be."[11]

What to do about stress

You have at your disposal a wide variety of skills and resources to help you develop a hardy personality and respond appropriately to pressure. Throughout your life, you already have picked up some skills that have helped you deal with

---

Plague #10

Ulcers, Colitis and Irritable Bowel Syndrome

In this modern era, several ailments affect our gastrointestinal tracts. The most widely known are ulcers. Colitis and its first cousin, irritable bowel syndrome, also are prevalent among Americans. (Almost 20 percent of the adult population suffer from one of these three problems.)

An ulcer is an open sore in the stomach or intestine's inner lining. The chief causes of ulcers are: heredity, stress, poor circulation and poor diet.

Colitis is a chronic inflammation and ulceration of the large intestine (colon). The specialized fibers in the colon become irritated, and the blood supply to these tissues is blocked. The irritation, lack of circulation and other changes cause pus-

and blood-oozing ulcerations. The exact cause of colitis is unknown, but family history, stress, a poor diet, drugs and food allergies are possibilities.

Irritable bowel syndrome accounts for one-half of all stomach complaints referred to doctors. It involves the small intestine and the large bowel. For every three women affected with this ailment, there is one male. It is most common in people who experience a great deal of stress (anxiety over children, marital discord, loss of a loved one), take drugs, use hormones or have a poor diet.

To help control or manage these ailments, a proper diet (low in fat and sugar), stress reduction techniques, exercise, and the avoidance of drugs and alcohol are important.

stress—some good and some bad. Some typical negative stress-abatement techniques are sleeping, drugs, alcohol, escape, and reacting with anger, hostility and frustration. Positive stress-abatement skills include communicating your feelings and being in touch with the stress signals your body sends out.

Here are some ideas to help you better handle the stressors of life.

Idea #1: Recognize that God is in control—NOT YOU.

Scripture from Genesis to Revelation speaks of our alienation from God and our need for redemption through Jesus Christ. If we trust in our own efforts, rather than in God, we will fail. As Jesus taught us, the problem, not the answer, lies within human's hearts.[12] (If you are not sure if you have placed your faith in Christ and are trusting in God, see appendix A.)

Idea #2: Adopt a positive mental outlook.

Many people think negatively. They put themselves down in almost all situations. They have a distorted view of life and things. Dr. David Burns, a psychiatrist for the University of Pennsylvania, explains some striking negative thought patterns:[13]

- **All or nothing thinking.** Many people evaluate themselves in black and white categories: they are all good or all bad. If you have this distorted view, when your child does something wrong, you deduce, "I am a born loser when it comes to parenting." That kind of thinking is perfectionistic and unrealistic. You probably have done many fine things as a parent.
- **Overgeneralization.** Let's assume you get turned down for a new job. An overgeneralization would be to say, "I am never going to get a new job. No one wants me." You've just oversimplified. Just because you received one rejection doesn't mean you're locked into losing all the time. Most home-run hitters lead the league in strike-outs. You're bound to fail at times, but the more you try, the greater your chances for success.
- **Mental Filter.** You find out that someone at church has spread a rumor about you. You react with, "You can't even trust Christians." You let one negative experience color your opinion of all Christians and affect your response to everything they say in the future. Stop and think for a minute of all the Christians who have proven themselves trustworthy.
- **Disqualify the positive.** Suppose your child, who is an average runner, wins a race and is within striking distance of the school record. Maybe you or the child think, *That was a fluke. It will never happen again.* That is distorted thinking. Most people who think this way have the uncanny knack of turning a compliment into a negative experience. That is tragic.
- **Jumping to conclusions.** There are two parts to this thinking. The first is the mind reading error. You pass a friend on the street and she doesn't respond.

You think "Boy, is she stuck up," or "I'll bet she hates me." In reality, your friend was lost in thought and didn't even see you.

The second is the fortune-teller error. Concerned, you call the friend when you get home. Her child answers the phone and you leave a message. She doesn't return the call. You conclude that you were right the first time: she no longer wants to be your friend. In reality, her child forgot to tell her you called.

- **Magnification.** While speaking at a PTA meeting, you mispronounce a person's name or a word. You panic. *Everyone will think I am a clod. How could I be so stupid.*

  Magnification causes you to exaggerate the importance of a simple mistake. You blow it out of proportion. Your error was no big deal—everyone mispronounces words and names, and makes mistakes.

- **Labeling.** Your teenage daughter flunks her first test in tenth grade geometry. She reacts, "I don't get geometry. It's stupid. I'll never need it, anyway."

  She made one mistake. Maybe she didn't study. Maybe she missed some important points in class. She shouldn't evaluate herself on the things she does. Giving yourselves negative labels is oversimplification and wrong, says Dr. Burns.

To overcome this negative thinking, start thinking positively. When you get up in the morning, tell yourself, *Today is going to be a great day! Thanks, God, for giving me life and today.* Approach each task in a new light. Look for things that are amusing. When you begin to think or say negative things, replace them with positive ones. Here are some examples:

Negative	**Positive**
1. I'm not any good—no one loves me.	1. I'm a child of God—He loves me.
2. I'm so unfit, I can't walk two miles.	2. I've walked one mile a week for three weeks. I'm not stopping now.
3. Why did I blow my diet last night?	3. I lost a battle last night with my diet, but I'm going to win the war. After all, I've been careful for the past two weeks.
4. I'm a failure—I just gained back three pounds.	4. I may have gained back three pounds, but during the past six months I've lost twenty-two pounds.
5. Not another sleepless night! I can't take it.	5. Finally, I have a chance to do some reading in peace and quiet.
6. I can't do anything right.	6. Nonsense! I do many things right. I just need more practice.

You may be surprised to find that a more positive approach can turn a wearisome situation into a pleasant one.

Idea #3: Develop a sense of humor and a play spirit.

Closely allied to a positive mental outlook is cultivating a sense of humor. When things are hectic, harried and pressured, keep things in perspective by viewing your world as Bill Cosby would in a comic monologue.

David Fink, a psychiatrist who has done extensive work in the area of stress and nervous tension, encourages his patients to take a "play spirit" into everything they do.[14] That is, approach each activity as if it were going to be playful and fun—as our children usually do. While that may sound simplistic, it is important. Our attitude often dictates how a situation affects us. If we go to work with a feeling of dread or boredom, chances are the day will meet our expectations.

It also is important to participate in activities that you consider play, in and of themselves. According to Fink, play is anything you do that you can drop as soon as it ceases to amuse. You can take it or leave alone. Some things you once thought were fun are now drudgery. Bowling leagues, coffee klatches, bridge nights and even running can turn into an obligation you can't or won't give up. You'd like to quit the softball team, but the guys are counting on you. You have to attend the neighborhood study group because, well, it's expected of you. Play can become work.

To remedy that, look for new ways to play. Return to basic, simple activities, perhaps even activities that are childish. Use the activities listed after this chapter. Or start a hobby or special project. Adults often abandon hobbies when they enter the work/family bandwagon. Interestingly, that's when stress usually becomes a problem. If you collected stamps in the sixth grade, dig out your old collection— it may rekindle interest and give you something to play with. If that doesn't suit you, try something on the creative side. Grab a brush, canvas and palette. Learn to play a musical instrument. The goal is not to become a world master, but to divert your attention from the doldrums while having a little fun.

Idea #4: Express feelings, or assert yourself.

Emotional health and a zest for living are impossible unless we acknowledge our feelings and learn to express them appropriately and use them effectively. Unfortunately, our culture does not respect emotions, and we are taught to hide, deny or repress our feelings, lest we "lose control" and "act irrationally."

This is particularly true in the business world, where directly expressing feelings usually is discouraged, and where the ability to deal with feelings is much less valued than the capacity to handle ideas. Nevertheless, as behavioral scientists have noted, many of the most desirable traits in business—as well as in personal life—are derived from emotions. These valuable qualities include creativity, motivation, loyalty, enthusiasm and cooperation.

When feelings are stifled, whether at home or on the job, the results may be disastrous. The person harboring "unacceptable" emotions cannot function fully and freely. Precious energy is wasted to create an "image" and to "play the game." Furthermore, if feelings are not shared and dealt with face-to-face, problems that have been "solved" by rational means don't stay solved for long. The underlying emotional conflict simply translates itself into other terms, erupting sooner or later into another crisis at work or home.

Experimental evidence suggests that a person who expresses negative feelings, rather than forcing them to remain "underground," later feels friendlier to the individual who aroused him or her. If the expression of anger, anxiety or frustration is not met with a counterattack, but is received with understanding and acceptance ("You seem upset. What's troubling you? . . ." "I know how you feel."), then the troubled person can work through the negative feeling and arrive at a more objective assessment of the situation. If the feelings are denied, they can become a barrier to working rationally, harmoniously and closely with others toward common goals.

Some people confuse assertive behavior with agressive behavior. Nothing could be farther from the truth. Assertiveness means stating your wishes clearly and forthrightly, without aggressive hostility and force. Consider this illustration:

You are at the checkout counter at your favorite supermarket. The clerk short-changes you by ten dollars. You can react in one of three ways:

Non-assertive: Say nothing. You probably will become angry at yourself for your not speaking out.

Aggressive: "Hey, lady, you gypped me." You're angry and she's angry. You both explode. Later, you both feel remorse for acting foolishly.

Assertive: "Miss, would you please count again? I think I have another ten dollars coming." You both feel good.

I believe the assertive method is the Christian response. Look at the apostle Paul. Many of his letters were to the early churches, refuting heresies, misunderstandings and criticisms lodged against him. While Paul told it "like it was," he began his letters praising the new churches for their devotion to God and their prayer life, and/or thanking God for them. Then he got down to the nitty-gritty. At the end, he promised to pray for the churches and asked them to pray for him. How can you dislike anyone who asks you to pray for him? He also wished for them peace, love and God's grace.

Paul was assertive. We should follow his lead.

Idea #5: Apply the three R's of stress management.

To supplement the previous four ideas, consider these important R's: rest, relaxation and recreation.

Rest. As you know, your body is in action constantly. Sometimes slow, sometimes fast, but it's always working. During sleep, you are revitalized because your nervous system no longer is stimulated as it is while you're awake. Your heart rate and respiration slow down, and your blood pressure drops. Your batteries are recharged during a good night's sleep.

Scientists feel that it's difficult to make up for lost sleep. So, rather than always playing catch-up, try to get your proper allotment each night. Sleep needs vary, but generally, most young people need eight to ten hours, while adults usually find seven or less sufficient.

Relaxation. We often misinterpret what type of break our bodies need. Flopping down in the hammock sometimes is good medicine, but many times it only postpones the problem. Try other methods. After studying various similar activities, we have concluded that the Family Stress Control Activities listed after this chapter are among the simplest and most effective ways to help soothe stress.

Recreation. To experience real recreation, first identify your needs and seek out resources to satisfy them. Look for restorative activities. For an activity to qualify as recreation, it must be active and not passive. You must be involved, and not merely a spectator.

Activities such as needlepoint, reading, golf and painting can be recreational, if you understand why you are participating in that activity. But if you suffer from extreme frustration because you can't paint as well as you would like, the recreation is not restoration and is of no value. Here are some guidelines:

—Choose an activity you enjoy.
—Think of each session as a reward, not an obligation.
—Don't overdo it—too much of anything is not healthy. Take it easy, especially in the early stages.
—Be proud that you are using stress to your advantage, rather than letting it abuse you.
—Don't race against the clock. Engage in the activity at a pace that suits your mood.

Assisters to Reduce Stress

In addition to these five ideas, consider these ways to help reduce stress and improve your response to it.

1. Clarify your values. I can't think of a more important step. Who's in charge of your life—you, your spouse, your child, your boss or God?
2. Trust in God and follow the leading of the Holy Spirit. "The mind controlled by the Spirit is life and peace" (Romans 8:6b).

3. Learn to recognize your stress signs. My first sign of stress is I'm short with people. Close at hand is restless sleep, dark circles under my eyes, and a feeling of pressure.
4. Pinpoint your chronic stress and bring it under control. I tend to mask my feelings. I've done such a good job at suppressing my feelings that I can go several weeks (I'm improving—it used to be months) before I recognize what I'm doing. I also take on more than I can handle—it's that old "over-work syndrome." In handling these things, I force myself to be more patient and deliberate and I remember that God loves me, as imperfect as I am. I don't have to do all things well. I just have to do well what God wants me to do. In other words, I strive to do His will, not mine.
5. Know when to stand your ground and when to give in. Ask yourself *Why must I win this argument or disagreement?* or *What am I trying to prove?* Dr. Robert S. Eliot of Menninger Clinic asks a simple, yet brilliant, question: "Is it worth dying for?"[15] That says it all.
6. Talk about your problems to someone. Find people with whom you can share your deepest thoughts. I have three. (1) God—I share everything with Him. (2) My wife. She is a source of inspiration, strength and patience as she listens to my innermost feelings, which are hard for me to share. (3) My dog, Happy, believe it or not. I discuss all kinds of things on my six-mile runs with her. Unfortunately, or fortunately, she doesn't talk back.

I think that the next three assisters will help you maximize items 1 through 6. They won't solve your problems, but they will help you unwind and put things in perspective. They can make you alert, vibrant, energetic and clear-thinking. Do not neglect them.

7. Get started on a physical fitness program today. See chapters 5 and 6.
8. Develop a plan to drop your addictions. Do not use drugs, alcohol, tobacco or, caffeine (including colas). See chapters 11 and 12.
9. Apply the three R's of stress management—rest, relaxation and recreation.

> "We are pressed on every side, but not crushed; perplexed, but not in despair; persecuted, but not abandoned; struck down, but not destroyed" (2 Corinthians 4:8, 9).

FAMILY STRESS CONTROL ACTIVITIES

Family stress is pervasive. Mom and Dad are under pressure at home and on the job. The children are uptight about friends, grades and sports, and they sense Mom's and Dad's feelings. The activities in this section are designed to help families understand the sources of stress, find ways to release stress, and experience methods of relieving pressures.

I've recommended the most appropriate ages for each activity but, again, everyone can benefit from participation.

I. *Your Perception and Reaction to Stress*

● **How Do You Feel?** (Ages 7–16)

Ask family members, "How do you feel when . . ."

a. You don't get your way?
b. You do something well?
c. Someone says, "You look fantastic"?
d. Someone criticizes you?
e. You lie to someone?
f. Someone teases you?
g. Someone hugs you?
h. You learn something new?

In their journal, have them describe a situation in which they acted differently from how they felt. What would have made them feel better in that situation?

● **Sleep** (Ages 9–16)

Have family members assess their sleeping patterns by answering these questions.

a. How long does it take you to get to sleep?
   1. More than an hour   1 point
   2. 30 to 60 minutes   2 points
   3. 15 to 30 minutes   3 points
   4. 15 minutes or less   4 points

b. How much sleep do you get?
   1. A lot less than I need, or too much   1 point
   2. A little less than I need   2 points
   3. A little more than I need   3 points
   4. Just right   4 points

c. How do you feel when you awake?
   1. Exhausted   1 point
   2. Tired   2 points
   3. Slightly tired   3 points
   4. Refreshed   4 points

d. During the past two weeks, how many nights did you wake up and have trouble getting back to sleep?
   1. Seven or more   1 point
   2. Three to six   2 points
   3. One or two   3 points
   4. None   4 points

e. During the past fourteen days, describe your sleep.
   1. Fitful and restless   1 point
   2. Some sleep problems   2 points
   3. Rare sleep problems   3 points
   4. Sound sleep   4 points

f. Describe your feelings throughout the day.
   1. Tired and sleepy   1 point
   2. Tired   2 points
   3. Enough energy to get through the day   3 points
   4. Energetic   4 points

Scoring

24 points   = Excellent sleeping habits
20 to 24 points = Good sleeping habits (Look at your lower scores. See what can be done.)
15 to 19 points = Fair sleeping habits (Can improve in some areas.)
14 points or less = Poor sleeping habits (Need to strongly consider how to reduce stress.)

● Holmes Stress Quotient (Ages 12–16)

To take stock of the amount of stress to which your family has been exposed over the past year:

a. Carefully read each statement under "Keeping Track of Your Stress."
b. If the statement describes a change you have experienced in the past year, circle the number to the right. If not, place an X through the number.
c. Add all your circled numbers. Record: _____.

d. If you scored more than 100 points, you may be more prone to developing disease.

e. In what area are you experiencing the most stress?

_____

f. In what area are you experiencing the least stress?

_____

g. List the areas in which you can reduce your stress score.

_____

● Keeping Track of Your Stress[1]

a. Changes: Has there been a change in . . .

	Parent	Child
1. Your eating habits?	8	8
2. The frequency of family gatherings?	8	8
3. Your sleeping habits?	8	8
4. Your social activities?	9	9
5. Your church activities?	10	10
6. Your recreational habits?	10	5
7. The school you attend?	10	10
8. Where you live?	10	10
9. The conditions or hours of your work or school?	10	10
10. Your living conditions?	13	13
11. The amount of responsibility at your job?	15	15
12. The frequency of family arguments?	18	18
13. Your line of work?	18	18
14. Your family's financial status?	19	10
15. A family member's health?	22	22

b. Financial and Legal Problems

	Parent	Child
1. Have you or one of your parents taken out a loan or signed a mortgage for less than $10,000?	9	4
2. Have you or one of your parents taken out a loan or signed a mortgage for more than $10,000?	16	8
3. Has your (or your parents') loan or mortgage been foreclosed?	15	8
4. Were you cited for a minor violation of the law?	9	9
5. Were you sentenced to a jail term?	34	34

c. Health Problems and Deaths

	Parent	Child
1. Has a close friend of yours died?	19	19
2. Did you experience a pregnancy or a new child in your home?	20	20

   3. Did you have an illness or personal injury?   27   27
   4. Has a close member of your family died (e.g.,
      grandparent)?   32   32
   5. Has your spouse died? Or parent?   50   50

d. Family Problems
   1. Did your spouse or parent start or stop a job?   13   26
   2. Did you have any trouble with your in-laws or
      grandparents?   15   15
   3. Did one of your children or brothers or sisters leave
      home?   15   15
   4. Has there been an addition to the family?   15   25
   5. Did you or your parents go through a marital
      reconciliation?   23   23
   6. Did you or one of your parents get married?   25   30
   7. Did you or your parents go through a marital
      separation?   33   33
   8. Did you or your parents get divorced?   37   37

e. School, Business or Personal Stress
   1. Have you taken a vacation?   7   7
   2. Have you had any trouble with your boss or teacher?   12   12
   3. Have you revised any personal habits?   12   12
   4. Have you started or finished school?   13   13
   5. Have you accomplished an outstanding personal
      achievement?   14   14
   6. Have you experienced any sexual difficulties?   20   20
   7. Have you had to make a business readjustment?   20   N/A
   8. Did you or one of your parents retire from work?   23   12
   9. Have you or one of your parents been fired from a job?   24   12

● Type A Behavior (Ages 12–16)[2]

To help family members determine if they fall into the category known as Type A (or highly stressful) behavior, have them circle the number that best characterizes their behavior for each item.

a. Casual about   1 2 3 4 5 6 7 8 Never late
   appointments
b. Not competitive   1 2 3 4 5 6 7 8 Very competitive
c. Never feel rushed, even 1 2 3 4 5 6 7 8 Try to do many things at
   under pressure   once; think about what
                                        I'm going to do next

d. Do things slowly   1 2 3 4 5 6 7 8   Do things fast (eating, walking, etc.)

e. "Sit on" my feelings   1 2 3 4 5 6 7 8   Express my feelings

f. Many interests   1 2 3 4 5 6 7 8   Few interests outside work

     Total Score _____

     Multiply by 3 _____

Interpretation

More than 120	Very strongly Type A
106–119	Definitely Type A
100–105	Type A, but the Type B in you may save your life
90–99	Type B, but with some Type A tendencies
Less than 90	Type B

● Family Discussion (Ages 9–16)

Discuss these statements after dinner.

a. Regardless of how much you want to be loved, it's useless to try and befriend someone who continually rejects you.

b. Face the fact that perfection is unattainable. Your highest goal is to be the best *you* can be.

c. Simplifying your lifestyle can add more pleasure to life than all the wealth and extravagance you've been struggling to obtain.

d. Before you waste a lot of energy trying to fight your way out of a situation, ask yourself if it's really worth the effort.

e. Focus only on what is pleasant in your life; forget anything painful or ugly.

f. When you face your most difficult hour, try to recall and dwell on a past success. A sense of frustration can totally immobilize you, so avoid it by concentrating on even the slightest bright spot in your past.

g. Never try to detour unpleasant tasks. Face them as soon as possible, so you can move on to more enjoyable things.

h. There are no pat answers or special success formulas to fit everyone. Choose from a wide variety of advice only those things that fit your unique personality.

● Your Sense of Humor (Ages 10–16)

Have family members read the statements below and circle the number that best characterizes their response for each item.

a. I rarely laugh. In fact I find it difficult to do so.   1 2 3 4 5 6 7 8   I laugh easily and heartily quite often.

b. I do not like to take the time to listen to jokes or humorous stories.   1 2 3 4 5 6 7 8   I enjoy listening to and/or telling jokes and funny stories.

c. I find humorous movies and/or plays a waste.   1 2 3 4 5 6 7 8   I enjoy watching humorous movies and/or plays.

d. In an embarrassing situation, I try to remove myself as quickly and quietly as possible.   1 2 3 4 5 6 7 8   When I find myself in an embarrassing situation, I usually try to find the humor in it.

e. I do not find humor in mistakes I make.   1 2 3 4 5 6 7 8   I can laugh at my own mistakes.

f. I rarely feel lighthearted.   1 2 3 4 5 6 7 8   Most of the time I have "a song in my heart and a smile on my face."

g. I feel that my self-concept could be improved substantially.   1 2 3 4 5 6 7 8   I have a strong self-concept and adapt very well to new situations.

h. I do not have a good sense of humor.   1 2 3 4 5 6 7 8   I have a strong sense of humor.

Add all the above figures. TOTAL SCORE _____.

Interpretation

40 or more	You seem to have a strong sense of humor.
39–35	You have a sense of humor, but are somewhat serious.
34–30	You are quite serious.
29 or less	You need to work on your sense of humor.

You may want to have a friend evaluate you as well. Compare your two perceptions, which may differ significantly. If you are dissatisfied, discuss ways you can improve your sense of humor.

● Stress and Interpersonal Relations (Ages 5–16)

While you are together as a family, have your children verbally complete these sentences:

a. I feel best when _____.

b. I feel worst when _____.

c. I really get mad when _____.

d. When I am mad, I _____.

e. My dad (mom) makes me angriest when _____.
f. My dad (mom) makes me happiest when _____.
g. When the teacher is angry, _____.
h. When I am angry, I _____.
i. Stress can _____.
j. I don't feel pressure when _____.
k. I'm happiest when _____.

● Stress and Health (Ages 7–16)

Discuss with all family members:
a. Who thinks that happy people are free of stress?
b. How many of you believe that stress can kill?
c. How many of you think that "feeling uptight" is another word for stress?
d. How many of you think that Mom's (Dad's) job produces a great deal of stress?
e. How many of you think that school makes you uptight (feel uncomfortable)?
f. How many of you believe that stress can raise your blood pressure?
g. How many of you think that stress can harm your heart?
h. How many of you think that one man's stress is another man's pleasure?

● Burn-out (Ages 14–16)

Have family members answer the following questions to discover if their environment increases their chances of burning out? If they count more than three Ts, they can reasonably conclude that their environment is stress-producing. Discuss your answers, and see if the family can come up with ways to reduce stress.

T F   a. My lifestyle is such that I find it extremely difficult to exercise three or more times a week.

T F   b. My friends and associates would laugh at me if I practiced relaxation techniques.

T F   c. My lifestyle is such that it is difficult for me to get to sleep each night at approximately the same time.

T F   d. I am angry, hostile and/or impatient a great deal of the time.

T F   e. My family, friends and associates have unreasonable expectations of me.

T F   f. My friends and associates frown on people who take extended vacations or do something for pure pleasure.

T F   g. I have to be busy all the time. I find it hard to just relax.

T F   h. I often feel rushed and harried. Most days, I have little time to think, because I am so busy.

T   F   i. I feel as though my life's goals have been blocked or not achieved.
T   F   j. I feel that my life is not full.

● Stress Continuum (Ages 9–16)

Have your children place themselves on this continuum and, if possible, explain why they selected their positions.

EASY GOING	⟨□□□□□□□□□□□□□□□□□□□□□□⟩	SUPER HYPE
Takes things in stride and does not need to do several things at once.		Does several things at once; is easily upset and high-strung.

Have family discuss where the child or adult placed themselves. Discuss differences.

● Assessing Relationships (Ages 10–16)

Ask family members to rate how well they get along with the following people. If a category does not apply, leave it blank.

Husband/wife	5	4	3	2	1	0
Mother/father	5	4	3	2	1	0
Your own children	5	4	3	2	1	0
Your brother/sister	5	4	3	2	1	0
In-laws	5	4	3	2	1	0
Your neighbors	5	4	3	2	1	0
Your immediate supervisor at work	5	4	3	2	1	0
Your co-workers	5	4	3	2	1	0
Those whom you supervise	5	4	3	2	1	0
Your minister/priest	5	4	3	2	1	0
Your landlord	5	4	3	2	1	0
Your friends	5	4	3	2	1	0

Ratings:
    5—Extremely well
    4—Quite well
    3—Average
    2—Not very well
    1—Quite poorly
    0—Terrible

Scoring:

Total the numbers you have circled. Then divide by the number of categories you rated. For example, if you rated only five columns, and the total rating was 15, your score would be 3.

1–2 You probably have too many negative relationships.
3–4 Most of your relationships are at least satisfactory, though they could use some improvement.
5 You enjoy your relationships and value improving them.

● **Draw Self** (Ages 5–12)

Have your children draw a picture of themselves and draw arrows to parts of their bodies they would like to improve. Then have the children draw a picture of how they would like to look.

● **Identify Sources of Stress** (Ages 12–16)[3]

To help family members more clearly understand why life may not be so enjoyable for them, have them check any of the following conditions that apply:

_____a. Too many people to relate to
_____b. Frequent overtime and long hours
_____c. Egotistical fellow employees or supervisors
_____d. Excessive deadlines to meet
_____e. Excessive technical and repetitive work
_____f. Deluge of seemingly senseless paperwork
_____g. Fear of the consequences of making mistakes
_____h. Excessive noise
_____i. Extreme smells, sights, heat and cold
_____j. Smoke and toxic substances in the air
_____k. Feeling of incompetence
_____l. Job seems meaningless and unchallenging
_____m. Lack of true friends to share feelings with
_____n. Current physical problems
_____o. Failing marriage
_____p. Poor money management resulting in excessive debt
_____q. Long drive to and from work in rush-hour traffic
_____r. Overcommitment to clubs, organizations, church and so on
_____s. Strained relationships with the children
_____t. Not enough time for recreation and hobbies

Additional Conditions

_____u.

_____v.

_____w.

_____x.

_____y.

Now go over the above list and select the three major sources of stress in your life:

a. _____

b. _____

c. _____

● **Feeling Upset** (Ages 5–16)

Set up a sheet of paper as shown, and ask your children to do the following:

Write down some things that have made you upset.   How did you feel?

	▷
	▷
	▷

● **Color Sad** (Ages 3–8)

Ask your children to show you what color sad is. Then ask them to tell you what sad looks like. Ask them to draw sad.

● **Color Glad** (Ages 3–8)

Ask your children to show you what color glad is. Then ask them to tell you what glad looks like. Ask them to draw glad.

II. *Specific Stress Control Activities*

● **Relaxation** (Ages 10–16)

In *Beyond the Relaxation Response,* Dr. Herbert Benson, a Harvard cardiologist, outlines a simple way for Christians to soothe the stress in the body:[4]

a. Sit quietly in a comfortable position.

b. Close your eyes.

c. Deeply relax all your muscles, beginning at your feet and progressing up to your face. Keep them relaxed.

d. Breathe through your nose. Become aware of your breathing. As you breathe out, say one of the following:
   — Words from Psalm 23:1: "The Lord is my shepherd."
   — Words from Psalm 100:1: "Make a joyful noise unto the Lord" (KJV).
   — Any of Jesus' teachings or words, such as: "My peace I give unto you,"[5] "Love one another,"[6] or "I am the way, the truth, and the life."[7]

e. Continue for ten to twenty minutes. You may open your eyes to check the time, but do not use an alarm. When you finish, sit quietly for several minutes, at first with your eyes closed and later with them open. Do not stand up for a few minutes.

f. Do not worry about whether you achieve a deep level of relaxation. Maintain a passive attitude and permit relaxation to occur at its own pace. When distracting thoughts come, try to ignore them by not dwelling on them, and return to repeating your phrase. With practice, relaxation should come with little effort. Practice the technique once or twice daily, but not within two hours after any meal, since the digestive processes seem to interfere with the elicitation of the relaxation.

Three R's (Adults; can be modified for ages 10 and up)

Rest—If you ignore this element, you may not have enough energy to keep up with your new lifestyle.

a. Go to bed one half-hour earlier than normal. If you aren't tired enough to sleep, use the time to read, write letters, talk with your spouse or listen to music.

b. If you are using a sleeping aid, such as a barbiturate or a tranquilizer, stop for at least a two-week trial period. If you have difficulty sleeping during that time, try some of these methods:
   1) Drink a cup of warm milk or herb tea one half-hour before retiring.
   2) Read something that is not related in any way to your work. Fiction is usually better for this than nonfiction.
   3) Exercise leisurely for ten minutes just before going to bed.

4) Take a hot bath before you retire.
5) Practice a relaxation technique while lying in bed.
6) Try falling asleep to soft music.
7) Do not have any coffee, tea, cola or chocolate after noon.

Recreation—Put the play back into your life . . . even if it means being a kid again.

a. Perform an aerobic activity (jogging, walking, swimming, and so forth) for at least twenty minutes a day three times a week).
b. Once each week, participate in a noncompetitive physical activity with your family or friends. Suggested activities include:

Free-form wrestling and tumbling	Canoeing or sailing
Imitate animal motions	Archery
Backyard obstacle course	Tree climbing
Playground equipment play	Horseback riding
Hiking or biking	Skating (ice or roller)
Sledding and tobogganing	Ping-pong and badminton
Skiing (snow or water)	

Note: Traditional recreational activities, such as golf, bowling, softball and so forth, are fine if a) competition does not become serious, b) a regular obligation does not turn it into a chore, c) relationships with family and/or friends do not play second fiddle to the activity.

Relaxation—Practice daily Benson's relaxation technique (described in the previous activity).

● Thinking Positive (Ages 9–16)

You've heard, "You are what you eat." Consider another expression: "You are what you think." Too often, we let negative thoughts shape the way we act. By replacing negative thoughts with positive ones, you can be happier and more productive.

Have family members replace the following negative statements with positive ones:

Example:
  Negative: I have to go to the dentist today. I hate dentists.
  Positive: I'll get to listen to headphones at the dentist today. I also will enjoy talking to the secretary, who is in my study group.
a. "Oh, no. The dog woke me up, and it's only 4:30 A.M."
b. "Today I have to do all that yard work."
c. "We've got to drive 300 miles today."

d. "There's nothing good on television."
e. "Nobody phones me to go out with them."

● Sleep (Ages 10–16)

To help family members determine the amount of sleep they need, have them do the following: for three days, go to bed one half-hour later than they normally do, and then answer the following questions:
a. Was I able to get more things done by staying up the extra half-hour?
b. Did I feel sufficiently rested throughout the day?
c. Was it difficult to stay awake for the extra half-hour?
   Now, have them try going to bed a half-hour earlier than their regular bedtime and answer these questions:
a. Did I have difficulty falling asleep?
b. Did I feel noticeably more refreshed the next day?
c. Did I run out of time to get things accomplished, due to the earlier bedtime?
   From this experiment, they can determine whether their present sleeping pattern is sufficient or whether they need a little more or less sleep.

● Belly Laugh (Ages 3–16)

Get the whole family and, if possible, relatives or friends involved in this activity. You'll need a large area.
   Have one family member lie on the floor on his or her back. The next person lies down, placing his or her head on the stomach of the first person. Each additional person does the same, until everyone is lying on their back with someone's head on their lap and their own head on someone else's lap (except for the first and last people). If possible, have everyone lie so that they form a circle. The first person then says "Ha." Everyone else takes a turn saying, "Ha." Then the first person says, "Ha, ha," which again is passed on. This continues until everyone is roaring with laughter.

● What Makes Me Happy? (Ages 5–16)

Have family members identify five to ten things that make them happy. Then take turns telling what makes you happy and why. For example, "Christmas always makes me happy because I get to see Grandma."

● What Makes Me Nervous? (Ages 5–16)

Have family members identify and share five to ten things or situations that make them nervous. They should tell what they do in the situation to feel less nervous.

Other family members can make suggestions, such as, "Whenever I have to speak in front of a group, I get nervous, too. I make good notes, and that helps."

● Doctor, Doctor (Ages 5–12)

Have family members take turns being the doctor for the others. The patient comes into the doctor's office with a problem, such as those listed below. The doctor tries to give helpful advice.

a. "I'm, afraid I'm going to fail at school. My marks are very good, but I'm never satisfied."
b. "I can't get to sleep at night. I lie awake worrying about my job."
c. "All my friends are good athletes, but I'm not. It bugs me that I can't be better."

● Center Stage (Ages 5–16)

Family members need to feel important. They need attention. But sometimes those who have something important to say don't get a chance to speak up.

Therefore, develop a schedule whereby each family member is given a night. That night at dinner, everyone is to ask that person how he is and what's going on in his life. If the person wants to talk about losing and finding his pet turtle, that's O.K. The last five minutes of dinner are reserved for other news. Someone else may want to share something important that happened that day. Then end the meal by giving thanks and praying, especially for the featured member.

● Mealtime Rules (Ages 3–16)

Mealtime can be very relaxing or very stressful. To add order and foster a more relaxed atmosphere, family members should identify some rules, such as:

a. Take turns reciting prayer before meals (everyone participates).
b. No starting until everyone sits down.
c. No reading at the table.
d. Take turns setting the table (schedule).
e. Take turns clearing the table (schedule).

● Thought-Provoking (Ages 7–12)

Write a thought-provoking statement on an index card. Place the card on the refrigerator where it can be clearly read. Keep it up about a week. After the week, everyone is to give their feelings about the statement. Sample ideas:

a. When you're in a bad mood, it's best to keep to yourself until the feelings go away.

b. When you feel sad or upset, it helps to talk with a friend.
c. Screaming and yelling is O.K. when you're mad, because it makes you feel better.
d. When you're unhappy, going out for a great big ice-cream sundae sometimes helps.

● Not-so-Trivial Pursuit (Ages 7–16)

This is a take-off on the popular board game, Trivial Pursuit. Family members record on a piece of paper the dates of the most happy moments in their lives, such as "June 3, 1962, Mom's high school graduation." After each person records three or four dates, family members take turns announcing a date. Everyone else takes turns guessing what occurred on that date. Once the event is guessed, or after two to three minutes, the family member relates the happy memory. This is a great family activity that makes everyone feel good.

● How to Relax (Ages 9–14)

Have family members list the situations that make them most angry, upset, tense, nervous or mad. Then match the following stress management techniques with the situations, and practice the stress management strategies, if necessary.
a. Go for a walk.
b. Do something extremely vigorous, such as run, swim or cycle.
c. Talk with someone.
d. Practice relaxation or prayer.
e. Play a musical instument.
f. Write a letter.
g. Practice deep breathing.
h. Engage in a favorite hobby.
i. Take an occasional nap.

Examples:
Situation I—Final Exams
    Technique a—Get up early and go for a walk.
    Or technique c—Study with a friend.
Situation II—Rush Hour Traffic
    Technique g—Practice deep breathing.

● Keep a Log (Ages 12–16)

For one week, have family members keep a log of their positive and negative relationships (following the format below.) At the end of each day and at the end of the week, they should read and reflect on their entries.

Example:

| **Monday** | | | |
Approximate Time	Person(s) Involved	Feelings Produced	Possible Reason
6:45 A.M.	Mother	Anger—some resentment	Tired; nervous about school work not completed.
8:15 A.M.	Friend at bus stop	Anger/frustration	His nasty comments.
9:30 A.M.	Teacher	Mild anger	She didn't warn me about the surprise test.
11:00 A.M.	Jim	Enjoyment	Ate lunch together. He listened to my story.

When you review your log, try to see if and how your feelings are caused by the person involved or some other factor. In the example, you might think the child had a reason to complain about his mother, friend and teacher, and that his only true friend was Jim. Actually, his mother, friend and teacher had nothing to do with his anger, and all three may have been very supportive.

Examine your positive and negative relationships to see what may contribute to them.

● Improve a Relationship (Ages 12–16)

Have family members identify one person with whom they would most like to improve their relationship.

Example: New boy who moved in down the street

List three things about that person that you think contribute to your poor relationship.

Never talks with me.

Spends too much time practicing the piano. Music is his "thing."

Has other friends.

List three things about yourself that you think contribute to the poor relationship.

Never really talked to him. I am shy.

I'm not very good at music.

I must work after school.

List three things over which neither of you has much control that seem to negatively affect the relationship.

No classes together.

His parents are demanding.

Neither of us can drive.

List five things you would like to try in an effort to improve the relationship.

Call him on the phone.

Invite him to church.

Learn more about music.

Have my parents invite him over.

Take a class with him.

Select the easiest option from this last list and try it during the next week.

Repeat this process for two other people. Remember, developing positive relationships takes time. Don't rush through this process. You may need to observe your relationships for a week or two before you can complete the questions.

● A Daily Kind Word (Ages 3–16)

Encourage family members to speak kindly or offer a word of encouragement to at least one person each day.

● A Weekly Family Powwow (Ages 3–16)

Hold a family powwow for the sole purpose of keeping the lines of communication open between all members. Encourage everyone to share feelings as well as petty problems that often arise. Spend some time in physical contact, either holding hands in a circle or embracing each other. End the session by singing or reciting an inspiring verse together, or praying together.

● Monthly Small Group (Ages 12–16)

Encourage family members to contact three to five people with whom they would like to engage in conversation and emotional involvement, and then form a small discussion/sharing group. During the first few meetings, they may have to initiate conversation by putting thought-provoking questions in a hat and having each member draw one. They should forego the usual party format of games, beverages, food and so on, and use the time to develop strong bonds of genuine friendship.

● Cultivate New Relationships (Ages 9–16)

If you or your child feel a little inhibited about initiating relationships, reach out and treat yourself to another exciting adventure. Try to develop and cultivate one new relationship, perhaps with a neighbor, co-worker, relative or student. Your goal is to allow the relationship to develop beyond the casual stage and into a close bond of friendship.

● Attack on "Stress Target" (Adults; also can be used for ages 12–16)

From the stress sources you selected on page 212, choose one as your target for one week. Plan an all-out attack that includes the following components:

a. Devise a realistic time schedule.

One simple way to do this is to use $3'' \times 5''$ index cards for each day of the week. On one side of the card, list your primary tasks and secondary tasks. On the other side, write a time schedule for the day. Example:

PRIMARY:	MONDAY
School Soccer practice Youth group	6:30 Wake-up 7:15 Leave for school 8:00–3:00 School 3:15–4:15 Soccer 4:15–5:00 Shopping
SECONDARY:	5:15–5:40 Run 6:00 Dinner 7:30 Church
Shopping Homework Run	9:00 Home Study 10:15 Bed

front   back

b. Approach primary tasks with a positive attitude.

As you write down your primary tasks, think or concentrate on the good results of finishing the task. For example:

Primary Task:

Complete the refinishing job I started on the kitchen table and chairs.

Positive Results:

1) The family won't have to eat on TV trays scattered throughout the house.
2) I can put my kitchen back in order.
3) It will give me a sense of pride and accomplishment.
4) It will give me time to enjoy something else.

c. Take time to confide in someone.

This, perhaps, will be the most difficult, but also could help you the most. Select someone you can trust and make it a point to spend some time with that individual for the sole purpose of sharing your feelings and emotions.

d. Take charge of your problems.

Write down one major problem you must face this week.

_____

Now list at least three ways to handle that problem. Do not include "ignore it" as an option.

_____

Select what you think is the best option and apply that solution to the problem.

e. Anticipate obstacles that may stop you.

Beat obstacles to the punch. If you think about them ahead of time, you already will have an idea of how to get around them. Write down any obstacles that you expect to stand in your way.

_____

_____

_____

f. Meet those obstacles head on.

Write down how you plan to get around any of the obstacles you selected.

_____

_____

_____

g. Recognize your own personal value.

Begin or end each day by thinking about things that make you proud of yourself. You can do this while on the bus, jogging or walking, or lying in bed.

● Help Yourself (Ages 10–16)

Have family members write down three problems they feel they need help with. They should pick the one they need the most help with and list as many creative solutions as they can think of for that problem.

Asking these questions might help:

a. What do I complain about the most?

b. What worries me the most?

c. What frustrates me the most?

d. What would I like to change about myself?

e. What would I like to do or accomplish?

● Dream (Ages 10–16)

Family members can try this daydreaming experiment when they feel upset:

a. Practice this activity on your own.

b. Sit comfortably, feet on the floor, eyes closed. Try to breathe in a relaxed manner. As you do this, concentrate on relaxing your muscles.

c. Now try to relax your mind by thinking about some pleasant memory, such as a picnic, a ballgame, a book, a good time with friends, or a vacation. This usually takes about a minute.

d. Try to experience the memory.

What did you feel during this experiment?

● Goal-Setting (Ages 10–16)

You and your children should set goals, writing down when you expect to achieve each one. Be specific; include the date. Then list the obstacles that may keep you from reaching your goals, and how you plan to get around these obstacles.

Example:

My goals:

—My daily goal is to run three miles.

—My weekly goal is to run fifteen miles a week (three miles, five times a week).

—My monthly goal is to run sixty miles a month.

—My ultimate goal is to run in the Boston Marathon.

Obstacles that might keep me from reaching my goals:

—Time

—Weather

—Fatigue

—Boredom

Dates I plan to achieve these goals:

—I will run three miles daily within thirty days.

—I will achieve my weekly goal of fifteen miles a week in two months.

—I will achieve my monthly goal in one year.

—I will achieve my ultimate goal in three years.

Ideas for getting around these obstacles:

—I will set aside a certain time that best fits my schedule. Right now, it seems like 5:00 to 5:30 P.M. every day would be good.

—I will read up on how to dress properly for cold, hot and humid weather. In very cold weather, I might run at a different time of day.

—I must be willing to take a day off when I'm not feeling well. (That's why I'm only counting five days a week.)

—To avoid boredom, I will try to run with a friend and will vary my route. I also will save inspirational newspaper stories, such as those about people who run in spite of their handicaps.

I achieved my goals on these dates:

a. Daily   _____   c. Monthly   _____

b. Weekly   _____   d. Ultimate   _____

III. *Trigger Stories*

Have family members discuss the following stories:

● Whose Fault? (Ages 12–16)

Jack was a very successful high school student—he earned good grades and was a top athlete. One day, his girlfriend broke up with him. He took it hard. His parents were very busy, and he didn't feel he could talk with them. He felt very lonely. He tried to talk with his best friend, but he didn't listen. Jack tried to kill himself but, fortunately, he failed. Why do you think he did it? How could you have helped him?

● Tough Choices (Ages 7–12)

You have no choice; you are going on a mission to outer space. This is a dangerous mission, and there is a good chance you won't return. You are allowed to bring six people. Who would you choose and why? You also can bring a small pack of personal things. What would you bring and why?

● Stealing and Your Sisters (Ages 7–12)

When you come home from school, your mother is waiting for you. She says your two older sisters told her that you took money out of their purses. (You didn't.) You try to explain that you did not even know they had money in their purses. Your mother doesn't listen to you. She takes you into the bedroom and disciplines you. How do you feel about your sisters? How should you treat them? Two days later, you see one sister taking money out of the other sister's purse. What could you do?

● Bobby's New Baby Sister (Ages 7–12)

Mother has just brought home a new baby sister. Mother had a difficult time in the pregnancy, and Bobby has not had much time to be with her. Now, he hopes that all this will change. But, when the baby comes home, he notices that he is no longer the center of attention. He doesn't even have his dad's attention. Both parents seem to devote a tremendous amount of time to his new sister. He resents it and his new sister. Why does he feel this way?

● Cheating (Ages 9–12)

Allyson is in fourth grade. She is a very good student in almost everything but math. She wants to please her mom and dad by getting good marks in school. One day, during a math test, she cheated, hoping to get a better mark. The teacher caught her and gave her a zero on the test. She was so afraid to tell her parents that she never showed them her report card. Instead, she forged her mom's signature. Just before Parents' Night, Allyson became very sick. She was terrified her parents would find out about her cheating. What should she have done to prevent her stress, and why?

• Mad, Angry and Tense (Ages 9–16)

Have family members write on small individual sheets of paper those events that make them most mad, angry, frustrated or tense. Place the pieces of paper in a hat. Have family members take turns drawing from the hat (one paper at a time). If they draw their own, have them put it back and select another. The person who draws the paper reads the situation and has thirty seconds to respond by saying, "If I were in a situation (describe), I would . . . ." Continue until all situations have been discussed. Keep this activity light by encouraging humor.

• Memorize Scripture Revealing the Character of God

Memorizing God's Word as a family activity can help us fill our mind with the greatness of God, His care for us, His faithfulness, His love, His role as our Father. These are sometimes called the attributes of God, and knowing how they apply in our stressful situations can bring real peace.

Select verses appropriate for the various age levels. Initiate a Scripture memory contest, awarding small prizes like special privileges. Engage in antiphonal reading, with you and the children reading by turn—and later quoting, back and forth at the table, verses that have been memorized.

A helpful book on the attributes of God is *Majesty: The God You Should Know*, by J. Sidlow Baxter. Since it contains a lot of Scripture, you may glean memory verses from it.

• Initiate Meditation on God's Promises

Once some Scripture has been memorized, lead the older children in a pattern of meditation on the promises of God. Though some consider meditation unbiblical, it has always been a spiritual discipline whereby the mind forces out the stressful thoughts and focuses on who God is and how He will work in our lives. We start with detachment from the pressures of the world and move to a richer attachment to God. An excellent resource for the promises of God is *Bible Promises: Key to Supernatural Living*, by Alice Chapin.

Chapter 15:
Managing Time, Setting Goals and Getting Started

"I press on toward the goal to win the prize for which God has called me heavenward in Christ Jesus" (Philippians 3:14).

Paul was a man with a mission. He knew that Christ stopped him on the Damascus road because he had a special purpose for him. To fulfill Christ's challenge, Paul set goals—missionary journeys that would take him to the ends of the then-known world. He planned and prayed to go to Jerusalem, Asia, Rome and Spain to proclaim God's message to Jews and Gentiles. And he pressed on.

Yet, Paul was seeking God's will, not his own, so he modified his goals when the Holy Spirit told him to do so. Paul wanted to go to Asia and Bithynia, but was blocked by the Holy Spirit. In a dream, he was begged to come to Macedonia. A lesser man might have shrugged off this advice. But, not Paul. He listened and obeyed God.[1] We can learn from Paul's example. If we pay attention, God will tell us what he has in mind for us and guide us to fulfill our purpose for His kingdom. And as He does, we, too, must set goals and use our time wisely—two skills that go hand-in-hand, and that some of us lack.

I'm convinced that many failures to stick to wellness programs are due to the absence of these skills. We flounder. We lack the ability to "press on." Or, though we agree with many things suggested throughout this book, we don't feel that we have the time to do them, or we feel guilty taking the time.

Don't feel guilty! You are a whole person—mind, body and spirit. Neglect one part and your entire being will suffer. Paul teaches about body parts working together.[2] While he was talking about the church, I think his illustration also applies to the mind, body and spirit interacting. Each part is a function, and it makes a contribution to the whole you. So take time to run, walk, lose weight, practice relaxation techniques, cook better and talk to your children. That time may increase your vigor. Besides, even our Lord took time to rest, away from the crowd.

Once you decide, through the guiding of the Holy Spirit, what you think is important, how do you find the time to do it? Through time management techniques, which help you maximize each minute. In essence, you end up working (or playing) smarter, not necessarily harder.

Time management techniques may seem oppressive, especially for the family. After all, home is where you are to relax—unwind. That's true. But effective use of your time is vital because, first, it gives you more time to relax. Second, it teaches your children to manage their time more effectively—a skill I wish I had learned when I was ten or twelve. Third, I think God wants you to be a good steward of your time, as well as your talents and financial resources.

As you plan your time, remember: you can't be all things to all people. I learned that lesson several years ago from my dad. He had several successful pastorates, but he always had a burning passion to start a new church. At the age of fifty-one, he had that opportunity. He became the first pastor of a mission church in Emmaus, Pennsylvania.

He attacked his new ministry with vigor, and the church prospered. When he was sixty-two, the church moved into a second building phase. New members flocked to the church, many carrying hurts and psychological problems. My dad, a good pulpiteer and counselor, was able to help. Those to whom he ministered asked him to help their friends, which he did. In time, my dad was being stretched. I should say "clobbered." Here he was, in his early sixties, working from 7:00 A.M. to 11:00 P.M., carrying many people's burdens. Soon his health began to falter. His sermons weren't as strong. He was easily distracted. Then came the crowning blow—his daughter-in-law (my first wife) became seriously ill with terminal cancer. Dad kept pushing. But his body wasn't thirty years of age; he needed a break. A wise Christian physician took my father aside and told him, "You can only do so much for God's kingdom." Knowing that my father grew up on a farm, this doctor then issued some down-home wisdom: "A person has to know how much of a garden he can take care of." Excellent advice. My father listened; his health and vitality returned. Today, at seventy-four, he is the picture of health, serenity and joy.

Most people are like my dad was. They have not assumed control over their own days. Many literally run through a busy schedule which others dictate. They try to get everything done at once, hoping to get a little room to breathe, someday. Life is busy for everyone, yet the ones who learn to manage their time effectively seem to find that room to breathe.

Time management consultant Alan Lakein views time management as a way of liberation.[3] It helps you more efficiently achieve goals at work and in private life, and it gives you more time for play, hobbies or other freedoms.

Areas of Your Life

Management of time applies to five broad areas of your life:

—work
—sleep
—relaxation
—family responsibilities
—social responsibilities

You can include your time with God under social or family responsibilities, or you may prefer to make a sixth category.

If you spend eight hours at work and seven hours sleeping, that leaves nine hours for church, reading, fun and games, right? Of course not. You have to mow the lawn, repair the leaky faucet, go shopping, take the kids to the dentist, pay the bills, get dressed, prepare meals. . . . That's where proper scheduling comes in. You have to do all of these things, and more, but you do not have to do them all at once.

Try this: Make a list of all your social and household obligations that aren't connected with your job, but must be done. Beside each one, put the approximate amount of time it takes to do them. Now underline those that are absolutely necessary, and put a question mark after the ones that you could omit. Using this list as a guide, make a schedule for each day of the week, setting aside time for each "absolute" activity. Do the most important or difficult things first. If there are not enough hours in the week to get everything done, cross out the ones that are followed with question marks, or delegate work to others (i.e. family members). Also, make sure you include time for relaxation and enjoyment.

Post your schedule in a place where you'll see it often, and follow it rigidly for one week. I think you'll find that it works. Why? Because without a plan, we often put things off until the last minute. Then when it's time to do them, we rush. The task seems extremely unpleasant. We get frustrated, experience more stress, tend to become immobilized and waste time. On the other hand, by scheduling our time more efficiently, we learn that being in control gives us a tremendous sense of satisfaction and accomplishment.

Setting Goals, Time Management

Time management is effective only if you have clearly defined goals. It is important to know what you want out of life.

I recommend that you set long-term goals (lifetime, a year, or anything in between) and then establish intermediate and short-term goals. The short-term goals should be activities you can do and which are directly under your control— a very important point. Let me illustrate. You may want a slimmer body (that's a general goal). Or you may be more specific and say you want to lose twenty-five pounds and keep the pounds off. That's a specific lifetime goal. To obtain this, you formulate a short-term goal, such as, "I want to lose a pound a week for the next twenty-five weeks.'' Your intermediate goal may be, ''At the end of three months, I want to have lost twelve pounds.''

The problem with these goals is that none are under your control. Your menstrual cycle, tendency to hold fluids, or muscle mass may not permit you to lose a pound a week. Or, by some quirk of your physiology, you may be able to lose only five, ten or fifteen pounds. Since you can't lose twenty-five pounds, you feel like a failure, even though you did the best your body would let you do.

To avoid that frustration, establish goals that are under your dominion. Going back to the above illustration, I would determine that I want a better-looking body. That's a general lifetime goal. Next, I would establish short-term goals that are under my control, such as: 1) Walk one to three miles a day, five days a week. 2) Cut 250 calories a day from my diet. 3) Learn assertiveness techniques to allow me to express my feelings when I don't want to eat certain foods.

My intermediate goals might be: 1) Run two to four miles a day, five days a week. 2) Maintain my reduction of 250 calories a day. 3) Develop my assertiveness techniques. 4) Learn how to cook with less fat.

In terms of specific long-term or lifetime goals, I would determine to: 1) Run from three to four miles a day and enter road races four times a year. 2) Eat mostly nutritious foods, i.e. the U.S. Dietary Guidelines. 3) Continue using my assertiveness techniques. 4) Like my body as it is, because I am doing all that is possible for it in terms of my time, ability and goals. All these goals offer me the satisfaction of reaching them, because they are within my grasp.

Again, (I can't emphasize this point enough), when attempting to improve your own or your family's health, set goals that are possible to control.

Determining Your Goal

List your primary lifetime goals. If you're not sure how to identify these, imagine you have only six months to live. Then make three lists: things you must do, things you want to do, and things you neither have to or want to do. After you finish writing, forget the third list and concentrate on the other two.

Some things on your two lists may be short-term and intermediate. Identify those to help you reach your long-term objectives. Make sure that the goals are obtainable for you.

It is easier to achieve your life goals when they are constantly in front of you. Jot them in a notebook. Then, each week, write down the steps you plan to take to accomplish those goals. You also can do this daily, as I do. I write down each night what I hope to accomplish the next day. I've found it best to tackle the toughest jobs first. If I wait, I fret about getting them done. They become a distraction.

Be Flexible

Just as the apostle Paul was redirected from some goals, we can expect changes and interruptions. One of my life's goals was to earn a doctorate in exercise physiology. I wanted to be finished by 1972, at the latest, but my wife became ill. I had to put my doctorate goal on the back burner for a time. I had a more important goal—a commitment that I had made ten years earlier: "In sickness and in health, and 'til death do us part." My wife needed me more than I needed a degree, so I made a new goal: Nurse my wife back to health. That goal was not under my control, however, but I resolved to comfort and care for her.

Interruptions are not always as catastrophic as an illness or death of a spouse. For example, when I was writing this book, I received a proposal request from a major magazine. It fit in with my long-term goals to be a writer and maintain financial independence. I had planned a six-week blitz to finish this book, but I could not let this chance of a lifetime go by. So I postponed my work on the book (a short-term goal) and took five days to write the proposal.

Thresholds

Many times, when people reach a goal, they think the battle is over. If they slip a bit, they feel defeated and, therefore, soon revert back to old behaviors.

That is tragic. We are not perfect. We need permission to fail. We need flexibility for extra upheavals in our lives that may temporarily thwart our goal-seeking.

Dr. Kelly Brownell, associate professor at the University of Pennsylvania School of Medicine and co-director of its weight control program, illustrates this point nicely. In experiments he conducted, he found it was best for dieters and exercisers to set an upper limit to what they could regain before they took action.[4] For example, a woman started running six months earlier and worked her way up to running three to five miles a day, three days a week (her lifetime goal). She made a pact with herself that she would never miss more than three days of running in succession. If she did, she would increase the number of days the next week. In other words, she gave herself a three-day threshold, which signaled the start of corrective action.

Below are some other examples of thresholds:

1. Do not go longer than three days without exercise.
2. Do not allow caloric intake to exceed 2,000 calories four days in a week.
3. Do not jog less than seven miles per week.
4. Do not have more than two colas a week.
5. Gain no more than five pounds over your present weight.
6. Do not go more than seven days in succession without doing a family fitness activity.

7. Do not allow candy in the house, except one day a week.
8. Do not allow the television on before 7:30 P.M.
9. Do not bring home work from the office more than twice a week.
10. Do not serve whole milk more than four times a week.
11. Do not talk about work at the dinner table.

Thresholds are important. They provide for some failure, while building new habits. Dr. Brownell also points out that you may experience relapses, especially during these high-risk situations:

Interpersonal factors include:
—an argument with a spouse
—someone nags about exercise
—pressure from the in-laws to eat more food
—attendance at a party where the hostess pushes food
—being at a wedding with lots of food
—children's birthday party with lots of cake and ice cream

Emotional factors could be:
—loneliness
—depression
—boredom
—nervousness about exams
—anger at the boss
—worry about finances
—worry about an ill child

Situational factors:
—too cold to exercise
—watching a ballgame
—visiting friends
—bowling night—everyone eats pizza
—catch the flu or a cold
—must watch the children for a week while spouse is gone—no free time

A Practical Application

Now the rubber meets the road. Let's give a concrete example of goal-setting:

Step #1:

Let's say your long-term goal is to get every family member to exercise aerobically four times a week for thirty minutes. That's a specific, controllable long-term goal. Write it on a sheet of paper or a file card.

The Kuntzleman Family Goal
All of us will exercise
a minimum of four times
a week (aerobically) for thirty minutes.

Save it! And come back to it once a week.

Step #2

Now establish short-term and intermediate goals. A short-term goal might be to take fifteen-minute family walks twice a week. An intermediate goal could be to take two thirty-minute family walks a week. Also have each family member, on their own, exercise areobically (walk, run, bike, swim, row, and/or do aerobics) for fifteen minutes once a week.

Put this on a card:

Short-term goal: Family walk twice a week for fifteen minutes (month #1)	Intermediate Goal: Family walk twice a week for thirty minutes plus one fifteen-minute aerobic exercise session on their own. (months #2 and #3)

Step #3

Plan ahead. Obviously, you will encounter obstacles. You'll need to recognize them and plan how to get around them. Also, determine target dates for achieving your goals and design or develop a reward for when you achieve them.

Record all this on a chart:

TABLE 19
Sample of Short-Term Goals and Problems

Short-Term Goal	Obstacles	How Get Around	Date Accomplished	Reward
Family walk twice a week for fifteen min.	Meetings, ballgames, television	All agree on best time of day and which days to reserve times.	Thirty days	Make up family T-shirt that says, "We Did It."

TABLE 20
Sample of Intermediate Goals and Problems

Intermediate Goal	Obstacles	How Get Around	Date Accomplished	Reward
Family walk twice a week for thirty min, plus one exercise session on own.	Meetings, ballgames, television. May not want to exercise alone.	Same as above, plus weekly check on individual activity. When accomplished, reward with extra dollars or blow money on ski weekend.	Within ninety days.	Family ski weekend.

Encourage everyone to stick to these by doing the following:

- *Chart progress.* Have an obvious place in the kitchen where family members and friends can see the progress being made. You can use a wall map or a calendar with dates designated.
- *Commit time.* Things take on an aura of importance if they're built into your schedule. You try to be at church at a certain time and eat dinner at a certain time. Do the same with exercise. Poll the family and figure out what time is best. Everyone may need to compromise.
- *Choose the best time.* With something like a family walk, after dinner seems best, since everyone is home. Find the time by keeping the television off for a half-hour.
- *Develop a schedule.* Don't skip all over the place with your time—morning one day, evening the next. Keep it at one particular time to build consistency and lessen the chance of forgetting.
- *Think the part.* Have motivational posters, pictures and/or sayings around the house. Tell everyone to think positively about exercise. No put-downs. Only positive talking and thinking.
- *Emphasize success.* Talk about the days you've exercised, not the days you've missed. Share your success with each other and friends.
- *Variety.* Don't always go the same direction; take a new route. Play games as you walk. How many different smells, cars, barking dogs, or mailboxes do you notice. Make up other games. Use your ingenuity. Let the kids create games.
- *Dress the part.* Have a walking outfit—special shoes, pants, coat, mittens—the works.
- *Enjoy.* Don't make it punitive. Keep it fun. Don't do it because it's good for you. Do it because you like the chance to be together, to talk, to relax, to play.
- *Don't overdo.* Exercise is pleasurable—not some macho event. Make haste slowly. Go at a pace and distance that is comfortable for all. Remember these guidelines:

a. You should be able to converse with someone beside you as you exercise. When exercising alone, use your imagination: Do you feel like talking? If not, you're exercising too fast for your present age or fitness level. This test is especially important during the first six to twelve weeks of exercising.

b. Your exercising should be painless. If you experience any jaw, chest or neck pain, slow down. If the pain doesn't stop, see your doctor.

c. If you seem excessively tired for an hour or longer after exercising, the exercise was too strenuous. Next time, go slower and easier. Your exercise should be exhilarating, not fatiguing. If you feel dizzy or lightheaded or your heart is beating too fast while you exercise, it's time to back off. If you have a strange hollow feeling in your chest, feel like vomiting, or are tired for at least a day after exercising, take it easy. If you can't sleep at night or if your nerves seem shot, you've been pushing too hard. The same is true if you've lost your zing or can't get your breath after a few minutes of exercise. These are your body's warning signs—listen to them.

Think Commitment. As a Christian, you know that a commitment is a commitment, and it's intensely personal. It is your responsibility to make this decision and then put it into and keep it in practice. Once you make the decision, no excuses are permitted, except that you choose not to make a healthful change.

"I do not run like a man running aimlessly; I do not fight like a man beating the air" (1 Corinthians 9:26).

Chapter 16
The Body Magnificent: Toward a Theology of the Human Body

"So God created man in His own image, in the image of God He created him; male and female He created them" (Genesis 1:27). (NIV)

We live in a world of paradoxes regarding health. As a society, we run, take vitamins, seek out healthy food, and practice relaxation techniques. We expend incredible time and resources to extend our life spans. Yet, we also eliminate millions of lives before they are born. We take all kinds of drugs and chemicals that destroy and pollute our bodies. We overindulge in rich food, sedentary activities, and fast-lane living. On one hand, we appear to be striving for immortality; on the other, we seem to be driven by a death wish.

Although not emphasized by the Christian church, a common theme throughout Scripture is God's vital concern about the human body and what we do with it. Clyde Van Valin, a bishop of the Free Methodist Church, has provided several ideas from Scripture that demonstrate this concern:[1]

1. God created man and woman in His image. He breathed life into man to make him a living being. God found His creation to be good, so he provided rules and regulations to protect and preserve the body.[2]

2. God intended for the body to live forever. He warned Adam and Eve not to eat from the tree of the knowledge of good and evil, under punishment of death. In essence, God was saying, "If you don't eat from it, you will live forever." Man chose death, rather than eternal life.[3]

3. God sent His Son, Jesus in a human body as a living sacrifice. This sacrifice would restore an original intention of creation—everlasting life.[4] Jesus' body and blood were given so you and I could be saved, free from sin.[5]

4. Jesus' ministry on earth focused heavily on physical ailments. Almost 20 percent of the 3,779 verses in the four Gospels deal with Jesus' healing ministry. Jesus' compassionate ministry communicated that God intends the human body to be whole and well.

5. God's plan of salvation includes the redemption, salvation, sanctification and preservation of the human body. Our flesh and blood of this life will pass away, but we will be resurrected. We will have a new body that will be enough like this earthly body to be recognized, but heavenly enough to be everlasting.[6] God raised Jesus' body from the dead with a glorified body; we are promised the same. Jesus will transform our lowly bodies to be like His glorious body.[7]

6. Paul tells us that the Christian's body is the temple of the Holy Spirit and belongs to Christ. No wonder Paul says to offer our "bodies as living sacrifices, holy and pleasing to God—which is your spiritual worship."[8]

7. The Christian's body is to be a servant, not master. We are not to give ourselves over to sin. Instead, we offer ourselves to God as an instrument of righteousness. We all have the option to turn our bodies over to sinful desires or to God, as His temple. We are not to be mastered by anything except Christ.[9] As Christ's, our bodies are to be servants to our fellow human beings. We are to make every effort to do what leads to peace and the buildup of others.[10] In other words, we use our bodies to serve God and others, not to serve ourselves. We do not indulge in sin, addictions and self-aggrandizement.

With this theology of the human body, we must take care that we do not get our priorities out of line—we must not worship the creation (our bodies). Neither are we to think that improving fitness, eating healthfully and controlling weight, addictions and stress are necessary for salvation. These things will not earn us God's love. God loves us whether we are fat, fit or fatigued. He has a wonderful plan for each of our lives, as imperfect as we are. If we recognize that we are sinners and separated from God, if we admit that Jesus is God's only provision for our sin, and if we accept Christ as our Savior and Lord, we will receive a spiritual birth. We will have a full and meaningful (abundant) life. When we repent, turn to God and trust Him to come into our lives to forgive our sins, we give God the opportunity to make us the kind of people He wants us to be. In so doing, we abandon our "Temple of Self." We fill it with the Holy Spirit. Then we can accomplish positive lifestyle changes.

I've offered these recommendations for fitness, food and control of weight, addictions and stress to you and your family to help you enjoy this earthly life more. These will improve your health, increase your energy, help your mental outlook and build family relations—all of which significantly affect your spiritual life. When I hurt emotionally because of too much stress, when I am tired because of not enough fitness and too much fat, when I am ill because I have violated God's health laws, my family and social relationships are shortchanged. I provide a poor Christian testimony for those around me. My spiritual growth and walk are stifled. My desire to keep God as my number one priority is impaired.

A balance is necessary. We must not allow a fascination with health and longevity to become a god, a "body worship." Our purpose is to glorify God, not our bodies. As we grow older, our bodily strength will fade away. But our soul should keep growing. Not surprisingly, the sufferings that weaken our bodies may be used to strengthen our souls. From a physical point of view, life may be a slow and inevitable slide toward death, but from a spiritual perspective, it should be a triumphant climb to life. We need not fear our age and physical decline, for they will bring us nearer to God.

How, then do we strike a balance? How do we revere, but not worship, our bodies?

As stated earlier, God has made provision for us to protect our bodies now and to preserve our bodies through the resurrection. Our lifestyles should reflect that concern. God intends to be glorified in the human body. In fact, the use and maintenance of our bodies may be our strongest witness that God is Lord of *all* aspects of our lives.

Therefore, we are accountable to the God who made us. What we do with our bodies is of utmost importance. What we put into them, what we do to them, and what we put on them. Our bodies are a means by which we demonstrate obedience and submission of our total beings to our Lord and Savior.

And when I meet God, I want to be able to say, "God, I present to you a body that is as strong, clean and free from disease as it possibly can be." Of course, some of us came into the world with less perfect bodies than others. That is not important. God expects us to do our best with whatever we have. The vessel cannot fault the Potter.[11]

Last, but not least, we are to recognize that to take care of ourselves requires discipline and commitment. Paul tells of an athlete who trains hard for a temporary crown. He also talks about Christians who seek God and run for a crown—a crown that lasts forever.[12] Paul, one such seeker of God, said he did not run or fight aimlessly. Instead, he trained his body to do what it should do, so that his mind and body were mastered. Like an athlete, he ran with purpose—commitment.

In this passage, Paul gives a brief philosophy of life. He saw the abundant life as a challenge—a hard fought battle. Paul says winning this battle requires discipline in three areas: 1) We must discipline our *bodies*. We tend to neglect the fact that spiritual depression often comes from nothing more than a lack of health and fitness. 2) We must discipline our *minds*. It is tragic that some of us refuse to think until we become incapable of thinking. We never can solve our problems by refusing to see them or running away from them. Nor can we grow by thinking negatively or destructively. 3) We must discipline our *souls*. We must recognize that we are sinful and separated from God, that Jesus Christ is God's only provision for our sin, and that we must receive Jesus as our Lord. Only then can we adequately face life's problems with calm endurance, knowing that God is in control. Then can we meet the challenge and experience the abundant life Jesus promised. And only then, in the power of the Holy Spirit, can we achieve wellness.

''I can do everything through Him who gives me strength'' (Philippians 4:13).

Appendix A
Have You Heard of the Four Spiritual Laws?

Just as there are physical laws that govern the
physical universe, so are there spiritual laws
which govern your relationship with God.

LAW ONE—God **Loves** You, And Offers A Wonderful **Plan** For Your
  Life

God's Love
"For God so loved the world, that He gave His only begotten Son, that whoever
believes in Him should not perish, but have eternal life" (John 3:16).

God's Plan
(Christ speaking) "I came that they might have life, and might have it abundantly"
(that it might be full and meaningful) (John 10:10).

Why is it that most people are not experiencing the abundant life? Because . . .

LAW TWO—Man Is **Sinful** And **Separated** From God. Therefore, He
  Cannot Know And Experience God's Love And Plan For
  His Life

Man Is Sinful
"For all have sinned and fall short of the glory of God" (Romans 3:23).
  Man was created to have fellowship with God; but, because of his stubborn
self-will, he chose to go his own independent way and fellowship with God was
broken. This self-will, characterized by an attitude of active rebellion or passive
indifference, is evidence of what the Bible calls sin.

(References contained in this Appendix should be read in context from the Bible wherever possible.)

Written by Bill Bright. Copyright © Campus Crusade for Christ, Inc., 1965. All rights reserved. Manufactured in the United States of America.

Man Is Separated

"For the wages of sin is death" (spiritual separation from God) (Romans 6:23).

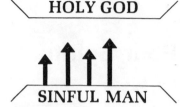

This diagram illustrates that God is holy and man is sinful. A great gulf separates the two. The arrows illustrate that man is continually trying to reach God and the abundant life through his own efforts, such as a good life, philosophy or religion.

The third law explains the only way to bridge this gulf . . .

LAW THREE—Jesus Christ Is God's **Only** Provision For Man's Sin. Through Him You Can Know And Experience God's Love And Plan For Your Life

He Died in Our Place

"But God demonstrates His love toward us, in that while we were yet sinners, Christ died for us" (Romans 5:8).

He Rose from the Dead

"Christ died for our sins . . . He was buried . . . He was raised on the third day, according to the Scriptures . . . He appeared to Peter, then to the twelve. After that He appeared to more than five hundred . . ." (I Corinthians 15:3-6).

He Is the Only Way to God

"Jesus said to him, 'I am the way, and the truth, and the life; no one comes to the Father, but through Me' " (John 14:6).

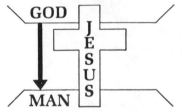

This diagram illustrates that God has bridged the gulf which separates us from Him by sending His Son, Jesus Christ, to die on the cross in our place to pay the penalty for our sins.

It is not enough just to know these three laws . . .

LAW FOUR—We Must Individually **Receive** Jesus Christ As Savior And Lord; Then We Can Know And Experience God's Love And Plan For Our Lives

We Must Receive Christ

"But as many received Him, to them He gave the right to become children of God, even to those who believe in His name" (John 1:12).

We Receive Christ Through Faith

"For by grace you have been saved through faith; and that not of yourselves, it is the gift of God; not as a result of works, that no one should boast" (Ephesians 2:8,9).

When We Receive Christ, We Experience a New Birth
(Read John 3:1-8.)

We Receive Christ by Personal Invitation

(Christ is speaking): "Behold, I stand at the door and knock; if any one hears My voice and opens the door, I will come in to him" (Revelation 3:20).

Receiving Christ involves turning to God from self (repentance) and trusting Christ to come into our lives to forgive our sins and to make us the kind of people He wants us to be. Just to agree intellectually that Jesus Christ is the Son of God and that He died on the cross for our sins is not enough. Nor is it enough to have an emotional experience. We receive Jesus Christ by faith, as an act of the will.

These two circles represent two kinds of lives:

SELF-DIRECTED LIFE
S—Self is on the throne
†—Christ is outside the life
●—Interests are directed by self, often resulting in discord and frustration

CHRIST-DIRECTED LIFE
†—Christ is in the life and on the throne
S—Self is yielding to Christ
●—Interests are directed by Christ, resulting in harmony with God's plan

Which circle best represents your life? Which circle would you like to have represent your life?

The following explains how you can receive Christ:

You Can Receive Christ Right Now By Faith Through Prayer

(Prayer is talking with God)

God knows your heart and is not so concerned with your words as He is with the attitude of your heart. The following is a suggested prayer:

> *"Lord Jesus, I need You. Thank You for dying on the cross for my sins. I open the door of my life and receive You as my Savior and Lord. Thank You for forgiving my sins and giving me eternal life. Take control of the throne of my life. Make me the kind of person You want me to be."*

Does this prayer express the desire of your heart?

If it does, pray this prayer right now, and Christ will come into your life, as He promised.

How to Know That Christ Is in Your Life
Did you receive Christ into your life? According to His promise in Revelation 3:20, where is Christ right now in relation to you? Christ said that He would come into your life. Would He mislead you? On what authority do you know that God has answered your prayer? (The trustworthiness of God Himself and His Word.)

The Bible Promises Eternal Life to All Who Receive Christ
"And the witness is this, that God has given us eternal life, and this life is in His Son. He who has the Son has the life; he who does not have the Son of God does not have the life. These things I have written to you who believe in the name of the Son of God, in order that you may know that you have eternal life" (I John 5:11-13).

Thank God often that Christ is in your life and that He will never leave you (Hebrews 13:5). You can know on the basis of His promise that Christ lives in you and that you have eternal life, from the very moment you invite Him in. He will not deceive you.

An important reminder . . .

Do Not Depend Upon Feelings

The promise of God's Word, the Bible—not our feelings—is our authority. The Christian lives by faith (trust) in the trustworthiness of God Himself and His Word. This train diagram illustrates the relationship between **fact** (God and His Word), **faith** (our trust in God and His Word), and **feeling** (the result of our faith and obedience) (John 14:21).

The train will run with or without the caboose. However, it would be useless to attempt to pull the train by the caboose. In the same way, we, as Christians, do not depend on feelings or emotions, but we place our faith (trust) in the trustworthiness of God and the promises of His Word.

Now That You Have Received Christ

The moment that you received Christ by faith, as an act of the will, many things happened, including the following:

1. Christ came into your life (Revelation 3:20 and Colossians 1:27).
2. Your sins were forgiven (Colossians 1:14).
3. You became a child of God (John 1:12).
4. You received eternal life (John 5:24).
5. You began the great adventure for which God created you (John 10:10; II Corinthians 5:17 and I Thessalonians 5:18).

Can you think of anything more wonderful that could happen to you than receiving Christ? Would you like to thank God in prayer right now for what He has done for you? By thanking God, you demonstrate your faith.

To enjoy your new life to the fullest . . .

Suggestions for Christian Growth

Spiritual growth results from trusting Jesus Christ. "The righteous man shall live by faith." (Galatians 3:11). A life of faith will enable you to trust God increasingly with every detail of your life, and to practice the following:

G Go to God in prayer daily (John 15:7).
R Read God's Word daily (Acts 17:11)—begin with the Gospel of John.
O Obey Gog moment by moment (John 14:21).
W Witness for Christ by your life and words (Matthew 4:19; John 15:8).
T Trust God for every detail of your life (I Peter 5:7).
H Holy Spirit—allow Him to control and empower your daily life and witness (Galatians 5:16,17; Acts 1:8).

Fellowship In A Good Church

God's Word admonishes us not to forsake "the assembling of ourselves together. . ." (Hebrews 10:25). Several logs burn brightly together; but put one aside on the cold hearth and the fire goes out. So it is with your relationship to other Christians. If you do not belong to a church, do not wait to be invited. Take the initiative; call the pastor of a nearby church where Christ is honored and His Word is preached. Start this week, and make plans to attend regularly.

Special Materials Are Available For Christian Growth

If you have come to know Christ personally through this presentation of the gospel, write for a free booklet especially written to assist you in your Christian growth.

A special Bible study series and an abundance of other helpful materials for Christian growth are also available. For additional information, please write Campus Crusade for Christ International, San Bernardino, CA 92414.

You will want to share this important discovery . . .

Appendix B
U.S. Recommended Daily Allowances (RDA) of Vitamins

Key

1 microgram (mcg)	= $\frac{1}{1000}$ of a milligram = 1 gamma
1,000 micrograms	= 1 milligram (mg)
1,000 milligrams	= 1 gram (g)
1,000 grams	= 1 kilogram (kg)

Vitamin	U.S. RDA
A	5,000 International Units (IU)
D	200 to 400 IU (5–10 mcg)
E	15 IU Men (10 mg) to 12 IU Women (8 mg)
K	70 to 140 mcg
B_1 Thiamine	1.4 mg Men to 1 mg Women
B_2 Riboflavin	1.6 Men to 1.2 mg Women
B_3 Niacin	18 mg Men to 13 mg Women
B_5 Pantothenic Acid	4 to 7 mg
B_6 Pyridoxine	2.2 mg Men to 2 mg Women
Biotin	1.3 mg
Folacin	1.4 mg
B_{12} Cyanocobalamin	3 mcg
C	60 mg

Vitamins and Their Relationship to Health

Fat-Soluble Vitamins

Those Most Likely to be Deficient	Sources	U.S. RDA	Known Health Roles	Deficiency Signs
A College students, cigarette smokers, drug users, marijuana smokers, alcoholics, nursing mothers and people living in polluted areas.	Carrots, peas, lettuce, sweet potatoes, tomatoes, liver, eggs, dairy foods, apricots, fresh fruits, squash, cantaloupe, butter, fortified margarine and broccoli.	5000 International Units (IU)	Vitamin A is important in the formation of the mucous membranes and skin. It helps prevent eye disorders. It's also important in bone and teeth formation.	Stunting of growth, impairment of vision, diseased conditions of the skin and membranes lining the respiratory passages and digestive and genital-urinary tracts, and abnormalities in enamel-forming cells of teeth.
D People with colds or the flu, pregnant women and heart disease patients.	Sunlight, fish liver oils, and fortified milk. Small amounts are found in butter, liver and egg yolk.	200 to 400 IU	Needed during periods of growth for bones and teeth, and required throughout life for calcium metabolism.	Weight loss, loss of appetite, cramps, poor bone formation and rickets.
E People who are exposed to air pollution, people who eat refined white flour, highly stressed individuals, diabetics, pregnant and lactating women, the aged, people using birth control pills, and heart disease patients.	Vegetable oils (cottonseed, safflower, sunflower, soybean), corn, almonds, peanuts, whole grains, wheat germ, nuts, legumes, eggs and sprouts.	15 IU Men, 12 IU Women	Acts as an antioxidant to reduce oxidation of vitamin A and polyunsaturated fatty acids.	Abnormal pigmentation and anemia.

Those Most Likely to be Deficient	Sources	U.S. RDA	Known Health Roles	Deficiency Signs
K People who take aspirin, antibiotic users, people on anticoagulants, those living in polluted environments, people who eat lots of frozen foods, patients recovering from surgery, and the aged.	Lettuce, spinach, kale, cauliflower, cabbage, other leafy, green vegetables, liver, egg yolk and soybean.	70 to 140 micrograms (mcg)	Necessary for proper blood clotting.	Prolonged clotting time.

Water-Soluble Vitamins

Those Most Likely to be Deficient	Sources	U.S. RDA	Known Health Roles	Deficiency Signs
B₁ Thiamine College students, cigarette smokers, drinkers, pregnant women, highly stressed individuals, those who do not eat regularly, arthritics, and those who eat white breads and refined white pastries.	Meat, fish, poultry, eggs, whole-grain breads and cereal, soybeans, beans, split peas, pork, oatmeal, yeast, wheat germ, sunflower and sesame seeds, and nuts, such as peanuts.	1.4 milligrams (mg) Men, 1 mg Women	Thiamine is important in regulating your appetite.	Fatigue, insomnia, irritability, loss of appetite, constipation. Heart-irregularity disturbances, digestive balances, muscle tenderness, weight loss, forgetfulness, lassitude, and mental inadequacy are all possible signs. Gross deficiency results in beriberi, a fatal heart disease.
B₂ Riboflavin College students, those who do not eat regularly, those who are depressed or highly stressed, the aged, and those using oral contraceptives.	Milk, cheese, liver, kidneys, fish, poultry, eggs, whole-grain breads and cereals, cottage cheese, oysters, beef, leafy vegetables, beans and peas.	1.6 mg Men, 1.2 mg Women	Is in enzymes that transport hydrogen as part of the metabolism of protein.	Irritation and cracks at corners of the mouth, scaly skin around nose and ears, some tongue and mouth itching and burning eyes, eyes sensitive to light.

Vitamins and Their Relationship to Health

Water-Soluble Vitamins

Those Most Likely to be Deficient	Sources	U.S. RDA	Known Health Roles	Deficiency Signs
B₃ Niacin College students, highly stressed individuals, heavy sugar users, hypoglycemics, users of antibiotics, and those eating large amounts of pastries and starches.	Meat, liver, fish, poultry, eggs, whole-grain breads and cereals, wheat germ, nuts, seeds, rice, beans and peas.	18 mg Men, 13mg Women	Function is related to protein metabolism.	Loss of appetite, nervousness, mental depression, soreness and redness of the tongue, abnormal skin pigmentation, ulceration of the gums, and diarrhea. Gross deficiency causes pellagra.
B₅ Pantothenic Acid College students, heavy sugar users, hypoglycemics, users of antibiotics, those under emotional stress, arthritics, workers in cold climates, and those eating refined flour products.	Whole-grain cereals, legumes, animal meats, eggs, wheat germ, peanuts and peas.	4 to 7 mg	Involved in release of energy from fat and carbohydrates. Used in adrenal gland function and is necessary to fight stress.	A deficiency is rarely seen unless your diet consists of highly processed food. Sore tongue, weakness, weight loss, headache, fatigue and muscle cramps are common.
B₆ Pridoxine College students, dieters, highly stressed individuals, pregnant women, lactating women, heart disease patients, the aged and alcoholics.	Liver, ham, lima beans, corn, sunflower seeds, wheat-germ, bran, potatoes, brown rice, and whole-grain bread, flour and cereals.	2.2 mg Men, 2 mg Women	Protein metabolism and health of central nervous system.	Loss of appetite, diarrhea, skin and mouth disorders, and blindness.

Biotin People with infections.	Liver, yeast, egg yolk, whole grains, nuts and legumes.	1.3 mg	Biotin is important in cellular metabolism and helps in the metabolism of fats, carbohydrates and proteins.	Anemia, muscular pain and skin disorders. Rare—eating a balanced diet provides 150–300 g daily. Some drugs, such as antibiotics, may destroy your body's own ability to synthesize biotin.
Folacin Highly stressed individuals, alcoholics, diabetics, those using sulfa drugs, pregnant women, women who experience excessive menstruation, and the aged.	Green, leafy vegetables, eggs, liver, kidneys, wheat germ and yeast.	1.4 mg	Assists in formation of certain body proteins.	Smooth red tongue, intestinal upsets, diarrhea, macrocytic anemia. Young red blood cells do not mature.
B$_{12}$ Cyanocobalamin Vegetarians, people suffering from irregular menstruation, frequent laxative users and the aged.	Present only in animal tissues—meats, poultry, fish, shellfish, eggs and milk products.	3 mcg	Red blood cell formation.	Anemia, tingling of hands and feet, back pain, mental and nervous change.
C Alcoholics, cigarette smokers, college students, users of antibiotics, people taking large amounts of aspirin, heroin addicts and the aged.	Citrus fruits, tomatoes, strawberries, cranberries, potatoes, raw greens, peppers, broccoli and cauliflower.	60 mg	Necessary for helping hold the cells together, including in the bones, teeth, skin, organs, and capillary walls.	Bleeding and receding gums, unexpected bruises, slow healing and scurvy.

Appendix C
U.S. Recommended Daily Allowances (RDA) of Minerals

Key

1 microgram (mcg)	= $\frac{1}{1000}$ of a milligram = 1 gamma
1,000 micrograms	= 1 milligram (mg)
1,000 milligrams	= 1 gram (g)
1,000 grams	= 1 kilogram (kg)

Mineral	**U.S. RDA**
Calcium	800 mg
Magnesium	350 mg Men to 300 mg Women
Phosphorus	800 mg
Potassium	1875 to 5625 mg
Sodium	1100 to 3300 mg
Sulfur	Unknown

Trace Mineral	**U.S. RDA**
Chromium	0.05 to 0.2 mg
Copper	2 to 3 mg
Flourine	Unknown
Iodine	150 mcg
Iron	18 mg
Manganese	2.5 to 5 mg
Selenium	Unknown
Zinc	15 mg

Minerals and Their Relationship to Health

Minerals:

People Most Likely to be Deficient	Sources	U.S. RDA	Known Health Roles	Deficiency Signs
Calcium People taking large amounts of vitamin A, C and D; heavy chocolate eaters; inactive and sedentary people; highly stressed individuals; people over 50 years of age; arthritics; people taking laxatives and heavy water drinkers.	Milk, dark green, leafy vegetables, small fish eaten with bones, all cheeses, dried beans and peas, broccoli, artichokes, and sesame seeds.	800 milligrams (mg)	It is necessary for hard bones and teeth, muscle contractions (especially normal heart rhythm), transmission of nerve impulses, proper blood clotting, and to activate a number of enzymes.	In children: stunted growth, retarded bone mineralization, poor bones and teeth, skeletal malformation (rickets). In adults: osteoporosis—brittle porous bones, resulting from demineralization.
Magnesium People who are on an unbalanced diet, such as a high cholesterol diet, high sugar diet, or a diet rich in meat; diabetics; those using diuretics; alcoholics; or those exposed to high levels of noise.	Whole grains, nuts, beans, green leafy vegetables. Processing may result in high losses of magnesium.	350 mg Men, 300 mg Women	Helps regulate body temperatures and protein synthesis.	Usually seen only in alcoholism when people are on a limited diet of highly processed foods. Weakness, tremors, dizziness, spasms, convulsions, delirium and depression.
Phosphorus Pregnant women, growing children, adolescents, cancer patients, arthritics, people with high levels of mental stress or significant tooth decay, and people who use a lot of laxatives or antacids.	Organ meats, meats, fish, poultry, eggs, milk, cheese, nuts, beans, peas and whole grains.	800 mg	Necessary (with calcium) to form and strengthen bones as part of the nucleic acids.	Seldom seen in humans eating a normal diet. Weakness, bone pain, loss of minerals (especially calcium from bones), poor growth.

	Sources	Amount	Function	Symptoms
Potassium People who use diuretics and laxatives, cortisone medication, excessive salt and excessive coffee. Also people suffering from migraine headaches, extreme stress, high blood pressure, hypoglycemia, diarrhea or alcoholism.	Fruits, dates, bananas, oranges, cantaloupes, tomatoes, vegetables (especially dark green leafy vegetables), liver, meat, fish, poultry and milk	1875 to 5625 mg	Major constituent of fluid inside cells. Along with sodium, it regulates water balance and nerve transmission. Necessary for protein synthesis.	Muscle weakness, nausea, depletion of glycogen, rapid heartbeat, and heart failure.
Sodium Those using diuretics or working in a hot, humid environment. Also those who have diarrhea.	Salt, salted foods, monosodium glutamate, soy sauce, baking powder, cheese, milk, shellfish, meat, fish, poultry, eggs, most packaged products.	1100 to 3300 mg	Major constituent of fluid outside the cells. Regulates water balance and nerve irritability.	Rare: nausea, diarrhea, abdominal and muscle cramps.
Sulfur Vegetarians, people suffering from inadequate protein intake, psoriasis or eczema.	Eggs, meat, milk, cheese, nuts and legumes.	Unknown	Part of proteins (especially in hair).	None found. A diet adequate in protein (several amino acids contain sulfur) will meet needs.

Minerals and Their Relationship to Health

Minerals:

People Most Likely to be Deficient	Sources	U.S. RDA	Known Health Roles	Deficiency Signs
Chromium Diabetics, hypoglycemics, the aged, people who sweat a great deal, vomit, or eat lots of sugar.	Corn oil, meats and whole grains.	0.05 to .2 mg	Metabolism of protein and synthesis of cholesterol.	Poor utilization of glucose.
Copper People who have suffered heavy loss of blood, are anemic and have a low red blood cell count.	Most foods, including organ meats, shellfish, nuts, dried beans, peas and cocoa. It is absent in dairy products. Copper is found in most unprocessed foods.	2 to 3 mg	Very important in the first few months of life. Important for nourishment of nerve wall and connective tissue.	Causes anemia in children. Unknown in adults.
Flourine Pregnant women, the aged and people with dental caries.	Water that is naturally or artificially fluoridated.	Unknown	Prevention of solid tooth formation and decrease in dental cavities.	Tooth decay in young children. Possibly osteoporosis in adults.
Iodine People who perspire a great deal, eat an excessive amount of raw cabbage or cauliflower, or live in an area where the soil is depleted.	Seafood; vegetables grown near the ocean where soil is rich in iodine; butter, milk, cheese and eggs if the animal's food has been rich in iodine; iodized salt.	150 micrograms	Influences growth, mental development, and depositing of protein and fat in the body.	Excess may depress thyroid activity and cause goiter.

Mineral / Who may need it	Food sources	Amount	Function	Deficiency symptoms
Iron Women during menstruation, pregnant women, and people who eat low amounts of vitamin C, have lost blood, experienced rapid growth or have peptic ulcers.	Liver, meat products, egg yolk, fish, green leafy vegetables, peas, beans, dried fruit, whole-grain cereals, and foods prepared from iron-enriched cereal products.	18 mg	Part of the hemoglobin in the blood, myoglobin in the muscles, parts of the cells, the cell nuclei, and many enzymes in the tissues.	Digestion problems, cell damage, anemia, excess skin pigmentation, lowered ability to handle glucose, cirrhosis of the liver.
Manganese Lactating women, the aged, diabetics, and people who eat lots of sugar and sugar products, refined products, or few vegetables.	Found in most foods, plant and animal. Whole grains, legumes and nuts are good sources.	2.5 to 5 mg	Necessary to unite complex carbohydrates, fats and cholesterol. Important for proper development of bones, the pancreas and tendon structure.	Rarely seen.
Selenium Cigarette smokers, and those living in areas of high air pollution.	Bran, whole-grain cereals, broccoli, nuts, onions, tomatoes and turnips.	Unknown	May prevent cancers to digestive tract and destroys fats in tiny blood vessels.	Fatigue.
Zinc Alcoholics, diabetics, pregnant women, men with prostate trouble, women taking oral contraceptives, those under a high amount of stress, and those on an unbalanced diet.	Wheat germ and bran, whole grains, dried beans and peas, nuts, lean meats, fish and poultry.	15 mg	Important in digestion, protein metabolism and synthesis of nucleic acids.	Rare in the United States. Can cause retarded growth, retarded sexual development, anemia and poor healing of wounds.

Notes

Preface

1. 1 Timothy 4:8 (KJV).
2. Matthew 6:25.
3. Matthew 6:27.
4. 1 Corinthians 6:20.

Chapter 1

1. J. L. Lynch, M.D., and W. H. Convey, "Loneliness, Disease and Death: Alternative Approaches," *Psychosomatics* 20 (October 1979):702–08.
2. George E. Vaillant, M.D., *Adapation to Life: How the Best and Brightest Came of Age* (Boston: Little, Brown and Co., 1977), book jacket.
3. Matthew 22:39.
4. Proverbs 16:16.
5. Jill Neimark, "Medical News," *American Health,* 3 (December 1984):14.
6. International Medical News Service, "Finds Children Are 'Enormously Competent at Self Care,' " *Pediatric News* 18 (October 1984):67.
7. Louis Harris and Associates, Inc., *Prevention in America: Steps People Take—or Fail to Take—for Better Health,* in Charles T. Kuntzleman and Debra Drake, *The Feelin' Good Report* (Spring Arbor, Mich.: Fitness Finders, 1984), pp. 172–75.
8. Daniel Yankelovich, *New Rules: Searching for Self-Fulfillment in a World Turned Upside Down* (New York: Bantam, 1982), pp. 57–59.
9. See Genesis 3:5.
10. See Romans 1:25.
11. Romans 5:2 (TLB).
12. See Romans 12:3–8.

Chapter 2

1. Nedra Belloc and Lester Breslow, "Relationship of Physical Health Status and Health Practices," *Preventive Medicine* 1 (1972):409–421.
2. Kenneth R. Pelletier, *Longevity* (New York: Delacorte Press/Seymour Lawrence, 1981), pp. 190–98.

3. Alexander Comfort, *A Good Age* (New York: Crown Publishers, 1976), p. 140; Charles T. Kuntzleman, *Concepts for Wellness* (Spring Arbor, Mich.: Arbor Press, 1982), p. 175; and Pelletier, *Longevity*, pp. 1–33.
4. See Matthew 6:27.
5. Luke 16:11.
6. Harvey Ebel, Neil Sol, Don Bailey, and Sid Schechter, *Presidential Sports Award Fitness Manual—The Total Guide* (Havertown, Penn.: FitCom Corp., 1983), vii–23; and Jack Kelly, "Our Bill for Health: $1,459," *USA Today* (11 October 1984), p. 1A.

Chapter 3

1. Louis Harris and Associates, Inc., *Prevention in America: Steps People Take—or Fail to Take—for Better Health*, p. A–12.
2. Frank I. Katch and William D. McArdle, *Nutrition, Weight Control, and Exercise*, 2nd ed. (Philadelphia: Lea and Febiger, 1983), p. 133.
3. Per Olaf Åshand, *Health and Fitness* (Ottawa: Information Canada, 1975), p. 8.
4. Richard Passwater, Ph.D., *Supernutrition* (New York: Dial Press, 1975), p. 19.
5. Charles T. Kuntzleman, *Concepts for Wellness* (Spring Arbor, Mich.: Arbor Press, 1982), p. 73.
6. Michael F. Jacobsen, *Eater's Digest: The Consumer's Factbook of Food Additives* (New York: Archer Books, 1972), p. 3.
7. Richard Hughes and Robert Brewin, *The Tranquilizing of America: Pill-Popping and the American Way of Life* (New York: Harcourt-Brace, 1979), p. 269.
8. Brent Q. Hafen and Brenda Peterson, *Medicine and Drugs: Problems and Risks, Use and Abuse* (Philadelphia: Lea and Febiger, 1978), p. 137.
9. Robert S. Mendelson, *Confessions of a Medical Heretic* (Chicago: Contemporary Books, Inc., 1979), p. 25.
10. Ivan Illich, *Medical Nemesis: The Expropriation of Health* (New York: Pantheon Books, 1976), p. 28.
11. John Naisbitt, *Megatrends* (New York: Warner Books, 1982), pp. 233–34.
12. Ibid.
13. Daniel Yankelovich, *New Rules: Searching for Self-Fulfillment in a World Turned Upside Down* (New York: Bantam, 1982), pp. 132–43.
14. Ibid., pp. 169–214; and Naisbitt, *Megatrends*, pp. 231–47.
15. Ibid.
16. *Healthy People: The Surgeon General's Report on Health Promotion and Disease Prevention* (Washington, D.C.: U.S. Department of Health, Education and Welfare, 1979), pp. 15, 53–69.

Chapter 5

1. 1 Timothy 4:8.
2. See Deuteronomy 34:1.
3. See 1 Kings 18:46; 19:1–4.
4. See Matthew 15:21.
5. See Luke 24:13–34.
6. See John 20:2.
7. Charles T. Kuntzleman and Debra Drake, *The Feelin' Good Report* (Spring Arbor, Mich.: Fitness Finders, 1984), pp. 35, 78.
8. Jane Brody, "Program Reverses Unhealthy Trend in Children," *The New York Times* (24 October 1984), p. 21.
9. Kenneth H. Cooper, Michael L. Pollock, R. P. Martin, S. R. White, A. C. Linnerud, and A. Jackson, "Physical Fitness Levels Versus Selected Coronary Risk Factors," *Journal of American Medical Association* 236 (12 July 1976), pp. 166–69.
10. Samuel M. Fox, "Relationship of Activity Habits to Coronary Heart Disease." In John P. Naughton and Herman K. Hellerstein, eds., *Exercise Testing and Exercise Training in Coronary Heart Disease* (New York: Academic Press, 1973), p. 13.
11. Alexander Melleby, *The Y's Way to a Healthy Back* (New Jersey: New Century Publishers, Inc., 1982), p. 3.
12. *Healthy People: The Surgeon General's Report on Health Promotion and Disease Prevention* (Washington, D.C.: U.S. Department of Health, Education and Welfare, 1979), pp. 119–38.
13. Ibid.
14. Wendy Murphy and the Editors of Time-Life Books, *Dealing With Headaches* (Alexandria, Va.: Time-Life Books, 1982), pp. 6–9.
15. Ibid.

Family Fitness Activities

1. Adapted from Brian J. Sharkey, *Physiology of Fitness* (Champaign, Ill.: Human Kinetics, 1982), p. 6.

Chapter 7

1. See Philippians 1:9,10.
2. Jean Mayer, *Health* (New York: D. Van Nostrand, 1974), p. 135.
3. *Healthy People: The Surgeon General's Report on Health Promotion and Disease Prevention* (Washington, D.C.: U.S. Department of Health, Education and Welfare, 1979), pp. 60–67.

Chapter 8

1. See Acts 10:15.
2. See 1 Timothy 4:4.
3. Mike Feinsilber and William B. Mead, *American Averages* (Garden City, N.Y.: Dolphin Books, 1980), pp. 283–85; and Frank I. Katch and William D. McArdle, *Nutrition, Weight Control, and Exercise,* 2nd ed. (Philadelphia: Lea and Febiger, 1983), p. 51.
4. Jane Brody, *Jane Brody's Nutrition Book* (New York: W.W. Norton, 1981), pp. 97–102; "Highlights," Ten-State Nutrition Survey, 1968–1970, Department of Health, Education and Welfare, no. HSM 72–8134; Charles T. Kuntzleman, *Maximum Personal Energy* (Emmaus, Penn.: Rodale Press, 1981), pp. 171–77; *The Lipid Research Clinic's Population Studies Data Book, Vol. 1, The Prevalence Study,* U.S. Department of Health and Human Service, Public Health Service, National Institutes of Health Publication, no. 82–2014 (1982); and *Washington Post* (27 May 1980), p. 7D.
5. David Ruben, *The Save Your Life Diet* (New York: Ballantine, 1975), p. 81.
6. Feinsilber and Mead, *American Averages,* pp. 283–85.
7. *Lipid Research Clinics Population Studies,* pp. 216–20.
8. Gerald S. Berenson, *Cardiovascular Risk Factors in Children* (New York: Oxford University Press, 1980), pp. 3–18.
9. Lipid Research Clinic's Program, "The Lipid Research Clinic's Coronary Primary Prevention Trial Results," *Journal of the American Medical Association* 251 (20 January 1984), pp. 351–74.
10. Berenson, *Cardiovascular Risk Factors,* pp. 3–18.
11. Brody, *Jane Brody's Nutrition,* p. 483.
12. Kuntzleman, *Maximum Personal Energy,* p. 26.

Family Food Activities

1. *Cooking Without Your Salt Shaker* (American Heart Association, 1978), pp. 12–13. (May be purchased from local chapters.)
2. Sheryl London, *Anything Grows* (Ammaus, Penn.: Rodale Press, 1984).
3. "What You Get Into When You Go Out for Dinner," *Executive Fitness Newsletter* 12 (30 May 1981):1, 2.

Chapter 9

1. See Deuteronomy 21:20; Proverbs 23:21; Matthew 11:19; and Luke 7:34.
2. Sally Ann Stewart, "When Is Obesity a Burden to Health?" *USA Today* (12 February 1985), p. 4D.
3. Frank I. Katch and William D. McArdle, *Nutrition, Weight Control, and Exercise,* 2nd ed. (Philadelphia: Lea and Febiger, 1983), p. 103.

4. Jean Seligmann, Marsh Zabarsky, Deborah Witherspoon, Lori Rotenbak, Mireya Schmidt, "A Deadly Feast and Famine," *Newsweek* (7 March 1983), p. 59.
5. Josh McDowell, *His Image . . . My Image* (San Bernardino, Calif.: Here's Life Publishers, 1984), p. 31.
6. "Letting Go of Leanness," *Executive Fitness Newsletter* 16 (19 January 1985):3.

Chapter 10

1. Psalm 139:14.
2. Charles T. Kuntzleman, *Diet Free!* (Emmaus, Penn.: Rodale Press, 1982), p. 27.
3. W. Bennett and J. Gurin, "The New Set Point Theory," *The Dieter's Dilemma* (New York: Basic Books, 1982).
4. Peter D. Wood, "On Playing More, Eating More and Being Slim," *Executive Health Report*, January 1985, pp. 1–2.
5. Frank I. Katch and William D. McArdle, *Nutrition, Weight Control, and Exercise*, 2nd ed. (Philadelphia: Lea and Febiger, 1983), p. 189.
6. Steven Findlay, "Sowing the Seeds of Adulthood Disease," *USA Today* (7 March 1985), p. 4D.
7. Ibid.

Family Weight Control Activities

1. Henry A. Jordan and Theodore Berland, *The Doctor's Calories-Plus Diet* (Chicago: Contemporary Books, Inc., 1981), pp. 20–24.
2. Jack D. Osman, "Teaching Nutrition With a Focus on Fitness," *Nutrition News* (April 1973), p. 3.

Chapter 11

1. Romans 7:24,25 (TLB).
2. Barbara Bisantz Raymond, "We're Often Our Own Worst Enemies," *USA Today* (10 October 1984), p. 6D.
3. Charles T. Kuntzleman, *Maximum Personal Energy* (Emmaus, Penn.: Rodale Press, 1981), p. 32.
4. Michael Rothenberg, "Effect of Television Violence on Children and Youth," *Journal of the American Medical Association* 234 (8 December 1975):1043–46.
5. "Relax: Runners Are Not Like Anorexics," *Executive Fitness Newsletter* 15 (27 October 1984):3.
6. Ibid.

Chapter 12

1. See James 4:10; 1 Peter 5:6.
2. 1 John 2:15,16 (TLB).
3. Galatians 5:17 (NAS).
4. See 1 Peter 5:7,8.

Chapter 13

1. Alvin Toffler, *Future Shock* (New York: Random House, 1970), p. 3.
2. Charles T. Kuntzleman, *Concepts for Wellness* (Spring Arbor, Mich.: Arbor Press, 1982), p. 97.
3. *Healthy People: The Surgeon General's Report on Health Promotion and Disease Prevention* (Washington, D.C.: U.S. Department of Health, Education and Welfare, 1979), pp. 60–67.
4. Hans Selye, M.D., *The Stress of Life* (New York: McGraw Hill, 1956), pp. 25–43.
5. Ibid.
6. Proverbs 29:22.
7. 1 Peter 5:7.
8. Meyer Friedman and Ray H. Rosenman, *Type A Behavior and Your Heart* (Greenwich, Conn.: Fawcett Publications, 1975), pp. 84–96.
9. Selye, *Stress of Life,* pp. 25–43.
10. Philippians 4:11.

Chapter 14

1. Romans 5:3–5 (TLB).
2. Maya Pines, "Psychological Hardiness," *Psychology Today* (December 1980), pp. 34–44.
3. Ibid.
4. Ibid.
5. "Hardiness: Why Some Executives Thrive Under Stress," *Executive Fitness Newsletter* 15 (18 August 1984):1.
6. See Revelation 3:15,16.
7. Romans 12:11.
8. Romans 8:28.
9. Hebrews 12:1–3.
10. William Barclay, *The Letter to the Hebrews* (Philadelphia: The Westminster Press, 1976), pp. 171–73.
11. Romans 5:2 (TLB).
12. See Mark 7:14–23.

13. David D. Burns, *Feeling Good—The New Mood Therapy* (New York: New American Library, 1980), pp. 40–41.
14. Charles T. Kuntzleman, *Maximum Personal Energy* (Emmaus, Penn.: Rodale Press, 1981), pp. 70–71.
15. Walter S. Ross, "Stress: It's Not Worth Dying For," *Reader's Digest* (January 1985), p. 77.

Family Stress Control Activities

1. Adapted from Thomas H. Holmes and R. H. Rake, "The Social Readjustment Rating Scale," *Journal of Psychosomatic Research* 11 (1967):213–18.
2. Adapted from Raymond W. Bortner, "A Short Rating Scale as a Potential Measure of Pattern A Behavior," *Journal of Chronic Disease* 22 (1969):87–91. Copyright 1969. Reprinted with permission from Pergamon Press, Ltd.
3. Adapted from Ron Clinton, *How to Prevent Burnout and Achieve Personal Well Being* (Detroit: Human Potential, 1980), p. 28.
4. Herbert Benson, *Beyond the Relaxation Response* (New York: Times Books, 1984), pp. 108, 122.
5. John 14:27 (KJV).
6. John 15:12 (KJV).
7. John 14:6 (KJV).

Chapter 15

1. See Acts 16:6–10.
2. See 1 Corinthians 12:12–26.
3. Alan Lakein, *How to Get Control of Your Time and Your Life* (New York: Signet Books, 1973), pp. 97, 146–47.
4. Campbell's Institute for Health and Fitness, *The Turnaround Lifestyle System* (Camden, N.J.: Campbell's Institute for Health and Fitness, 1985), pp. 17–18.

Chapter 16

1. This chapter was inspired by a 1985 conference at Spring Arbor College hosting Kenneth Vaux, Ph.D., Lyn Cryderman; Phillip Yancey; Charles Kuntzleman; and several Spring Arbor College faculty members. Additionally, Free Methodist Bishop Clyde Van Valin made available an unpublished paper called, "The Renewal of the Theology of the Human Body."
2. See Genesis 1:27; 2:7; 9:4–6; Exodus 20; and Leviticus.
3. See Genesis 2:17; and 1 Corinthians 15:21.
4. See John 12:47–50; Romans 5:21; and Galatians 6:8.
5. See Matthew 26:26–29.

6. See 1 Thessalonians 4:13–17; John 11:25; and 1 Corinthians 15.
7. See Acts 2:36; Romans 8:23; and Philippians 3:20,21.
8. Romans 12:1.
9. See Romans 6:11–14; 1 Corinthians 6:12.
10. See Romans 14.
11. See Romans 9:20.
12. See 1 Corinthians 9:24–27.